D0098136

Especially for

.............................................

From

.............................................

Date

.............................................

Michelle Medlock Adams

# Encouraging
## *Words*
### for
## *Mothers*

*Daily Devotions to Lift Mom's Soul*

BARBOUR
PUBLISHING

© 2004 by Barbour Publishing, Inc.

Previously published as *Daily Wisdom for Mothers*.

ISBN 978-1-64352-759-8

Published by Barbour Publishing, Inc., 1810 Barbour Drive, Uhrichsville, Ohio 44683, www.barbourbooks.com

*Our mission is to inspire the world with the life-changing message of the Bible.*

Printed in China.

# Introduction

Let's face it. Life is busy—especially for moms. When I was mother of two young girls, I found it challenging some days just to make time for a shower, let alone time to spend with God. I'm sure you face the same thing—you desire a deeper relationship with the Lord, but you don't have hours to spend in His Word every day.

That's why this book is perfect for moms like us. I wrote it with you in mind. Within these pages you'll find a quick, easy-to-read devotional for each day of the year. A scripture and a short prayer complete each day's reading. Every month we'll tackle a different aspect of being a mom—so by the end of the year, we'll have become stronger and wiser in every area of our lives!

January's theme is "Casting Your Cares"—dealing with the worries, expectations, and obligations of being a mother. In February, the topic is "Loving Unconditionally," learning to show love to your children no matter what. March is all about "Taking the Time" and treasuring every moment of raising our children—even the 2 a.m. feedings. April's theme is "Becoming Mother of the Year"—giving up the quest for perfection and learning to see yourself as God sees you. In May, we'll spend time considering "Having a Thankful Heart" and learning to appreciate the everyday blessings, big and small. June's topic is "Dreaming Big Dreams" and allowing yourself to have dreams of your own—even in the midst of soccer practices and bake sales. In July, it's "Surviving the Good, the Bad, and the Ugly," learning to lean on God when being a mom seems too hard.

August's theme, "Taming the Tongue," is about allowing God to use your words to edify and speak wisdom into your children's lives. For September, we'll discuss "Daring to Discipline" and following God's leading on the path to raising godly kids. October's topic is "Living to Give"—embracing the motherhood role and giving it all you've got! In November, we'll encourage "Praying More" and learning the importance of time on your knees as it relates to your children. Finally, in December, the topic is "Giving Your Kids to God." We'll explore trusting God totally with our children and teaching our kids about having a real relationship with Him.

I hope that you'll look forward to your devotional time each day. Grab a soda or a cup of java and spend some time with God today. Maybe you can squeeze it in while the kiddos are napping. Or maybe your best time with God is right after you put the children to bed at night. It doesn't really matter—whenever you sit down with this book, it'll be the right time. I pray that God will open your eyes and your heart as we take this daily journey together.

MICHELLE MEDLOCK ADAMS

# January 1

*"Come to me, all you who are weary
and burdened, and I will give you rest."*
MATTHEW 11:28

Ahhh. . .rest. Who wouldn't love a day of rest? But let's face it. Mothers don't really get a day of rest. If we rested, who would fix breakfast? Who would get the children ready for church? Who would do the laundry so your son can wear his lucky socks for the big game on Monday?

No, there's not a lot of rest in a mother's schedule. But that's not really the kind of rest this verse is talking about. The rest mentioned in this verse is the kind of rest that only Jesus can provide. Resting in Jesus means feeling secure in Him and allowing His peace to fill your soul. That kind of rest is available to all—even mothers.

So in the midst of the hustle and bustle of your life (even if you're elbow deep in dishwater), you can rest in Him. Start by meditating on the Lord's promises and His everlasting love for you. Make a mental list of the things in your life that you are thankful for, and praise God for each one. Allow His love to overwhelm you—and rest.

—————————— MOM TO MASTER ——————————

*Lord, help me to rest in You—even when
I'm overwhelmed with the "to-dos" of each day.
I want more of You in my life. I love You. Amen.*

# January 2

*Cast all your anxiety on him because he cares for you.*
1 PETER 5:7

Ever have one of those days? The alarm clock didn't go off. The kids were late for school. The dog threw up on the carpet. You spilled coffee down the front of your new white blouse. Ahhh! It's one of those "Calgon, take me away!" days, right?

But it doesn't have to be. No matter how many challenges you face today, you can smile in the face of aggravation. How? By casting your cares upon the Lord. That's what the Lord tells us to do in His Word, yet many of us feel compelled to take all of the cares upon ourselves. After all, we're mothers. We're fixers. We're the doers of the bunch. We wear five or six fedoras at a time—we can handle anything that comes our way, right?

Wrong! But God can. When the day starts to go south, cast your cares on Him. He wants you to! As mothers, we can handle a lot, but it's true what they say—Father really does know best. So give it to God. C'mon, you know you want to.

--------- MOM TO MASTER ---------

*Lord, help me to turn to You when my troubles seem too big to face alone and even when they don't. Help me to trust You with all of my cares. I love You, Lord. Amen.*

# January 3

*God is our refuge and strength, an ever-present help in trouble.*
PSALM 46:1

*"Mom!"* Allyson shrieked.

It was one of those "mom cries" that sends mothers into an instant panic. I heard my then five-year-old screaming for me, but I couldn't find her.

"Mom, hurry!"

Finally, I found her. She was way up in our live oak tree that stood in our front yard. . .and she was stuck. Trying to remember how to climb a tree, I inched my way up. Finally, when I could reach her, she clung to me like she'd never clung before. Once we were safely on the ground, I reminded Allyson that she wouldn't have been stuck in our tree if she'd been obedient. After all, she wasn't supposed to leave the backyard, and she certainly wasn't supposed to climb our tall tree—not without help.

Allyson's tree trauma is similar to how many of us walk with God. We do our own thing—and when we get stuck, we holler, "Help, God, and hurry!" After He rescues us, we cling to Him until we're safe. Then we go about our own lives until we need Him again.

Wouldn't it be better if we just stayed close to God all the time—not just in troubled times? Then we wouldn't have to holler. He'd already be there.

—————————— MOM TO MASTER ——————————

*Father, help me to stay near You all the time. Amen.*

# January 4

*"Can any one of you by worrying
add a single hour to your life?"*
MATTHEW 6:27

You might remember that catchy 1980s song "Don't Worry, Be Happy." (I bet you're singing it right now, aren't you?) You know, there's a lot of truth in that silly little song.

So many times, as mothers, we think it's our job to worry. After all, if we don't worry about the children, who will? Someone has to worry about their grades, their health, and their futures, right?

Well. . .not exactly. God tells us in His Word that worry is a profitless activity. Worrying about our children may feel like a natural thing to do as a mother, but in reality it's sin. Here's why. If we are constantly worrying about our kids, that means we're not trusting God to take care of them. It's like saying to God, "I know that You created the universe, but I'm not sure You know what's best for my children. So I'll handle these kids, God."

When you put it that way, it sounds ridiculous, doesn't it? We would never say that to God, yet each time we give in to worry, that's the message we're communicating. So do like the song says, "Don't worry, be happy." God's got you covered!

———————— MOM TO MASTER ————————

*Father, I give all of my worries to You.
I trust You with my children. I love You. Amen.*

# January 5

*All you need to remember is that God will never let you down;*
*he'll never let you be pushed past your limit; he'll always*
*be there to help you come through it.*

1 CORINTHIANS 10:13 MSG

Overwhelmed. Yes, sometimes I feel like that's my middle name—Michelle Overwhelmed Adams. I bet you share that feeling sometimes too, don't you?

Being a mom is the toughest job any of us will ever have. Sometimes the demands are so great, I'm not sure I can do it all. From laundry to parent-teacher conferences to homework help—it's a lot to pack into one day. And, as grateful as we are to be mothers, we still get stressed.

Whether you work outside the home or at home—you're busy. When you feel that overwhelming sense of "I don't think I can do one more thing today" taking over—stop! Breathe deeply and remember that God promised He'd never give you more than you can handle. Isn't that good news?

So when you're on your way to Walmart at 10 p.m. to retrieve art supplies for your child's project that is due tomorrow—don't sweat it! Don't let the stresses of the day overwhelm you. Just smile and know that God has equipped you to handle anything.

―――――――――― MOM TO MASTER ――――――――――

*Please be the Lord over the little and big things*
*in my life. Thank You, God, that I don't have*
*to feel overwhelmed today. Amen.*

# January 6

*I call on you, my God, for you will answer me;*
*turn your ear to me and hear my prayer.*
Psalm 17:6

When Allyson was only three, she encountered an eight-legged friend who wasn't so friendly. That spider left his mark—a large, black circle on my little girl's right calf. I hadn't noticed the bite that morning because Allyson had dressed herself. But shortly after I arrived at work, the phone rang.

"Michelle, you need to get Allyson to a doctor right away," urged my day care provider. "I think she's been bitten by a brown recluse."

Quickly, I drove to the day care, scooped up Allyson, and headed for the doctor's office. Panicked, I called my husband and unloaded. Then I called my mother and cried some more while Allyson sat calmly in her car seat—no tears, no fears.

Then I heard her sweet little voice say, "Don't cry, Mama. I prayed, and Jesus is taking care of me."

In all of the confusion, I had neglected to call on the Great Physician. Thankfully, Allyson hadn't forgotten. She knew who to go to, even if her spastic mother didn't.

Allyson taught me a lot that day. She showed me that prayer should be instinctive. God should be the first one we "call" in every situation. Make sure He is first on your speed dial.

—— MOM TO MASTER ——

*Lord, help me to pray without ceasing—*
*especially where my children are concerned. Amen.*

# January 7

*"For I know the plans I have for you," declares the LORD,*
*"plans to prosper you and not to harm you,*
*plans to give you hope and a future."*
JEREMIAH 29:11

Do you ever feel like you're not doing enough for your children? Sure, you enrolled them in ballet, karate, and gymnastics, but you forgot to sign them up for soccer—and now it's too late! The recording in your head begins playing, "You're a bad mother."

I hear that same recording. Sometimes it plays nonstop.

I worry that I'm not providing my children with the opportunities that will bring success. What if they don't make the middle school soccer team because I didn't sign them up for summer soccer camp? What if they miss out on those academic scholarships because I didn't spend enough time reading with them when they were little?

What if? What if? What if?

You know, God doesn't want us dwelling in the land of "What If." He wants us to trust Him with our children. He wants us to quit "what if-ing!" God has a plan for their lives— better than you could ever imagine. So relax. You're not a bad mother because you missed soccer camp sign-ups. If you've given your children to God, you've given them the best chance to succeed that you could ever give them!

—————— MOM TO MASTER ——————

*Lord, I give my children to You. Thank You,*
*God, for Your plans. Amen.*

# January 8

Are you a planner? Are you a list maker? I think most mothers have to-do lists longer than their legs. You know, my list making became so addictive that I found myself making lists during our pastor's sermon on Sunday mornings. Of course, it looked like I was taking notes, but I wasn't—I was planning out my week.

The pastor was preaching about spending more quality time with God, and I was scheduling a fifteen-minute devotional time for Him somewhere on Thursday. Pretty sad, huh?

Well, I'm happy to say that there is life after lists. I am a recovering to-do list maker. It was a gradual process, but now I can actually sit through a sermon and truly focus on what the pastor is saying.

I've found such freedom in trusting God with my daily activities. Sure, I still have reminder sticky notes scattered around my house, but now I'm not ruled by a list. I've learned there is sweet rest and freedom in trusting God with my day.

So before your feet hit the floor each morning, simply pray, "God I give this day to You." Let Him make your list. Trust me, His list is easier to accomplish and much more fulfilling.

--------- MOM TO MASTER ---------

*Lord, I commit this week to You. Help me to plan
wisely and follow Your leading. Amen.*

# January 9

*I can do all this through him who gives me strength.*
PHILIPPIANS 4:13

Remember that powerful song "I Am Woman" performed by Helen Reddy? I was just a youngster when it hit the charts, but I remember my mother belting out the lyrics: "I am strong. I am invincible. I am *woman!*"

She sang that song with such passion. I didn't understand that emotion then, but I certainly understand it now. Aren't those empowering words?

There are some days when I can't muster the courage to sing, "I am woman, hear me roar." In fact, I feel more like singing, "I'm a worm on the floor." How about you? Do you ever feel less than powerful?

Well, I've got good news, and it's even better than Helen Reddy's song. God's Word says that we can do *all* things through Christ who gives us strength. *All* means all, right? So no matter how you feel today, you can accomplish whatever is on your plate. See, you don't have to *feel* powerful to *be* powerful. God in you is all-powerful, and He will cause you to triumph. After all, you are more than a woman—you are a child of the Most High God. Now that's something to sing about!

——————— MOM TO MASTER ———————

*Thank You, Lord, that even when I feel powerless,*
*You are powerful. Help me to be courageous for You. Amen.*

# January 10

*"Be still, and know that I am God."*

PSALM 46:10

It was late, and the storm raged on.

*Where is she?*

Abby, my then nine-year-old, had gone to a theme park with her best friend. I had felt okay about letting her go—but that was before the tornado warnings had been issued. Now I just wanted her home—crouched in the hall closet with the rest of us. I wanted to know she was safe. I wanted to hug her. I wanted to protect her.

My husband, Jeff, and I prayed that God would watch over her. Still, worry filled my heart. I needed to know she was all right.

*Why don't they call?*

Just then, the front door opened. Abby was home.

In those prior moments of worry, I had heard that still, small voice saying, *"Be still, and know that I am God."* But I couldn't be still. My mind was filled with horrible thoughts and doubts. I wanted to trust God, but this was my baby!

Isn't that ironic? As moms, we're sometimes afraid to trust God with our children. But what we fail to realize is this: He loves them even more than we do. He loved them before we ever held them in our arms. We can trust Him with our kids.

––––––––––––––– MOM TO MASTER –––––––––––––––

*Thank You, Lord, for watching over my children—even when I can't be there for them. Amen.*

# January 11

*I will say of the LORD, "He is my refuge and
my fortress, my God, in whom I trust."*
PSALM 91:2

Somewhere deep within all moms lurks "Warrior Mom: Protector of Her Young." And when Warrior Mom surfaces— look out!

My Warrior Mom alter ego surfaced not long ago when a little girl began bullying my oldest daughter. I was just about to call this child's mother and give her a piece of my mind when I heard: *"Giving her a piece of your mind won't bring peace."*

Still, I longed to verbally annihilate this woman for raising such a mean-spirited daughter. But God prompted me to pray for them. Of course, that was the last thing I wanted to do. Warrior Mom isn't a prayer, she's a fighter! But I listened to that still, small voice and prayed. Do you know what happened? Abby and that little girl became friends, and later I was given the opportunity to pray with her mother during a family crisis.

If I had acted on my Warrior Mom instincts, I would never have had the opportunity to pray with this family. God didn't need Warrior Mom to handle the situation. He just needed me to follow His leading. So the next time Warrior Mom is awakened in you, remember that God has a better way.

---

## MOM TO MASTER

*Thank You, Lord, for taking care of
my children better than I can. Amen.*

# January 12

*There is a time for everything,*
*and a season for every activity under the heavens.*

ECCLESIASTES 3:1

If they gave an award for "World's Coolest Mom," my friend would win. She's nice and fun, and she throws the most elaborate birthday parties for her little girl. From games to treats to goodie bags—her parties rock!

Just before her daughter's seventh birthday, my friend was at it again. But in the midst of party planning, her daughter kept asking, "Mama, will you play with me?"

After saying no several times, my frustrated friend answered, "I can't play right now. I'm busy planning *your* birthday party. Now, isn't that more important?"

Her little girl looked up at her and thoughtfully said, "No. I'd rather cancel the party and just have you play with me. That's the best present."

Even as my friend shared the story with me, tears came to her eyes. Her daughter didn't care about an elaborate birthday bash. She simply wanted her mom's attention.

Many times in our quest to be the perfect mom, we lose sight of the big picture—our children need our love and attention more than anything. So stop trying to *plan* the perfect party games and actually *play* some games with your kids today. It's time.

——————— MOM TO MASTER ———————

*Lord, help me to make time for the most important*
*people in my life, and help me to keep things in perspective. Amen.*

# January 13

*"The LORD does not look at the things people look at.
People look at the outward appearance,
but the LORD looks at the heart."*

1 SAMUEL 16:7

I'm sure you know her. She's the mom who has a flat belly, long legs, and perfect hair. Admit it, you occasionally wish she'd fall into a cotton candy machine and gain thirty pounds. Her very presence makes you feel less than attractive, doesn't it?

Guess how I know these things? Because I know a Miss America mom too, and I feel like one of Cinderella's ugly stepsisters whenever she's around.

Comparing yourself with others is never a good thing, and it's not a God thing either. God isn't concerned with whether or not your belly is as trim as it was before childbirth. His Word says that He looks on the heart, not on your outward appearance. He's more concerned with the condition of your heart, not the cellulite on your legs. Of course, that doesn't mean we shouldn't strive to be the best we can be—both inside and out—but it certainly relieves some of that pressure to be perfect.

Give your jealousies and feelings of inadequacy to God and find your identity in Him. He loves you just the way you are—even if you're not Miss America.

——————— MOM TO MASTER ———————

*Father, help me not to compare myself with others.
Help me to see myself through Your eyes. Amen.*

# January 14

*You shall rejoice in all the good things the LORD your God
has given to you and your household.*

DEUTERONOMY 26:11

"Rejoice in the Lord always. Again I will say, rejoice!" (Philippians 4:4 NKJV). That's what the Word says, but that's not always the easiest task—am I right? What about when your child's teacher says something ugly about Junior during your parent-teacher conference? Or, how about when another driver pulls right in front of you and steals your parking spot at the grocery store? Or when your toddler knocks over your red fingernail polish, spilling it all over your bathroom rug? Not wanting to rejoice too much at that point, are you?

Daily aggravations will be a part of life until we get to heaven. That's a fact. So we just have to learn how to deal with those aggravations.

Here's the plan: today if something goes wrong—stop, pause, and praise. I don't mean you have to praise God for the aggravation. That would be kind of silly. I'm saying just praise God *in spite of* the aggravation. Before long, the "stop, pause, and praise" practice will become a habit. And that's the kind of habit worth forming! So go on, start rejoicing!

——————————— MOM TO MASTER ———————————

*Father, I repent for the times when I have been less
than thankful. I rejoice in You today. Amen.*

# January 15

*As far as the east is from the west,*
*so far has he removed our transgressions from us.*
PSALM 103:12

"So I'll put you down for two dozen chocolate chip cookies, okay?" asked the perky voice on the phone.

"Sure," I mumbled. "I can bring those on Friday."

If only she'd called after I'd had my morning diet soda, I could've come up with an excuse. But it was too late now. I'd have to produce the cookies.

Friday arrived and I still hadn't baked them. So I did what any resourceful mom would do—I drove to the Walmart bakery. After purchasing a box of cookies, I cleverly transferred them to one of my own storage containers.

Those cookies were a hit. Everyone commented on my wonderful baking ability! I just smiled. I couldn't bring myself to confess my secret. Allyson knew I hadn't baked them, but she kept quiet.

I had gotten away with it, but I'd been a poor witness for my daughter. Later that night, I apologized to Allyson, admitting my wrongdoing.

"It's okay, Mom," she said. "We all make mistakes."

Boy, that's the truth, and I surely make my share of them. I'm thankful that God wipes the slate clean each time we repent. That's good news no matter how the cookie crumbles.

——————— MOM TO MASTER ———————

*Thank You, God, for wiping the slate clean.*
*Help me to do better. Amen.*

# January 16

*For as high as the heavens are above the earth,*
*so great is his love for those who fear him.*
PSALM 103:11

Honor Day. That should be a wonderful, happy day, right? Well. . . this particular Honor Day was not so fun. It was the first Honor Day that my daughter, Abby, who was normally a straight-A student, had ever gotten a B on her report card.

Of course, we assured Abby that a B was good. Still, it was traumatic for my nine-year-old daughter. She ran off the stage in tears, and I chased after her. I hugged her and said those magic words: "Do you want to go get a chocolate doughnut and a soda?"

She nodded, and we were off.

Abby and I both lived through the first B on her report card—sad as it was. She felt bad even though we were quite proud of her 88 percent in math.

So many times as a mother, I feel like I've just received the dreaded B on my "Mom's Report Card." Ever been there? You've tried really hard to do everything right, but in the end, your best didn't feel good enough? On those days, I'm thankful that my heavenly Father is there with a spiritual chocolate doughnut and soda to cheer me up. It's nice to know that He loves us no matter what—just like we love our kids.

—————————— MOM TO MASTER ——————————

*Thank You, God, for loving me unconditionally. Amen.*

# January 17

*Trust in the LORD with all your heart and lean not on your
own understanding; in all your ways submit to him,
and he will make your paths straight.*

When I was eight years old in vacation Bible school, I memorized the above scripture. At the time, my motivation for learning this important passage was a blue ribbon. Ahhh. . .the lure of a shiny blue ribbon! Now, more than twenty years later, I've lost that ribbon, but those words are still imprinted on my heart. They pop into my mind at the times when I need them the most.

Today, as the mother of two little girls, I try to motivate my children to memorize scripture too. We recite verses on the way to school every morning, which has become a fun way to start the day. Sometimes we try to see how fast we can say the verses. Other times we make up songs with them. With every recitation, we're putting more of God's Word in our hearts.

As a mom, that's so comforting to me, because I know that those memory verses will pop into their minds whenever they need them most. God's Word will be there for them even when I can't be—and that's even better than a shiny blue ribbon!

——————— MOM TO MASTER ———————

*Thank You, God, for Your Word.
Please help my children to love Your Word
even more than I do. Amen.*

# January 18

> *"Martha, Martha," the Lord answered, "you are worried and upset about many things, but few things are needed— or indeed only one. Mary has chosen what is better, and it will not be taken away from her."*
>
> LUKE 10:41–42

Do you remember when you were pregnant? In the midst of weird food cravings, swollen ankles, and raging hormones, you spent time dreaming of your baby. You wondered things like: *What will he or she look like? What will be his or her first words? Will he or she be healthy? and How will I ever care for a tiny baby?*

I think every mother worries. It seems like the natural thing to do. Most first-time moms worry that they won't be equipped with the appropriate parenting skills needed to be a good mom. Then the baby comes—and with it, a whole new set of worries. As the child grows, the worries grow too. Sometimes, the worries can become almost suffocating.

When I feel overwhelmed with the worries that accompany motherhood, I realize I've forgotten to figure God into the equation. With God, all things are possible—even raising good kids in a mixed-up world. God doesn't expect mothers to have all the answers, but He does expect us to go to Him for those answers. So if worries are consuming your thoughts—go to God. He not only has the answers, He *is* the answer!

--- MOM TO MASTER ---

*God, I trust You with my children, and I give You my worries. Amen.*

# January 19

*Jesus answered, "I am the way and the truth and the life."*
JOHN 14:6

Do you ever get lost? I am what you might call "directionally challenged." My children think it's pretty funny, seeing their old mom talking to herself in the front seat, repeating directions in chant-like manner, and praying quite a lot. Still, it seems that no matter how I try, I get lost on a regular basis. Of course, in my defense, Texas *is* a big place, and you can never return the same way you arrived. It's never a matter of simply reversing the directions.

Getting lost used to really frustrate and frighten me. Now I consider it more of a fun adventure. I find that something good usually comes from it. For example, recently when I lost my way, I discovered this great garden shop with the most beautiful iron bench. Now that bench adorns our yard—it was meant to be! Other times, these extended trips in the SUV give us more family time—precious moments to laugh and share.

You see, it's all in the perspective. I no longer worry when I'm lost. I just enjoy the journey. Life is the same way. There's no sense worrying your way through each day—just enjoy the trip. After all, if we know Jesus as our Lord and Savior, we're on the right road because He is the Way!

———————— MOM TO MASTER ————————

*Thank You, God, for guiding my every step. Amen.*

# January 20

*. . .fixing our eyes on Jesus, the pioneer and perfecter of faith.*
Hebrews 12:2

When we were trying to break Abby from her pacifier, this verse took on new meaning for me. I'd never fully understood the meaning of the word *fixed* until I witnessed Abby's fixation on her pacifier. We thought we had thrown away every one of them. I'd pitched at least fifteen of them, but still Abby found the last one. There it sat atop her dresser, slightly hidden by a basket of hair bows. When I walked into her room, she was standing on her rocking chair, reaching toward her "pacy," and staring intently at her prized possession.

I picked her up, grabbed the pacifier, and quickly tossed it into the kitchen sink. I didn't think Abby had seen me, but she had. For the next hour, she stood beneath the sink, reaching upward, crying for her pacifier. Her eyes were fixed. In fact, they were fixed until she finally fell asleep right there on the kitchen floor.

Her determination really spoke to me. I thought, *If only I could be as determined to keep my eyes fixed on Jesus as Abby is to keep her eyes fixed on that pacifier, my faith would not falter.* Even today that image of Abby's pursuit of her pacifier stays with me, reminding me to stay fixed on the Father.

—— MOM TO MASTER ——

*Lord, help me to keep my eyes fixed on You. Amen.*

# January 21

*Dear children, do not let anyone lead you astray.*
1 JOHN 3:7

Do you ever worry about the friends your children are making? I do. I often wonder, *Will they be good influences on my children? Will they hurt my children? Do they know Jesus as their Lord and Savior? Will they be lifelong, trustworthy friends?*

While I don't know the answers to all of these questions, I do know one thing—Jesus will be their lifelong Friend. They will always be able to count on Him. He will come through for them time and time again. He will stand by them no matter what. How do I know these things? Because He's been there for me when nobody else was.

I discovered early in life that friends sometimes let you down—even your best friends—because they're human. If you put your hope in friends, disappointment and hurt are inevitable. But God is a sure thing.

I realize that I can't pick my children's friends, and I know that I can't protect them from the hurt that comes from broken friendships and disloyalty. But there are two things I can do—I can teach them about Jesus, and I can pray that the Lord sends them godly friends. You can do the same for your kids. You can start today.

———————— MOM TO MASTER ————————

*Lord, please send my children good friends.*
*I'm thankful that You are their best*
*Friend and mine. Amen.*

# January 22

*"Love each other as I have loved you."*
JOHN 15:12

"Stop it!" Allyson wailed.

"You stop it, stupid head!" Abby screamed.

And on and on it went. . .

There are days when I wonder if my girls will ever be friends. Sure, they love each other because they have to—they're sisters. But will they ever *like* each other?

I think all moms wonder that same thing—especially after witnessing an hour or two of nonstop fighting between their children.

Then, just about the time I've given up and think my kids are doomed to be enemies, the Lord gives me a glimpse of their true feelings. Another child comes against one of them, and the other sister steps up in her defense—just like that! Or, I find them asleep, side by side on the living room floor. That's a scene that always makes me smile.

The Lord knew what He was doing when He put our families together. He knew that our kids would fight, and He knew they'd need each other. And here's another comforting thought—God loves your children even more than you do, and He desires for them to be buddies too. So the next time your children are bickering, don't get discouraged. Just thank the Lord for His love in your home.

—————— MOM TO MASTER ——————

*Lord, thank You for my children.*
*Please help them to appreciate each other more. Amen.*

# January 23

*Many are the plans in a person's heart,*
*but it is the LORD's purpose that prevails.*
PROVERBS 19:21

Stage mothers. They aren't bad people. They're just overzealous. A few years ago, I was in charge of the annual elementary talent show at my daughters' school, and I encountered moms who verbally assaulted me over their children's placement in the program. (Did I mention it was a volunteer position?) At the time, I couldn't understand their irrational behavior. I thought, *These moms must be nuts!* Little did I know that I also had a nutty stage mother inside *me*.

Later, while watching my daughters' gymnastics team practice, I made casual conversation with another mom until she huffed and puffed that my daughters were taking too many turns, causing her daughter to miss practice time. Immediately, the stage mother in me arose. I should've let it go, but I didn't. She may have huffed and puffed, but I blew her house down.

At once, I understood why those moms had attacked me over the talent show details. Their abominable behavior had been motivated by an intense love for their children—same as mine. The only way to control the stage mom in all of us is to realize that God is the best director. He doesn't need our input. He has a starring role for our children—if we'll only take our places backstage.

——————— MOM TO MASTER ———————

*Lord, please direct my children in all things. Amen.*

# January 24

Do you know that worry never changed a single thing? Worry never turned a single thing around. (Well, it's turned a lot of hair prematurely gray, but that's about it.)

You know, worriers are called "worrywarts." Think about that—a wart isn't exactly a beautiful sight. No, it's an eyesore. What do we do with warts? We put medicated drops on them and make them disappear. That's exactly what we should do with our worrywart personalities—make them disappear.

While there's no magic "worrywart potion" on the market, you have easy access to one you might not have considered—God's Word! It will obliterate worry if you'll only believe it. If you truly believe that "No weapon formed against you [or your children] shall prosper" (Isaiah 54:17 NKJV), then you shouldn't waste time worrying about unforeseen tragedies. God has got you covered! Isn't that comforting? Doesn't that make the worrywart inside of you shrink and wither away? It should!

God must have known we'd worry. I think that's why He put so many scriptures about worry in His Word. Find those today and meditate on them. Worry never changed anything, but God's Word always does.

---

## MOM TO MASTER

*Father, I give my worries to You. Amen.*

# January 25

LORD, *I know that people's lives are not their own;*
*it is not for them to direct their steps.*
JEREMIAH 10:23

We had just moved cross-country, and now we had to find a school for Abby, who was starting kindergarten in the fall. Several of my coworkers suggested a Christian school nearby. My husband and I met the principal and completed all of the necessary paperwork for Abby's enrollment—still, I wasn't sure. At my urging, we also investigated the public elementary school, just minutes from our home.

Abby didn't care where she attended school as long as she could take her Little Mermaid lunchbox. But Jeff and I worried. We didn't want to make a wrong decision. We prayed about which school would be best for our girls, but neither of us felt that we'd received a definite answer from God. I was hoping the clouds would part and Jesus would utter the right choice. That never happened, so we went with our gut instinct and chose the public school. It was a wonderful decision, although at the time, we weren't sure.

I often worry when we have to make big decisions concerning our children. I'm so afraid I'll stray from the path that God has for us, but you know what I've discovered? Even if we stray, God finds us.

## MOM TO MASTER

*Father, I trust You with all my decisions. Amen.*

# January 26

*"I, the LORD, have called you in righteousness;*
*I will take hold of your hand."*

ISAIAH 42:6

Even as they grew, I instinctively grabbed Abby's and Allyson's hands when we crossed the street. At ages ten and eight, my girls did not think this was cool, but I couldn't help myself. By taking their hands, I felt I was protecting them from traffic, strangers, and all other dangers. I bet you do the same for your children. As I often told my daughters—it's a mom thing.

I was reaching for their hands until they left the nest. But you know what? That's not such a bad habit. In fact, if I could get in the habit of reaching out to God and taking hold of His hand more often in my day-to-day activities, I'd be farther down the road in my faith walk.

I'm not sure why I neglect to reach for His hand when I'm crossing the busy streets of life. I guess, like my daughters, I think I'm mature enough to handle it on my own. Or, as my mother would say, I get "too big for my britches." I'm so thankful that we have a loving heavenly Father who reaches down to take our hands when we need Him the most. If you haven't taken hold of God's hand in a while, why don't you grab it today?

———————— MOM TO MASTER ————————

*Father, I take hold of Your hand today. Amen.*

# January 27

*Look in the scroll of the LORD and read.*
ISAIAH 34:16

Just saying the words, "It's devotion time," used to make my girls roll their eyes. In a world of PlayStation, Blu-rays, iPods, and computers—keeping our kids' attention on what's important is a tough task. So we try to make our devotion time into a question and answer game. This ensures our children will pay attention because no one wants to lose the Bible Quiz game!

This game tactic works for our family devotion time, but getting our children to have their personal devotional time is even tougher. That worries me. You know what else worries me? I once heard a preacher say, "Your children may not be reading their Bible regularly, but you can bet they are reading you." Ugh! I sure hope they weren't reading me the other day when that lady took my parking spot at Walmart.

As you know, we're not supposed to worry. So I gave my worries to God over this situation. Daily, I asked Him to help me live out my faith. If my life was an open book before my girls, I wanted to make sure it was full of God's Word. How about you? Encourage your kids to read God's Word and then live your life according to His Word. That's a one-two punch against the devil!

—————— MOM TO MASTER ——————

*Father, help me to live out Your Word*
*before my children. Amen.*

# January 28

Did you ever have a pet rock? Those of a certain age all did. I remember painting them, gluing funny eyes on top, and naming each one. Crazy, isn't it? And can you believe that pet rocks are actually making a comeback? My girls are loving them! Of course, I know it's just a phase they'll soon outgrow. When the next fad rolls around, they'll throw their pet rocks into their desk drawers, never to be seen again.

That's how fads are—totally hot one minute and completely forgotten the next. In a world of fad diets, fad fashions, and fad everything else, I want to make sure that my children don't think of God as a passing fad. I know you wish the same for your kids. So how can we ensure that our children will view God as a steadfast part of their lives? If only there were a magic pill we could give them that would guarantee they'd love God until the end of time.

Well, there's no pill to give them, but we do have God's Word to feed them. We can also let our children see us loving God and His Word. Most importantly, we can pray that our kids will always love God—the real Rock.

--- MOM TO MASTER ---

*Father, help my children to love You more*
*than anything or anyone else. Amen.*

# January 29

It amazes me sometimes just how much I worry. The Bible clearly says to cast all of your cares on Him, yet I choose to keep those cares to myself. By nature, I'm a fixer; I'm a doer. And sometimes that works against me. While my self-sufficient nature enables me to get a lot accomplished, it also causes me to worry over things that I should hand over to God.

Are you a worrier too? To some extent, I think all moms are worriers. Worrying just seems to be part of our job description, right underneath the "take care of your children until you die" part. While worrying may come naturally to you, it's not God's will for your life. He wants you to live in perfect peace, and worrying is a peace destroyer. It's the opposite of peace. So why not give your worries to God today?

It won't be easy at first, but you can do it. Here's the plan: The very minute that your thoughts turn into worries, say aloud, "I cast (fill in the blank) on God right now." Pretty soon, casting your cares will become a habit and worrying will be a thing of the past.

--------- MOM TO MASTER ---------

*Father, transform my thinking.*
*Help me to quit worrying and simply*
*trust You with every part of my life. Amen.*

# January 30

*"Therefore do not worry about tomorrow,*
*for tomorrow will worry about itself."*
MATTHEW 6:34

"No worries."

I've been told that is a common Aussie expression. Well, if that's true, I'd say those folks down under are right on top of things. What a great attitude! If only I could look in the face of trouble and say, "No worries." Instead, I usually list all of my worries and wallow around in them for a while.

You know, as Christians, we really should be able to look in the face of trouble and say, "No worries." After all, if we're really trusting our heavenly Father, we won't have any worries. Now, I didn't say we wouldn't have any problems. As long as we're on this earth, there will be trouble. God tells us that in His Word, but He also tells us not to fret over them. That means it's actually possible to encounter stress and problems and still have no worries. That should be our goal.

If we could live like that, we'd be better wives, better mothers, better daughters, better friends, better Christians—better everything! Life would simply be better if we stopped worrying. Worrying is a time stealer, so put worry in its place! The next time you encounter trouble, say, "No worries!" and mean it!

——————— MOM TO MASTER ———————

*Father, help me to have a "no worries"*
*attitude from now on! Amen.*

# January 31

*Plans fail for lack of counsel, but with many advisers they succeed.*

PROVERBS 15:22

Vacation is supposed to be a fun time, right? But if you're a planner or a list maker like me, even vacations can stress you out and cause worry.

Once, we took our girls to Disney World in Orlando. I ordered the free vacation planning video. I purchased the *Disney World Vacation Planning Guide*. I visited numerous Disney World websites, collecting research. I even called six different families who had recently been to Disney World and interrogated them.

While research and planning have merit, I went overboard. I became so involved that I began overanalyzing every decision about the trip. It stole my joy. Instead of eagerly anticipating our family vacation, I became burdened with the responsibility of planning the "best Disney vacation ever." I drove everyone in our house totally nuts! Finally, my husband (seeing that I was on overload) hired a travel agent to plan the vacation for us. Whew! It was off my shoulders, and I could rest in the fact that an expert was on the job.

Well, we have a life expert *always* on the job—God. So the next time you get overloaded with the cares of the world, call on Him. He will take care of everything, and He doesn't even charge a commission!

——————— MOM TO MASTER ———————

*Father, I give all of my "to-dos" to You. Amen.*

# February 1

*Satisfy us in the morning with your unfailing love.*
PSALM 90:14

Let's face it. There are days when it's tough to show love to your children. Of course, you always love them—they're your kids! But if you're like me, there are days when you don't particularly love everything about them.

We had one of those days when my in-laws were in town and I had asked the girls to be on their best behavior. That *so* did not happen. They fought nonstop. At one point, Ally actually had Abby in a headlock. I threatened, spanked, grounded, and hollered until I was totally defeated. By day's end, I was sure I had to be the worst mother in the world.

As I kissed my girls good night, I wanted so badly to hit the rewind button and start the day over again. Unfortunately, that was impossible. As I moped down the hallway to my bedroom, I took heart in one thing—God does have a rewind button! He lets us start over every time we fail. So the next time your children are acting less than lovely and your love walk has become more of a crawl, ask God to hit the rewind button.

—————————— MOM TO MASTER ——————————

*Lord, help me to love my children even when they act unlovely.*
*Help me to love them like You love me. Amen.*

# February 2

*"My grace is sufficient for you,
for my power is made perfect in weakness."*

2 CORINTHIANS 12:9

It's the mother's curse. I'm sure your mom has used it on you before: "I hope you have a child just like you when you grow up!" And chances are—you did! In my case, I had two. You know what's interesting about raising children that are exactly like you? You tend to see all of your faults in them. It's as if there is a gigantic magnifying glass, constantly revealing their weaknesses, which happen to be the same weaknesses that you struggle with on a daily basis.

This, of course, is the breeding ground for fighting, resentment, and hurt. So as mothers, we have to break that "mother's curse" and celebrate our children. We need to smash that magnifying glass that focuses in on their flaws and love our kids—weaknesses and all. Ask the Lord to help you see your children as God sees them. And ask Him to help you see yourself through His eyes too.

In other words, give your kids and yourself a break. Don't expect them to be perfect, and don't expect perfection from yourself either. God loves you and your kids—flaws and all. Remember, His power is made perfect through our weakness.

------- MOM TO MASTER -------

*Lord, help me to nurture my children's strengths and
pray over their weaknesses. I give them to You. Amen.*

# February 3

*God is love. Whoever lives in love lives in God, and God in them. This is how love is made complete among us.*

1 John 4:16–17

Remember that popular '70s song "Love Will Keep Us Together"? I was in grade school when it hit the radio airwaves, and I can remember singing it at recess with my gal pals. We knew every word by heart. Well, there's a lot of truth in that title, especially where our families are concerned.

Life gets complicated, and families fall apart. It happens. It even happens to Christian families. It may have happened in your own family. But I'm here to tell you that love is the answer. When nothing else will, love will keep your family together. No, I'm not talking about that fair-weather kind of love. I'm talking about the God kind of love—an everlasting, unconditional love from heaven.

So even if your teenager has left home or turned his back on God, love will draw him back. Not the sermons you've preached nor the rules you've enforced—only love will turn your situation around. Let God's love live big in you. Let God's love be the superglue in your family, binding you with one another for a lifetime. Live the love and reap the results.

## MOM TO MASTER

*Father, I ask that Your love flow through me to my children. Amen.*

# February 4

*"Love each other as I have loved you."*
JOHN 15:12

"You love Allyson more because she's a blond like you!" Abby, then nine, screamed at me as she slammed the door.

Following Abby's logic, that statement would've been inaccurate because I'm only blond thanks to Clairol. (I don't even remember my natural color, but I think it's closer to Abby's brown locks.) At any rate, I had a problem that ran much deeper than the color of my roots.

I was baffled, befuddled, bewildered, and all those other *b* words too.

I had always tried to treat my children equally. I certainly didn't love one daughter more than the other. I thought I had the "no favoritism" thing down. Apparently, that was not true, as Abby had so eloquently let me know.

As I pondered Abby's feelings of mistreatment, I checked into "Hurt Hotel." Indignant, I huffed, *How could she say such a thing?* Then I took a "guilt getaway" and said a few "Woe is me, I'm a bad mom" mantras. Finally, I hit my knees in desperation. That's where I found answers and insight that gave me hope for a better tomorrow. I may not always get it right where my kids are concerned, but if my heart is right, God will cover me. He'll help me to show them just how much I love them. He'll do the same for you.

———— MOM TO MASTER ————

*Father, help me to love my children*
*like You love me. Amen.*

# February 5

*Knowledge puffs up while love builds up.*
1 CORINTHIANS 8:1

There should be a retreat reserved for all mothers of "tween" girls. As it turns out, once a girl hits age ten, mothers are stupid. I know this firsthand because I became an official member of the Stupid Mom Club. It's not a membership I like very much, and I constantly tried to prove that I don't belong in the club. I found myself saying things like: "Do you know that I was on the honor roll all through school? I never even got a B until high school!" Or, "I am three times your age, and I know more than you'll ever know!"

Ever used that one?

Of course, all of that self-elevating talk accomplished absolutely nothing. I could talk until my lips fell off, but my words didn't change how Abby viewed me. God's Word, though, could! Proverbs 31:28 says, "Her children arise and call her blessed." Oh yeah! I was living for that day, how about you? During your prayer time, say, "Lord, I thank You that my children arise and call me blessed," and watch your kids' attitudes change. Soon, we'll all be out of the Stupid Mom Club. That's a promise!

--- MOM TO MASTER ---

*Father, give me patience to love my children—even when they don't treat me nicely. Help me not to take it personally. Amen.*

# February 6

*"I have loved you with an everlasting love."*
JEREMIAH 31:3

Looking down into the face of my first newborn baby, I couldn't imagine loving anyone more than I loved her at that moment. She was everything I had dreamed of during those nine months of pregnancy. Jeff and I did all of the annoying baby talk and silly noises that all new parents do. We were absolutely captivated by her every sound, move, and facial expression. We adored her!

So when I discovered I was pregnant with Baby Number Two on the eve before Abby's first birthday, I wondered, *Will I ever love another child as much as I love Abby?* I was worried. I just couldn't fathom loving another child as much as I loved "Baby Abbers," as we affectionately nicknamed her.

Then Allyson Michelle Adams came into this world on August 15, 1994—bald and beautiful. I looked into her sweet face and fell in love all over again. Jeff and I discovered that we could love another baby just as much as our first. We always tell our girls, "You are *both* our favorites!" Do you know that is exactly how God sees us? He doesn't love you or me more than anyone else—we're all His favorites! Meditate on that today and embrace the Father's love.

———————— MOM TO MASTER ————————

*Father, help me to accept and celebrate*
*Your love for me. Amen.*

# February 7

*Love is patient.*
1 CORINTHIANS 13:4

Have you ever really meditated on the Love Chapter—1 Corinthians 13? I had to memorize the entire passage when I was a member of our church's high school Bible quizzing team. Even now, years later, I can still quote the entire chapter. I wish I lived those verses as well as I can recite them.

You know which one really gets me? Love is patient. Uh-oh! Patience is one of those virtues that you admire in others but you're sure is not an option for you, right? This is especially true when it comes to our kids. It seems they know exactly which buttons to push. If you're in a hurry, Junior will lose your keys. If you're expecting company, your daughter is sure to spill nail polish on the carpet. If you're on the telephone, every child suddenly needs your undivided attention.

Let's face it—moms get a patience test every day. I've often failed that test. That's why I'm so thankful that God offers "make-up exams." Through His Word and His unconditional love, we don't have to fail those patience tests anymore. The Lord can help us walk in love—even patience—if we'll only ask for His intervention. So ask Him today.

—————————— MOM TO MASTER ——————————

*Father, fill me with more of Your love,*
*and help me to have more patience—*
*especially with my family. Amen.*

# February 8

*Do not let any unwholesome talk come out of your mouths,*
*but only what is helpful for building others up according*
*to their needs, that it may benefit those who listen.*
EPHESIANS 4:29

Have you ever been around a parrot? I've never owned an actual parrot, but I do have two little "parrots" running around my house. Abby and Allyson repeat much of what I say—good and bad. I bet you have some parrots in your house too.

Recently, my youngest daughter overheard one of my "girl-friend gab sessions" and later repeated something I'd said. In her cute little eight-year-old voice, she said, "Bite my hiney," to her sister! Goodness, it had sounded so harmless when I'd said it, or had it? Either way, my parrot had repeated something that was what the Bible might call "unwholesome or unlovely talk." I was busted!

This parrot episode has made me watch my speech a lot more carefully, looking for unlovely talk and asking the Holy Spirit to keep a watch over my words. It's not only about setting a good example for my children; it's also about truly living love in every area of my life. Catty remarks, unwholesome talk, and sarcasm really have no place in our conversations—not if we're really living the God kind of love. So walk and talk love, and give your parrots something worth repeating.

―――――――――― MOM TO MASTER ――――――――――

*Father, put a watch over my mouth.*
*Help me to walk and talk love. Amen.*

# February 9

*[Love] always protects, always trusts,*
*always hopes, always perseveres.*
1 CORINTHIANS 13:7

One time, our pastor preached a sermon I'll never forget. His topic? Love. I've heard hundreds of sermons about love, but I'd never heard it preached quite like this. He said, "Love always believes the best in others."

Yikes! Just when I thought my love walk was shaping up, he zapped me! I wrote it down this way in my journal: "Love always believes the best—especially in my children."

It's a tough world out there and getting tougher all the time. Our children are faced with many challenges. Sometimes we're the only ones believing the best in them. We're the only ones cheering them on to victory. We're the only ones making them feel special. Sometimes we're the only ones on their side.

Believing the best in our children doesn't mean turning our heads when they act inappropriately. Rather, it means giving them the benefit of the doubt. If they say they turned in their homework and yet you receive a note that says they didn't, you believe them, assuming the teacher has misplaced it. Then pray with your child that the teacher will find the missing homework. You know, if we believe the best in our children, we'll get the best from our children.

---

### MOM TO MASTER

*Father, thank You for my precious children.*
*Help me to always believe the best in them. Amen.*

# February 10

*Follow God's example. . .and walk in the way of love.*
Ephesians 5:1–2

Valentine's Day is just around the corner. Department stores are splashed in red and pink. Radio stations are playing sappy love songs. And heart-shaped boxes of chocolates are calling your name! Love is in the air, so why not celebrate it?

If you're married, schedule a sitter and steal some time away with your mate. Drink flavored coffee at your favorite café or pop some popcorn and rent *An Affair to Remember*. Just enjoy each other. If you're a single mom, don't let Valentine's Day be a sad holiday for you. Instead, celebrate the love you share with your children! Take the kids out for a night of bowling or catch a kids' flick together. Tight on cash? Simply stay home and read funny poetry books or play fun board games as a family. Just spend quality time with each other.

This is also a great time to send a special note to your grown children, letting them know how much they mean to you. Go ahead. You have an excuse to be mushy! It's Valentine's Day, so spread the love, share the love, and celebrate the love! And, by all means, eat a few pieces of chocolate too!

---

## MOM TO MASTER

*Lord, thank You for placing such wonderful people in my life.*
*May they always know this week—and always—*
*how much I love them. Amen.*

# February 11

*Love is patient, love is kind.*
1 CORINTHIANS 13:4

It never failed. Whenever I got on the telephone, suddenly my children needed me. It was almost instantaneous. As soon as the receiver went to my ear, my daughters appeared. It was one of those "mom phenomena."

One afternoon while I was on a long-distance phone call with my best friend, the clamoring for my attention began. One after another, my girls interrupted. All at once, I lost it. I put my hand over the phone (so that my best friend couldn't hear me holler), and I shot out some verbal bullets. It was ugly.

Both daughters retreated to their bedrooms to sulk and recover from my outburst. As I hung up the phone, I realized how unlovely I had acted. The Bible says that love is patient and kind, and I hadn't been either of those things.

Funny, I had practiced patience and kindness all day long with friends, coworkers, and strangers, but I couldn't show my children the same love aspects. I repented to God, and then I asked for my daughters' forgiveness. It's easy to act ugly, but it takes work to walk in love—especially with our children. Love is a choice. Choose to show your family love today.

## —— MOM TO MASTER ——

*Father, help me to walk in love—especially
where my children are concerned.
Help me to be more like You. Amen.*

# February 12

*I trust in God's unfailing love for ever and ever.*
PSALM 52:8

We use the word *love* an awful lot. "I *love* your new purse," or "I *love* that dress on you," or "I *love* Hershey's Kisses." I bet if you kept track, you'd find yourself using the word *love* more than a dozen times each day. Because we use it so much, *love* has lost some of its punch, some of its luster, some of its meaning.

But real love—the God kind of love—is so much more than the "love" that has become so clichéd in our culture. The God kind of love is an everlasting love. His love stretches as far as the east is from the west. His love is deeper than the deepest ocean. His love is higher than the highest mountain. His love covers a multitude of sins. His love is unconditional. His love is truly awesome!

Now, that's the kind of love I want to walk in. How about you? I want to receive the Father's love, and I want to extend His love to others—especially to my children. As moms, we should have the aroma of love. So if your love aroma is a little funky (like that green cheese in the back of the fridge), ask God to refresh your love today!

—————————— MOM TO MASTER ——————————

*Lord, I pray that Your love—the real thing—
shines in me and through me. Amen.*

# February 13

*In the beginning God created the heavens and the earth.*
Genesis 1:1

"Love makes the world go round." I've heard that expression all of my life, but I've never really pondered its meaning. . .until this week. I flippantly said it, and my ten-year-old gave me a blank stare and uttered, "Huh? What does that mean?"

Here's what I concluded after a few serious moments of reflection. The world's kind of love doesn't make the world go round. In fact, the kind of shallow, temporary love the world has to offer makes the world go crazy, not round. But the God kind of love—*that* is the kind that makes the world go round. It keeps it spinning when nothing else will.

If your world is no longer going round, if your household is less than heaven on earth, if you've forgotten what it feels like to experience unconditional love, run into the Father's arms right now. Your heavenly Father longs for the opportunity to "love on you" in the same way that you adore loving on your children. So spend some time with the Father today. His love not only makes the world go round, His love *created* the world! Awesome!

———————————— MOM TO MASTER ————————————

*Father, I want more of Your love. Wrap me in Your arms today
that I might experience the kind of love that truly
makes the world go round. Amen.*

# February 14

*"Love your neighbor as yourself."*
LEVITICUS 19:18

Love is a verb, but sometimes we forget that in today's society. Since February is the month we celebrate love, I thought it might be nice if we activated love in our various communities. Here's the plan for "Activation Love." Do at least one "love in action" activity each day for the rest of this month. It doesn't have to be a big thing. Small gestures such as calling a relative just to say "I love you" count.

Here are some other ideas to get you started: Enlist your kiddos' help and volunteer at a nearby soup kitchen one Saturday. Go grocery shopping for the church shut-ins and deliver the bags of food as a family. Buy some dog and cat food, and drop it off at your local humane society or animal shelter. Begin a letter-writing campaign this week, and write letters of appreciation to the president, the servicemen and women of this nation, the pastoral staff at your church, the teachers at your children's school, etc.

You'll be surprised how much your kids will enjoy "Activation Love." You'll be doing good works on behalf of the Father, and you'll be teaching your children that love truly is an active verb. So go for it! Put your love to work!

————————— MOM TO MASTER —————————

*Lord, help me to love others the way*
*You love me. Amen.*

# February 15

*Oh, how I love your law! I meditate on it all day long.*
Psalm 119:97

Don't you just love *The Grinch Who Stole Christmas* by Dr. Seuss? Do you remember the scene where the Grinch's heart grows ten times bigger? Then the Grinch who once wore a scowl wears a big Grinchy smile! Doesn't that make you feel warm and fuzzy inside?

Well, that scene is played out in my life every time I spend time in God's Word. Many mornings I wake up like the Grinch, scowling as I try to find a cup of coffee to revive me. I stumble through the morning, saying as little as possible, until I finally get time alone with God. During those moments, my heart grows ten times bigger in order to make room for all of my Father's love. After I get my "love fill-up," I'm ready to face my family again and give out the love I've just received.

As moms, we can't run on empty love tanks. We are expected to give love all day long, so if we don't have a full supply, we'll start to resemble old Mr. Grinch. If your love tank is low today, pull up to the Word of God and spend some time with the Lord. His love is waiting for you, and it's premium stuff! Ready? Begin fueling.

————————— MOM TO MASTER —————————

*Lord, fill up my love tank until it is overflowing. Amen.*

# February 16

*A gentle answer turns away wrath.*

PROVERBS 15:1

I once saw a T-shirt with the printing LOVE IS MY FINAL ANSWER on it. I thought that was pretty good. Think about it. When you answer with love, you give strife no place to go.

There was a time that Abby wanted to go boating with her friend. Normally we would say yes to this request, but this was a holiday weekend. And, according to the news reports, there would be many alcohol-filled boaters on the lake. We just didn't have peace about it, so we told Abby, "No, not this time."

Abby *really* wanted to go, so she began retaliating in a big way. It was ugly. As she huffed and puffed, I decided to try out the "love answer." So I said, "Abby, honey, we love you too much to let something bad happen to you. There will be lots of drunken boaters out there today, and we just aren't willing to take that chance. You are too precious to us." To my surprise, she was okay with that answer. While she was disappointed that she couldn't go to the lake, she understood our reasons and resumed normal behavior. Wow! I didn't even have to raise my voice or threaten to ground her!

Let love be your final answer today. It really works!

––––––––––––––– MOM TO MASTER –––––––––––––––

*Lord, help me to make love my final
answer in every situation. Amen.*

# February 17

*Show me the wonders of your great love.*

PSALM 17:7

Do you have unstoppable love? Do you have the kind of love that overflows to everyone around you? I wish I could answer yes to those questions, but I'd have to say, "Not really." But that is my desire.

A firefighter at our church recently shared with us that firefighters use a piece of equipment called a deluge nozzle for really big fires. This nozzle puts out fifteen hundred gallons of water per minute. Now that's a lot of water!

Wouldn't it be neat if they could invent a deluge love nozzle, guaranteed to put out fifteen hundred gallons of love per minute? Then, each time I feel impatience, irritability, or frustration rising up inside of me, I could just reach for the deluge love nozzle and spew some love around. I can hear it now—I'd start to holler, and my kids would say, "Hurry! Get Mom her deluge love nozzle!"

Well, there may not be a deluge love nozzle in existence, but we have something even better—Jesus Christ. He's our secret weapon of love. And He can cause you to spew more love than even a deluge nozzle. So call on Him today. He has enough love to totally soak your family.

—————— MOM TO MASTER ——————

*Lord, thank You for being my secret love weapon.*
*Help me to share Your love today. Amen.*

# February 18

*[Love] bears all things.*
1 CORINTHIANS 13:7 NKJV

"Mommy, guess what Abby did?" Allyson asked in a sing-songy voice.

My then blond-haired, blue-eyed, six-year-old couldn't wait to tattle on her big sister. She was almost bursting with the news, hoping to get Abby grounded for her misdeed.

"I don't know what Abby did, but before you tattle on your sister, you'd better be sure it's worth it," I interjected. "Because I ground the one who is exposed, *and* I ground the tattler."

Allyson's eyes didn't look quite as bright as she pondered the temptation to tattle. Slowly, she retreated to her bedroom. Her desire to expose her sister had passed, and I was glad. Tattling is a bad habit that extends way beyond childhood—as adults we call it gossiping. Both are despicable in God's eyes.

Tattling and gossiping are roadblocks in many of our love walks. Exposing each other's shortcomings and failures is the exact opposite of love, because love bears all things. The word *bears* in that sentence means "covers." So the next time your little tattlers run up to you with some juicy information about another sibling, turn 1 Corinthians 13:7 loose on them. Your words may not be effective, but God's Word packs quite a punch! Tattling and gossiping have no place in our homes. Let love root them out!

--------- MOM TO MASTER ---------

*Lord, help me to raise my children to walk in love. Amen.*

# February 19

*I trust in God's unfailing love for ever and ever.*
PSALM 52:8

Sometimes it's harder to walk in love than others. Can I get an "Amen!" on that? There are days when my love walk has quite a limp. On those days, I often wonder how God can still love me. Ever wondered that yourself? I'll think back over something I've said or done that was less than lovely, and my insides cringe.

This is especially true when it comes to my children. Of all the people in my life, I want to make sure I show my kids that unconditional, always-there-for-you kind of love. So when I fail to accomplish that goal, my heart hurts. But it's in those times that I sense the Father's presence in a big way. I can literally feel His love wrapping around me like a cozy sweater.

No matter how many times I fail, God still loves me. And, on those days when I know I'm definitely not in the running for Mother of the Year, that's good to know. God loves us even more than we love our children. In fact, the Word says that we're the apple of His eye. I like that. So the next time your love walk becomes more of a crawl, remember—God adores you.

--- MOM TO MASTER ---

*Heavenly Father, thank You for loving me
even when I am less than loving. Amen.*

# February 20

*"I have loved you with an everlasting love."*
JEREMIAH 31:3

"I love you more than a million red M&Ms."

That's one of our favorite lines from a contemporary movie. It's what the daughter says to her mom in the beginning of *What a Girl Wants.*

My daughters and I have come up with a few of our own "Love you more thans. . . ." Here are our top five:

1.  I love you more than a bag of Hershey's Kisses.
2.  I love you more than a fluffy, fuzzy puppy.
3.  I love you more than McDonald's french fries.
4.  I love you more than shopping at Limited Too.
5.  I love you more than a snow cone with extra flavoring.

This is such a fun game to play on road trips. (It's especially effective to stop petty fights in the backseat, as well as discontinue comments such as "Mom, she's touching me!") Also, it's a great way to say "I love you" in a nonmushy, kid-friendly way. As my girls inch toward those preteen years, they tend to become embarrassed by just about everything—especially affection-showing parents.

So find lots of new ways to say you love your children today. Then have each child come up with a new way to express love to our heavenly Father. There's nothing quite like a day of love.

—————— MOM TO MASTER ——————

*Lord, I love You more than _____. Amen.*

# February 21

*[Love] is not self-seeking.*
1 CORINTHIANS 13:5

Love means putting others' needs and desires before your own. Of course, as moms, we are well aware of that fact. When my girls were toddlers, they had many needs and desires. In fact, it seemed that one of them needed something from me all the time. If I had taken a shower by 3 p.m., I was doing well.

Especially when our children are little, we get to learn firsthand that aspect of love. And some days it's not easy. There were times when I prayed, "Please, God, just let them nap at the same time today so I can take a long, hot bath." (Hey, I would've paid a thousand dollars for a bubble bath back then!) Those were precious times, but boy, they were busy times too!

Maybe you're living those busy days right now. Maybe you're reading this and thinking, *Precious days? I want to escape!* Well, don't despair. God cares about your crazy, busy days. He knows that this "mom gig" isn't an easy job. He wants to give you rest and peace, and He is well pleased with your well doing. So the next time you hear "Mommy!" and you want to run the other direction—take heart! You are growing in love.

---

### MOM TO MASTER

*Lord, help me to appreciate even the busiest of days
and help me to show Your love today. Amen.*

# February 22

Remember memorizing "Love your neighbor as yourself" back in Sunday school? That was an easy one to learn but not so easy to apply. In fact, there are days I still have trouble with that love commandment.

I recently had one of those days when I volunteered to oversee the annual talent show at my daughters' school. It was scary! Every stage mother came out of her closet and decided to make herself known. Either their children were in the wrong part of the show or they didn't like the way I ran dress rehearsal. Talk about a love challenge! I did not want to "love my neighbor" at that juncture. Actually, I wanted to throttle my neighbor and repent later. Ever been there?

I discovered that sometimes love means biting your tongue really hard. But it's in those times that we find out how much love we truly have inside of us. It's sort of like a tube of toothpaste. If there is toothpaste inside the tube, toothpaste comes out when you squeeze it. Well, when we are squeezed under pressure, if love is on the inside of us, love comes out. But if we have other junk in there, that comes out too. So build yourself up in love. Trust me, you'll need it later!

———————— MOM TO MASTER ————————

*Lord, help me to love all of Your people. Amen.*

# February 23

*"People look at the outward appearance,
but the LORD looks at the heart."*
1 SAMUEL 16:7

"Can't Buy Me Love" is a catchy little song with a power-packed message. Of course, kids don't always agree with its message. When my husband told our daughters he wouldn't buy them a go-kart, they cried and said, "You just don't love us!"

Maybe you've heard that same retaliation in your home. It's a common kid manipulation but totally ineffective and way off base. In fact, the reason we wouldn't buy our daughters the go-kart is because it was dangerous for them to have one in our neighborhood. It wasn't that we didn't want to get them one; it's that we wanted to protect them from dangers they didn't understand.

God is like that too. As our heavenly Father, He has to say no to some of our requests. He sees those hidden dangers that we don't. But when He says no, occasionally I'll come out with that old manipulation that never works: "You didn't answer my prayer, so You must not love me." Of course, that is not true. I know that in my heart, but sometimes I pray out of hurt. I'm so thankful that God looks on the heart, not the hurt. Show your kids that same mercy the next time they say, "You just don't love me."

---- MOM TO MASTER ----

*Lord, help me to show Your mercy to my children. Amen.*

# February 24

*"Love your neighbor as yourself."*
LEVITICUS 19:18

Did you know this commandment is listed nine times in the Bible? I've used it several times in this devotional. It's just so good. I've probably read this scripture a hundred times, but I usually focus on the "Love your neighbor" part; however, the verse doesn't stop there. It says, "Love your neighbor *as yourself*." That means that we have to love ourselves before we can really love others.

I don't know about you, but since I've had children, things have shifted. There are definitely parts of my body I don't love anymore. And there are things I'd like to change about my personality too. I wish I were more patient and more organized. Bottom line—there are a lot of days that I don't love myself. How about you? It's hard to love ourselves. We tend to focus on all of our imperfections. We hone in on all of our faults.

If you have trouble receiving a compliment or if you are constantly belittling yourself—you need to get in the "self-love mode." Ask God to fill you up with His love and help you to see yourself through His eyes. When I look at myself through His eyes, I look great! It's like the best airbrush job ever! So love yourself today. It's not a biblical suggestion. It's a commandment!

—————— MOM TO MASTER ——————

*Lord, help me to love myself today. Amen.*

# February 25

*But from everlasting to everlasting the LORD's love*
*is with those who fear him.*

PSALM 103:17

There are some days when I can't see past the end of my nose. Life is just so busy! Deadlines, overflowing laundry baskets, soccer practice, grocery shopping. . . Tomorrow seems an eternity away, and I can't even wrap my mind around the concept of eternity. So when I read a verse that says God's love is with us from everlasting to everlasting, I don't always get it.

Lately when having my Bible study time, I've been asking God to turn off the to-do list part of my brain so that I can really hear God's voice through His Word. And you know what? It works! Suddenly, His Word leaps off the page, and all at once, I get it! This has now become one of my very favorite verses! To think that someone—especially the Creator of the universe—could love me forever and ever is so great! What a wonderful promise!

As moms, we don't have a lot of time to meditate on God's Word, so we have to make the most of those moments with the Master. Ask God to help you really focus as you read the Bible. Ask Him to show you what He has especially for you on that day. It's exciting!

—————————— MOM TO MASTER ——————————

*Lord, help me to meditate more on Your Word. Amen.*

# February 26

*"For I, the* LORD *your God, am a jealous God."*
EXODUS 20:5

Remember your first love? I married my high school sweetheart. I remember the first time we held hands. I remember the first time we kissed. I remember the exact outfit I was wearing when he first said he loved me. I remember it all! Even after years of marriage, I still smile and get all sappy when I hear "our song" on the radio.

God wants us to love Him even more than we love our spouse and children. He tells us that He is a jealous God. He wants us to remember those special times with Him—the moment you gave your heart to Him, the miracles He has performed in your life, the times He came through when no one else could. He wants us to sing praise songs to Him as a love offering. He says if we won't praise Him, the rocks will cry out. I don't want any rock doing my praising for me. How about you?

Start today and keep an "I Remember" journal. Record what God does for you each day—even the smallest things. It'll be sort of a daily "love letter" to the Father. If you've grown cold to God, you're sure to fall in love with Him again.

———————— MOM TO MASTER ————————

*Lord, help me to keep You as my first love. Amen.*

# February 27

*"Truly I tell you, if you have faith as small as a mustard seed,*
*you can say to this mountain, 'Move from here*
*to there,' and it will move."*

MATTHEW 17:20

The girls are at it again. I find it rather ironic that I'm writing about love while my daughters wrestle on the ground. Obviously, God has a sense of humor. Deep down, beneath their "I'm too cool for words" attitudes—they do love one another. I occasionally see glimpses of that love. It's sort of like the morning mist—there for a few moments and then gone almost instantly. Still, their love for each other remains—buried within them somewhere.

On the days when I can't see even a shadow of that love, I continue to thank the Lord that it's there. Abby will call Allyson a "stupid head," and Allyson will give Abby a crack on the head. After I discipline them, I raise my hands and I say, "Thank You, Lord, that my girls love each other. I thank You, God, that they will be lifelong friends." Sometimes, I say it purely out of faith because there is no evidence of that love, but faith of a mustard seed is all I need—that I have! Put your faith to work today, and watch the love grow in your home.

———————— MOM TO MASTER ————————

*Thank You, Father, that my children love*
*You and each other. Amen.*

# February 28

*Love one another deeply, from the heart.*
1 PETER 1:22

"Mommy, will you always love me?" Abby asked, looking up at me with her big green eyes.

"Of course, I'll always love you," I said, kissing her on the head. "That's what mommies do."

Abby smiled, satisfied with my answer.

At that moment, I thought, *I hope she will always be able to feel my love—no matter what.* Or, if she can't feel my love, I want her to feel God's love. His love is much more far-reaching than mine.

Today's world is very unsure. In fact, it's crazy many days. In the hustle and bustle of day-to-day life, our children need our affirmation. They need to know that we'll always love them. And more importantly, they need to know that their heavenly Father will always love them. So take this opportunity to tell them that you love them and that God loves them even more than you do—and that's a lot!

Love is the answer. Even if your children wander from "the straight and narrow path," love will bring them back. If you're discouraged today because your children don't seem to be accepting your love or embracing God's love—hold on! God's love has a way of penetrating even the hardest of hearts.

――――――― MOM TO MASTER ―――――――

*Thank You, Father, for Your love.*
*Help me to show Your love to my children. Amen.*

# February 29

*"Look at the birds of the air; they do not sow or reap or store
away in barns, and yet your heavenly Father feeds them.
Are you not much more valuable than they?"*

MATTHEW 6:26

"Mommy, hurry!" Abby called from the middle of the driveway.
"It's a baby bird!"

Sure enough, right in the middle of our driveway was a sweet,
fluffy, baby dove. He was probably five weeks old. He had all of
his feathers, but the dainty dove still couldn't fly. After calling the
Texas Wildlife Headquarters, I was instructed to move the bird
into a makeshift nest in a hanging basket near the tree where he
had fallen. As I planned my emergency bird rescue, I rushed to
the front door to watch our little feathered friend. That's when I
saw one of the most beautiful sights I'd ever seen—the mother
dove nuzzling her baby bird—right in the middle of our driveway. She was protecting her baby at all costs.

We would do the same for our children. We'd give our life
for our kids, wouldn't we? Do you know that's how God feels
about us? He adores us! He cares about each one of us. When we
fall out of our respective nests, He is right there, hovering over
us, protecting us, loving us.

—————— MOM TO MASTER ——————

*Thank You, Father, for always being there
for me—protecting me and loving me. Amen.*

# March 1

*You too, be patient and stand firm.*
JAMES 5:8

When one of my best friends had her second baby—Baby Aimee—she was so precious and innocent and tiny. Every time I hold a newborn, I'm still amazed. For nine months we wait and dream and anticipate, and then finally the baby comes. At that moment, when you see your sweet baby for the first time, all of those months of waiting are so worth it.

Waiting is not easy, especially when you're waiting for something as monumental as the birth of a child. But even if you're waiting on God to perform a miracle in some other area of your life, it's tough. We're not a patient people. When days turn to weeks and weeks turn to months and months turn to years, you can't help but wonder if God is still working on your behalf. But rest assured, He is! Just as your children were born when they were ready, your dreams and miracles will hatch at their appointed times. So hang in there and wait with joy. Whenever you are able to finally embrace whatever it is you're believing God for, it will be more than worth the wait!

--------- MOM TO MASTER ---------

*Lord, thank You for giving me the patience*
*to wait with joy. I love You. Amen.*

# March 2

*"As long as the earth endures, seedtime and harvest, cold and heat, summer and winter, day and night will never cease."*
GENESIS 8:22

Somehow that verse is comforting to me. Just knowing that God can keep all of the earth's functions—seasons, temperatures, etc.—in order, makes me feel good. Often, I find myself stressing about time-related issues, such as: *Am I spending enough quality time with my children? Will I meet my book deadline? Will I have enough time to lose ten pounds before my next high school reunion?*

I once heard a preacher on the radio talking about time management, and he asked, "Are you spinning your wheels or are you on a roll?"

*Well*, I thought, *it depends on which day you ask me!*

Some days I have it all together—everything is running on schedule and I feel in complete control. (Okay, realistically I have only three days a year like that.) Most of my days are filled with unexpected visitors, last-minute hair appointments, school activities, and putting out fires. Can I hear a collective "Amen"?

But we can rejoice in knowing that if God can keep the world spinning, He can certainly handle the tasks before us each day. So the next time you're running in circles, call on Him.

—————————— MOM TO MASTER ——————————

*Lord, I recognize Your ability to keep everything in order. I give every part of my life to You. Amen.*

# March 3

*Jesus said, "Let the little children come to me,*
*and do not hinder them."*
MATTHEW 19:14

I once read an article that said children spell love T-I-M-E. As I pondered that statement, I had to agree. Sometimes, as parents, we think that our kids spell love M-O-N-E-Y because our society has become so materialistic, but in reality, kids just want to be with us. Abby and Ally would rather spend an afternoon watching old Doris Day movies on my big bed than practically anything I could give them. They actually enjoy being with me, and that's something I am so thankful for. I realize that as they get older, that may not always be true, so I want to take advantage of each and every opportunity to snuggle together, eat buttery popcorn, and watch Doris Day work her onscreen magic with Rock Hudson.

Find some activities that you and your children enjoy doing together, such as going hiking, going fishing, doing crafts, reading stories, baking cookies, playing board games. . . . Just find some common ground and make time for your children. Even if you have to "pencil in" a day of baking cookies with kids in your daily planner—do it! Don't just say you love your children—show them! Spend some time together.

——————— MOM TO MASTER ———————

*Father, I want to thank You for every moment I get to spend*
*with my children. Help me to treasure this time. Amen.*

# March 4

*Rejoice always.*
1 THESSALONIANS 5:16

Slowly you open one eye, trying hard to focus on the clock—2 a.m.

*How could she be hungry again?* you wonder.

As the baby wails on, you stumble down the hallway in your fuzzy slippers and tattered bathrobe. Such is the life of a mommy.

We are a rare breed. A royal sisterhood. A mommy sorority. We operate on only a few hours of sleep, never finishing a meal, and usually juggling ten balls at once. Let's face it—this mom thing is no easy gig, which is why moms can be occasionally crabby—especially moms of newborns. C'mon, admit it! You've bitten a few heads off in your lifetime too! I can remember thinking, *I can't do this one more day! God must not have known what He was doing when He made me a mom.* But you know what? He did know.

I found out that He had equipped me with everything I needed to be a good mom. And He was more than happy to help me make it through when I felt my weakest. He will do the same for you. No matter how dark your dark circles are. No matter how ugly you've acted today. No matter what—God loves you and believes in you.

——— MOM TO MASTER ———

*Father, help me not to be crabby*
*as I learn how to be a mom. Amen.*

# March 5

*"For I know the plans I have for you,"*
*declares the L*ORD*, "plans to prosper you and not to*
*harm you, plans to give you hope and a future."*
JEREMIAH 29:11

Our family once went to MGM Studios in Walt Disney World in Orlando—such fun! We rode the Tower of Terror. We went upside down several times on Aerosmith's Rock 'n' Roller Coaster. We had a total blast!

As evening fell, we only had time for one more ride. That's when I read the description of the Disney Animation Tour. I knew that as a budding artist, my ten-year-old Abby would love it! I would have rather gone on the Tower of Terror again, but I knew Abby would be greatly inspired by the animation tour. So that's what we did. We watched clips from classic Disney movies. We listened to actual artists talk about the process of making animated films. We saw drawings from an upcoming movie. It was interesting, and for Abby, it was magical. It confirmed something inside of her.

The whole way back to the hotel, we discussed the beauty of Disney art. Abby talked passionately of how God would someday use her art. I was so thankful that we hadn't missed the opportunity to fan Abby's dream. Why not look for ways to encourage your children's dreams today?

—————————— MOM TO MASTER ——————————

*Father, help me to fan the dreams*
*You've placed within my children. Amen.*

# March 6

*Whoever heeds discipline shows the way to life.*
PROVERBS 10:17

"That's it. You're in the time-out chair!" I hollered to my then four-year-old Allyson. She had rolled her eyes at me one too many times that afternoon. Slowly, she cowered over to the time-out chair, positioned in the corner of her room. She detested time-out. Just hearing the words *time* and *out* in the same sentence made her cringe. But as much as she hated it, she spent a lot of time in that little wooden chair. Her rebellious streak simply took over from time to time.

I find myself in God's time-out chair almost as often as Allyson frequented hers as a preschooler. It seems I also have a rebellious streak. But God's time-out chair isn't a place where He puts you to punish you; rather, you put yourself there when you disobey Him. It's a place where the blessings of God no longer flow. I don't like it there any more than Allyson liked her little wooden chair. But the best thing about God's time-out chair is you can get up at any time. All you have to do is repent and move on. So if you're in the time-out chair today, don't worry. Your chair time is almost up.

—————————— MOM TO MASTER ——————————

*Father, help me to follow You all the time. Amen.*

# March 7

*"Is not wisdom found among the aged?*
*Does not long life bring understanding?"*
JOB 12:12

As we strolled through our local Walmart, my then three-year-old Abby found a stuffed animal that she just couldn't live without. I told her no, and that was it. Abby threw herself on the floor and proceeded to have the mother of all tantrums. Ally, who was one at the time, let out some sympathy cries, adding to the scene. Once Abby's breathing returned to normal, we headed to the checkout lane.

It was at that exact moment when I saw this sweet elderly man from our church. He looked into the faces of my little girls and whispered to me, "They are so precious. These are the best years of your life. Treasure each moment!"

I smiled politely, but on the inside I was thinking, *Are you kidding me? Did you just see the tantrum I had to deal with back there? Give me a break!* That was more than seven years ago, but his words have stayed with me.

Those were precious years. I can see that now. Sometimes, when I was elbow deep in dirty diapers, I couldn't see it. So if you're in the middle of your children's preschool years, take some advice from the wise old man at my church—treasure each moment.

───────── MOM TO MASTER ─────────

*Father, help me to treasure each moment*
*with my children. Amen.*

# March 8

*Let the wise listen and add to their learning.*
PROVERBS 1:5

Listening. It's almost a lost art form in today's world. Yet, according to the International Listening Association, "Being listened to spells the difference between feeling accepted and feeling isolated." Wow, that's pretty strong, isn't it?

In professional circles, I am a good listener. I understand the importance of listening to my colleagues, yet I sometimes fail to listen to my children. I find myself interrupting them, trying to get them to "get to the end of the story" while I am still young. But that's not what I should be doing as a caring, accepting mom. The Lord convicted me about this very thing not long ago, and I've been working on my listening skills ever since.

Are you a good listener? Do you really give your kids your full attention when they are talking to you? Do you nod your head and smile, letting them know that you're truly into what they are saying? If not, you may need to ask God to help you improve your listening skills too. If we fail to listen to them now, we'll be sorry later when they no longer choose to tell us things. So go ahead. Open up your ears and your heart and listen to your children!

--------- MOM TO MASTER ---------

*Lord, please help me to listen to my children
the same way You listen to me. Amen.*

# March 9

*He gives strength to the weary
and increases the power of the weak.*

ISAIAH 40:29

Are you too busy? Is your calendar so marked up that you have to pencil in potty breaks? Moms are busy people. That's just a fact of life, but if we allow ourselves to become too busy, we'll miss out on quality time with our families. We'll be running around so much that we won't know if we're coming or going. Even good things can be bad if they take us away from our families.

For instance, if volunteering to head up the crafts committee for this year's vacation Bible school consumes so much of your time that you can't play with your kids an entire month of the summer, it's not a good thing. Or if teaching the ladies' Bible study on Tuesday nights conflicts with going to your son's baseball games all spring—you might need to step down from that leadership role.

Like the catchy antidrug campaign slogan, I've had to learn to "Just say no!" to some things. It's not my nature to say no. I am usually the first one to jump in and volunteer—many times at the expense of my husband and children. But I'm doing better these days. So if you're like me, learn to "Just say no!" Your family will thank you.

―――――――――― MOM TO MASTER ――――――――――

*Lord, help me to make wise decisions
where my time is concerned. Amen.*

# March 10

*Oh, how I love your law! I meditate on it all day long.*
PSALM 119:97

Don't you just love to soak in a big bathtub full of bubbles? The beautiful bubbles tickle your toes, and the fresh, flowery fragrance fills the room. It's one of my most favorite things to do. If I could, I would soak in the tub so long that my entire body would become pruney. There's just nothing like a bubble bath—it's pure heaven! It's time well spent, as far as I'm concerned. Soaking in bubbles totally de-stresses me and brings a quiet rest to my soul. And what mom doesn't need more of that in her life?

Do you know what else brings peace and rest? Soaking in God's Word. When you spend time in the Word of God, it transforms you from the inside out. It replaces stress with peace; sickness with healing; anger with compassion; hate with love; worry with faith; and weariness with energy. Soaking in God's Word every day will keep you balanced and ready to tackle whatever comes your way. It's time well spent. You'll become a better person—a better wife and a better mom. And you won't even get pruney in the process.

———————— MOM TO MASTER ————————

*Lord, thank You for Your Word. Help me to
soak it in more and more each day. Amen.*

# March 11

The joke around our house is, "I bought a book about time management. I just haven't had time to read it." As a fellow mom, I'm sure you can relate. We have about a hundred things to do before noon! Listen, I'm all for time management. I have interviewed experts about time management and written very informative articles using their comments and advice; however, I am not very efficient when it comes to actually practicing time management principles.

I truly want to do better, but I feel overwhelmed before I even get started. I rush around in a thousand directions—wrapping presents a minute before we're supposed to leave for the birthday party, making my bed while I brush my teeth, etc. You get the idea. Then one day it dawned on me—God is a great time manager. He can get a lot done in a short amount of time. I mean, hey, He made the entire world in a week!

At that moment of revelation, I asked God to help manage my time. I asked Him to reveal the activities, volunteer positions, assignments, and friendships that needed to go. Then I asked Him to replace that "free time" with things He would have me do. And you know what? He really knows what He's doing.

---

## MOM TO MASTER

*Lord, help me to be a better time manager. Amen.*

# March 12

*The LORD has done it this very day;*
*let us rejoice today and be glad.*
PSALM 118:24

"Kodak moments." Aren't they great? I love to look through photographs from past vacations, honor days, field trips, sporting events, family gatherings, holidays, and more! And, when I have time, I enjoy scrapbooking—to really showcase our precious pictures. As I was putting together a recent scrapbook for my father, I noticed that almost every picture I'd taken featured smiling, happy folks. Some were posed "cheesy" pictures, but even the candid shots showed intense happiness. Whether it was Abby finishing her round-off back handspring series at the last gymnastics meet or Ally enjoying some fresh watermelon—happiness just oozed from each photograph.

Like the old commercial said, those are the moments you cherish. Sometimes, you have to hold on to those happy memories to make it through until the next Kodak moment. Life is difficult, and traumatic events can uproot your entire life in an instant. So we need to live each day mindful that these are precious times—special moments with our loved ones—treasured times that are gone like the mist in the morning. Enjoy each moment with your children—even the not-so-pleasant ones—and thank God for the Kodak moments.

——— MOM TO MASTER ———

*Lord, I thank You for filling my life*
*with Kodak moments. Amen.*

# March 13

*"By this everyone will know that you are my disciples,
if you love one another."*
JOHN 13:35

When was the last time you slowed down long enough to make mud pies with your kids? When was the last time you read funny poetry by a candlelight pizza dinner? If it's been awhile, then plan a special day to do nothing but fun stuff with your children. Of course, this works much better if your kids are willing to spend an entire day with you. Once they reach puberty, Mom is sort of on the "nerd list." But if you still have little ones or tweens running around, why not host an all-out fun-filled day?

Begin with pizza for breakfast. Watch funny family films in your jammies until noon. Then, if the weather is nice, take a bike ride together or go on a scavenger hunt in a nearby park. Play board games until nightfall. Finish the day with devotions and prayer time. Just bask in each other's presence, soaking it all in.

At the end of the day, you will have made some magnificent memories. When your kids are old, they'll look back on that day and smile. They may not remember exactly what you did, but they'll remember the love.

## —— MOM TO MASTER ——

*Lord, help me to spend more quality time
with my family. Amen.*

# March 14

*And pray in the Spirit on all occasions
with all kinds of prayers and requests.*

EPHESIANS 6:18

I once saw a bumper sticker that said, *Seven days without prayer makes one weak.* At first I thought it was a typo, but then I realized it was a clever play on words. The more I thought about it, the more I liked it—and the more convicted I became.

I'm really diligent about reading my daily devotions. I regularly go to church. But then I started evaluating my prayer life. Wow—it seemed almost nonexistent.

I started thinking about the times I had spent more than a few minutes in prayer, and it was always at a time when I was going through bad stuff. In other words, I only spent quality time talking to God. We always need him whether we recognize it or not. I spent all of my prayer time asking Him for stuff. I would throw in "Thank You, Lord, for such and such" every now and then, but most of my time was spent requesting His intervention. I rarely took time to listen to hear whether He had something He wanted to say to me in that still, small voice.

Is your prayer life rushed and one-sided? If it is, don't despair. Just begin spending quality prayer time with the Father today. He's been waiting for you.

――――――― MOM TO MASTER ―――――――

*Lord, I want to hear from You. I love You.*

# March 15

*The living, the living—they praise you, as I am doing today;*
*parents tell their children about your faithfulness.*
ISAIAH 38:19

"There's no time like the present."

That's what my mother always used to say when she wanted me to clean my room. Then I found myself using that very same line on my girls. Of course, they looked at me the same way I used to look at my mom when she used that expression on me. (Yes, I rolled my eyes at my mom too!) Still, the fact remains that it's a true statement. There really is no time like the present.

So if there is something you've been longing to do or someplace you've been dreaming of going or someone you've been wanting to visit—go for it. Do it today. Seize the moment! What are you waiting for?

We're not promised tomorrow, which is why we need to live each day as if it were our last. Love a little more. Laugh a little more. Hug your kids more. Serve God with all of your heart. Don't let the sun go down without telling your family how much you love them. Make sure your kids know how much Jesus loves them. Think of today as a gift from God—because it is.

---

## MOM TO MASTER

*Thank You, God, for every minute of every day. Amen.*

# March 16

*Jesus said, "Let the little children come to me,
and do not hinder them."*

MATTHEW 19:14

"No."

That was always the answer I received from one of my former bosses. No matter what idea I'd offer—even if it had been the best suggestion in the world—his answer was always, "No." I nicknamed him "Negative Ned." Though I tried to joke about it, his negativity almost crippled me on the inside.

After being shot down so many times, I quit offering suggestions. I quit sharing my thoughts. I went into my "survival mode" with all of my defenses up. God eventually freed me from that supervisor, but I learned a lot during those months of drifting in the "Sea of Negativism." Those lessons have stayed with me, and I often think of Old Ned when I'm parenting.

As moms, it seems our duty to say no. And sometimes, no is the correct response. But don't be so quick to always say no, or your children will quit asking you stuff. They'll go into their survival mode and put up their defenses—just like I did with my boss. As moms, we should take time to really listen to our kids' requests before saying no. If we don't, we just might become "Negative Nellie."

——————— MOM TO MASTER ———————

*Lord, help me to be open-minded and
approachable—especially with my children. Amen.*

# March 17

*"Do not judge, or you too will be judged."*
MATTHEW 7:1

"You're not like other moms," commented one of my daughter's friends. "You rock!"

That may be the highest compliment I've received in my first thirtysome years. Abby's friend thought it was cool because I knew all of the words to Aaron Carter's song, "That's How I Beat Shaq."

Okay, so that's not exactly a spiritual hymn, but the point is, I had taken the time to be interested in my nine-year-old daughter's musical preferences. While scanning her CDs for offensive language (which results in an immediate eject), I discovered that some of her music was kind of fun. I borrowed a few of her CDs and began listening to them when I power walked. Hey, you've never lived unless you've power walked to an upbeat song!

Besides discovering some fun new tunes, I also discovered something else—taking time to know your kids and their likes and dislikes is very cool. It brings you closer to them. It puts you right in the middle of their world and helps you better understand their turf, their dreams, their struggles, and more. I highly recommend it. It's exciting and fun. And you might just find out that you really like that SpongeBob guy after all. (It's okay; I'll never tell.)

───────────── MOM TO MASTER ─────────────

*Lord, help me to better understand my kids*
*and their preferences. Amen.*

# March 18

*"I have swept away your offenses like a cloud,*
*your sins like the morning mist."*
ISAIAH 44:22

Do you remember that great song by Cher called, "If I Could Turn Back Time"?

Okay, that's about the only line from the entire song that I actually remember, but that line is really good, isn't it? I mean, have you ever really pondered the concept of turning back time? What would you do differently? (Besides that terrible mullet hairstyle you had in the '80s, what else would you change?) What would you keep exactly the same?

I wrote an entry in my journal about this very topic, and I discovered some key things. I wouldn't change any of the big decisions I'd made—choosing to follow God, choosing to marry Jeff, choosing to go into journalism, having children early in our marriage. But my journal entry was filled with little regrets and misguided priorities. I wrote, "If I could turn back time, I would spend more time playing in the sandbox with my girls. I would spend more time enjoying my children instead of just caring for them."

Well, we can't turn back time, and there's no sense living in regret. God doesn't want us to do that. But we can begin correcting those things today—spend more lazy afternoons with your kids. The housework will wait—time won't.

––––––––– MOM TO MASTER –––––––––

*Lord, help me prioritize my life. Amen.*

# March 19

*Don't let anyone look down on you because you are young.*
1 TIMOTHY 4:12

They say that once you learn to ride a bike, you never forget. I beg to differ. Okay, so I haven't really ridden a bike (unless you count the stationary ones at the YMCA) in about fifteen years. But when we bought our daughters two new, shiny bikes, I wanted one too! Suddenly, I had to have one. So my husband bought me a beautiful silver bike—with gearshifts and everything!

I could hardly wait to get home and try it. The girls thought it was really funny seeing their old mom on a new bike, but they were supportive in between giggles. Abby showed me how to use the gearshifts while Ally reviewed the whole kickstand thing with me. The bike felt quite foreign as I shakily began down our driveway. My heart pounded with fear. It was as if I'd never ridden a bike in my whole life. Thankfully, my children were there to teach me all of the skills I had forgotten.

You know, we're never too old to learn, and sometimes we neglect to recognize the teachers living in our own homes. Our kids may be younger, but in some ways they are much wiser. Why not let your kids teach you something today?

——————————— MOM TO MASTER ———————————

*Father, help me to never get too old*
*to enjoy my kids. Amen.*

# March 20

It was the last day of horse camp, and all of the parents were on hand to see the campers' presentation of the skills they'd learned that week. Smiling proudly, Abby rounded the corner on her horse. Then, all at once, the old, stubborn horse stopped. She simply wouldn't budge. Abby ever so gently kicked the horse in the ribs. Still, the horse wouldn't go. Then Abby whispered, "Walk on, Prissy. Walk on." Finally, the horse started moving forward. Every time the stubborn animal stopped, Abby would simply say, "Walk on," and the horse would begin moving again.

As I watched Abby maneuver that large animal around the ring, I learned something—encouragement is vitally important. Each time our kids start to get off that straight and narrow path, we should softly whisper, "Walk on." By encouraging our children, we can give them the confidence to move toward their dreams, to conquer their fears, and to fulfill the destiny that God has for each of them. Sometimes all they need is a little nudge and a soft, encouraging word to move forward.

Sure, offering encouragement takes time, but it'll be time well spent. So why not look for opportunities to whisper "Walk on" today? Like Abby's horse, your children will respond positively.

--------- MOM TO MASTER ---------

*Father, help me to ever so gently encourage my children. Amen.*

# March 21

*Be very careful, then, how you live—not as unwise but
as wise, making the most of every opportunity.*
EPHESIANS 5:15–16

Did you know that there are 1,440 minutes in every day? Our
youth group at church recently changed its name to "14:40" to
signify that our kids are learning to follow God every minute
of every day.

"Make the most of the minutes!" our youth pastor shared.

Wow. That's good, isn't it? If we really lived every minute
for God, wouldn't this be a different world? As our youth pastor
spoke passionately about "14:40," my heart started beating so
hard that I thought it would pound right out of my chest. I got
excited, challenged, and convicted all at the same time. Now it's
a daily goal around our house to make the most of those 1,440
minutes. The girls have really embraced the idea. It causes them
to think about their decisions and actions throughout the day. It
does the same for me.

Sure, we miss it. There are minutes in our day that we wish
we could do over, but God knows our hearts. He knows that we
are focused on making the most of the minutes for the Master.
Why not start a 14:40 campaign in your house?

——————————— MOM TO MASTER ———————————

*Father, help me to make the most of every minute today.
Help me to live each minute for You. Amen.*

# March 22

*Make the most of every opportunity.*
COLOSSIANS 4:5

It was my thirteenth birthday, and I was very much into drama. I loved being in plays. I loved going to the theater. And I loved *Annie*. It was my all-time favorite musical, and it was coming to Bloomington, Indiana, on my birthday! I knew tickets would be scarce, but my heart was set on going. My mom knew it, and she must have called every ticket vendor in the entire state of Indiana to track down tickets. After weeks of sleuth work, she was finally able to nab three fifth-row tickets to the show. I will never forget that night. I'm not sure if it was so special because the show was wonderful or if it was because I knew how hard my mom had worked to make that night possible.

Each time my daughters' birthdays roll around, I think about that *Annie* birthday. Even if we can't purchase expensive tickets to a Broadway musical every year, we always try to make each birthday celebration very special. I bet you do the same. Or, if you haven't made a big deal of your children's birthdays in the past, it's not too late. You'll have an opportunity every year! Start planning now. Let your children know that you are thankful to be their mother.

——————————— MOM TO MASTER ———————————

*Lord, help me to make my children feel loved every day—especially on their birthdays. Amen.*

# March 23

*And my God will meet all your needs according
to the riches of his glory in Christ Jesus.*
PHILIPPIANS 4:19

Abby and Allyson were drawing pictures of our family, and Abby proudly displayed her artwork on the fridge. When I passed by later in the day, I saw the picture of me that she had drawn. It broke my heart. There was a picture of Daddy fishing with them and there was a picture of me typing at my computer.

"Oh no!" I cringed. "Is that how they see me? As just a writer at my computer—never having any time for them?" I panicked. I cried. And then I prayed. I asked God to work a financial miracle in my life so that I wouldn't have to work so many hours and miss out on the fun family stuff. God was faithful to answer my prayer. I have been able to turn down some of the lesser-paying, more time-consuming jobs, still make the car payment, and have more time with my children.

God will do the same for you. The Bible says that He is no respecter of persons. So if it's your desire to work fewer hours to be with your children more, just ask God. He has the answer.

―――――― MOM TO MASTER ――――――

*Lord, please work a financial miracle in my life that would
allow me to spend more time with my family. Amen.*

# March 24

*Jesus Christ is the same yesterday and today and forever.*
HEBREWS 13:8

As I waited for Abby's highlights to process, I read a hair magazine. I was so relieved to discover that "Big Hair Is in Again!" Finally, my '80s "do" was back in fashion!

In fact, the '80s were coming back with a vengeance! Allyson told me about a new kind of pants she liked. She described them like this: "They have zippers and pockets all over them, and they make this weird swishy noise when you walk."

I said, "You mean parachute pants?" *Ding. Ding. Ding.* That was the right answer! I cannot believe that parachute pants were back in style. (I thought they were a fashion fiasco the first time around!) It's really true what they say—if you hang on to something long enough, it will eventually come back in style.

Isn't it good to know that no matter if you're sporting a mullet, the "Rachel," or a classic bob, Jesus loves you? His love never changes. In fact, He is always in season. His Word is as current and applicable today as it was a century ago. So even if our clothing, hairdos, and musical preferences are considered "totally uncool" by our offspring, we can offer them the One who will never go out of style—Jesus.

——— MOM TO MASTER ———

*Thank You, Lord, for being my Savior all the time. Amen.*

# March 25

*They are like a breath; their days are like a fleeting shadow.*
PSALM 144:4

Attention shoppers! Christmas is only nine months away. Hurry! Hurry! You don't want to be caught in that last-minute yuletide frenzy.

Okay, so in reality, few people begin shopping for Christmas in March. Oh sure, there are some of those eager beavers who start shopping for the next Christmas on December 26, but most of us wait until Thanksgiving dinner is settled in our tummies before we hit the malls, right?

As far off as December 25 may seem, it's just around the corner. Time has a way of slipping by us. It's like the introduction to *Days of Our Lives* says—"like sands through the hourglass. . ."

It seems like only yesterday that we were celebrating birthdays at Chuck E. Cheese. Now, we're having boy-girl skating parties. What happened to those years? They sneaked past me when I wasn't looking. Wouldn't it be great if we could keep our children little forever? But we can't, so don't miss one moment of their growing-up years. We can't get those years back. Enjoy them as much as you can right now. (Oh, and go ahead and start buying a few Christmas presents each month to avoid the retail rush!)

— MOM TO MASTER —

*God, help me to make good use of my time,*
*cherishing every moment with my kids. Amen.*

# March 26

*"To God belong wisdom and power;*
*counsel and understanding are his."*

JOB 12:13

"You are ruining my life!"

That's what the daughter screamed at her mother in the remake of Disney's *Freaky Friday*. We took the girls to see that movie, and all of us enjoyed it—especially me. I could totally relate to the mother in the film. I too am a member of the "You've ruined my life" club. Abby has told me that more than once.

You know, on days when your beloved child looks you in the face and says, "You're ruining my life," you don't want to be nice. Actually, you want to be defensive. You want to say, "Listen, kiddo, do you have any idea what I do for you every single day? You couldn't make it without me!" (And yes, I have said those things.)

But what the mother discovers in *Freaky Friday* is that she lacks understanding where her daughter is concerned and vice versa. Once the mom and daughter see things through the other's eyes, understanding comes. If you're also a member of the "You've ruined my life" club, ask God to give you understanding so that you can see things through your kids' eyes. If you do, I have a feeling your membership in that club will soon expire.

——————— MOM TO MASTER ———————

*God, help me to understand my children*
*the way You understand me. Amen.*

# March 27

*"But my salvation will last forever,
my righteousness will never fail."*
ISAIAH 51:6

Okay, admit it. You watched every episode of the very first *American Idol* season, didn't you? Well, if you didn't, I'll bet your kids did. It was an amazing journey. Of course, we Texans were quite thrilled when our home girl Kelly Clarkson won the coveted title. My daughters and I jumped and cheered as if we'd won!

Soon after, Kelly released her single "A Moment Like This," and it became an instant hit. Like millions of other Americans, we scrambled to the store to buy our copy, and we played it over and over again. I love these words: "A moment like this, Some people wait a lifetime, For a moment like this, Some people search forever. . . ."

There are very few "Moments Like This" in life. We treasure those monumental moments, such as our first prom, graduation day, our wedding day, the births of our children. Those are tender times. But do you know what the most special "Moment Like This" moment is? The day you made Jesus the Lord of your life.

Make sure you celebrate all of the "Moments Like This" with your children. But most importantly, make sure your children experience that most important moment so they won't be searching forever.

─────── MOM TO MASTER ───────

*God, help me never to miss a special
moment with my children. Amen.*

# March 28

*Finally, brothers and sisters, whatever is true, whatever is noble,*
*whatever is right, whatever is pure, whatever is lovely,*
*whatever is admirable. . .think about such things.*

PHILIPPIANS 4:8

"What time is it, kiddies?"

"It's time for *Cowboy Bob's Corral!*"

Even today, decades later, I can still remember the theme song to the *Cowboy Bob's Corral* kiddy show that aired on Channel 4 in southern Indiana in the 1970s. It was my very favorite show. I loved Cowboy Bob's horse. I loved the cartoon segments. And I loved how Cowboy Bob closed every show with, "Remember, if you can't say anything nice, don't say anything at all." Then he'd ride off into the sunset, and I'd wave good-bye to Cowboy Bob until the following afternoon.

Those were great afternoons spent with Cowboy Bob. Every show, that crafty old cowboy would sneak in moral advice, and we'd soak it all up, because if Cowboy Bob said it, it just had to be true.

Cowboy Bob has long since retired, and my kids headed home from school just in time to watch *Lizzie McGuire*—with me. Are you monitoring your kids' TV shows? If not, you should be. I don't mean you should become the TV gestapo, but you should find out what they're watching and what they'll be remembering twenty-five years from now.

--- MOM TO MASTER ---

*God, help me to help my children make*
*good viewing choices. Amen.*

# March 29

*"But when you pray, go into your room,*
*close the door and pray to your Father, who is unseen."*
MATTHEW 6:6

Do you have a sort of bedtime ritual with your children? Some parents read a storybook to their children every night. Other parents share a Bible story or two. Some even make up their own stories to share. Whatever your bedtime routine might be, I hope that prayer is part of it.

Saying a bedtime prayer with your children is one of the most important things you can do for them. It accomplishes several things, such as teaching your kids to pray by hearing you pray aloud, giving prayer a place of importance in their lives, making prayer a habit for them, drawing the family unit closer, and enriching their spiritual side. To put it in the words of my daughter Allyson, "Prayer rocks!"

We spend so much time just doing "stuff" with our kids—running them to soccer practice, helping with homework, playing board games—and all of that is good. But if we don't figure prayer time into the daily equation, we're just spinning our wheels. Prayer time is a precious time. Don't miss out on it even one night. It's a habit worth forming!

——————— MOM TO MASTER ———————

*Father, help me to teach my children*
*the importance of prayer time. Amen.*

# March 30

*Remember the days of old; consider the generations long past.*
DEUTERONOMY 32:7

Do you ever take a stroll down memory lane and take your kids with you? If not, you might want to put on your mental walking shoes and head down that path. Trust me, they'll like it!

My girls love to hear about "the olden days." They love to hear stories of when Jeff and I were high school sweethearts. They almost hurt themselves laughing when I share my most embarrassing moments. And they especially love the story about the time I met Shaquille O'Neal.

Funny, isn't it? Our children enjoy hearing about our youth. Sometimes I think our children believe we were born old. So when we share stuff from our past, they feel more connected to us. When my children found out that I was a cheerleader in high school and college, they were blown away! All of a sudden, Abby said, "Cool! Can you teach me?"

Sure, that does wonders for the old ego, but more than anything else, it establishes a line of communication that wasn't there before. It gives you a common ground with your kids. So go ahead. Share some funny stories from your youth. Your kids will love it.

------ MOM TO MASTER ------

*Thank You, Lord, for giving me such wonderful memories that I can share with my children. Amen.*

# March 31

*"If it is the Lord's will, we will live and do this or that."*

JAMES 4:15

I zipped past my father carrying an armload of dirty laundry. A few seconds later, I zipped past with a basket of clean laundry. Ten minutes later, I was wrapping Allyson's birthday presents while talking on the phone. As soon as I put down the receiver, my father sighed.

"You are too busy, honey," he said, sitting in the La-Z-Boy chair watching *The Price Is Right*.

I realized that I had totally ignored my precious visitor while trying to accomplish the tasks on my to-do list that morning. My seventy-nine-year-old dad had just wanted me to sit down and spend some quality time with him and Bob Barker. So I did. I let the answering machine get the rest of my calls, and I watched TV alongside my dad, making conversation on commercial breaks. Dad has suffered several strokes over the past three years, so every moment we have with him is a precious one.

There are times when those to-do lists serve us well, and there are other times when we need to crumple them up and toss them into the trash. That morning taught me something—don't be too busy with life to enjoy life. It's all about prioritizing, really.

—— MOM TO MASTER ——

*Lord, help me to prioritize my day in a way
that is pleasing to You. Amen.*

# April 1

*For where envy and self-seeking exist,*
*confusion and every evil thing are there.*
JAMES 3:16 NKJV

Once I was asked to cohost the Christmas party for my daughter Allyson's first-grade class. I felt overwhelmed—especially since I was cohosting with "The Perfect Mom." She was June Cleaver, Carol Brady, and Donna Reed all rolled into one. As she talked of creative crafts, groovy games, and adorable homemade treats, I realized my ideas were not nearly "Martha Stewart-y" enough. I quickly retreated and took direction from her.

I helped her create the Winter Wonderland party, but inside I was having a pity party. As I cleaned up the leftover goodies, Allyson threw her arms around my waist and squeezed her biggest squeeze.

"Thanks for coming today, Mommy," she said.

I hugged her back. In her eyes, I was a success. She didn't care that I couldn't get my snowman cakes to stand up. She didn't care that none of the games were my ideas. She loved me—flaws and all.

That's how God is. Many times we compare ourselves to others and feel we don't measure up, but God loves us—flaws and all. I may never be "The Perfect Mom," but as long as I'm the best mom I can be—that's enough.

——————— MOM TO MASTER ———————

*Lord, help me to keep my eyes on You and not on my shortcomings.*
*I repent for feeling jealous sometimes. Amen.*

# April 2

*"Come to me, all you who are weary and burdened,
and I will give you rest."*
MATTHEW 11:28

There were days when I'm sure the side of my SUV must have said TAXI. We ran to gymnastics. We raced to cheerleading practice. We rushed to art class. We hurried to Girl Scouts. We ate fast food on the way to computer class.

I wanted to stand up and say, "Stop the world from spinning! I want to get off!"

There is such pressure these days to make sure our children are in every extracurricular activity that sometimes I wonder if it's all too much. Have you been wondering the same thing?

We're moms. It's only natural that we desire to give our children the best. So it's no wonder we sign them up for all of these wonderful extracurricular opportunities. But be careful. Make sure you're not pushing and nudging your children right into burnout. We don't want our kids to be so overwhelmed with activities that they have no time to be kids. They only get one childhood. Ask God to help you enhance their growing-up years without overwhelming them with "stuff." Even good stuff, if there's too much of it, can be bad.

——————————— MOM TO MASTER ———————————

*Lord, help me not to pressure my children with too much "stuff." But help me to encourage the gifts that You have put inside them. Amen.*

# April 3

*I can do all this through him who gives me strength.*
PHILIPPIANS 4:13

As I climbed into bed, I felt lower than a snake's belly. I knew I had blown it.

My mind replayed all of the times I'd lost my temper with the girls throughout that day. Granted, Abby and Allyson had acted absolutely awful, but I had acted even worse. I wanted to bury my head under the covers and hibernate for at least six months.

Nobody likes to fail, but until we get to heaven, we're going to fail. We're going to have bad days. We're human! I think, as moms, we sometimes forget that fact. We set such high standards for ourselves—so high that they are unattainable by humans. So if you've been feeling lower than a snake's belly lately, take heart! God isn't mad at you. He loves you—temper tantrums and all. Just repent for your wrongdoings and ask Him to help you do better today. You can start fresh right now.

Determine to love more than you yell and laugh more than you nag. If you can do those two things today, you can go to bed tonight feeling really good! You may not be able to do those things in your own strength, but God can help you. Just ask Him.

—————————— MOM TO MASTER ——————————

*Father, I ask for Your forgiveness.*
*Help me to be quick to love, not quick to yell. Amen.*

# April 4

*Be perfect, be of good comfort, be of one mind, live in peace;*
*and the God of love and peace shall be with you.*
2 CORINTHIANS 13:11 KJV

Dictionary.com defines *perfection* like this:

*perfection* (per-fek-shuhn) *n.* A quality, trait, or feature of the highest degree of excellence.

Wow. If I am supposed to be "excellent" all the time, I'm in a heap of trouble. There are some days when I might earn that "Blue Ribbon of Excellence," but there are a lot of days when I wouldn't even qualify for an honorable mention. How about you?

That's why I like the Christian definition of perfection a lot better. One inspirational author defines "Christian perfection" like this: "loving God with all our heart, mind, soul, and strength."

Now that seems more doable to me. In other words, I don't always have to "get it right," but if my heart is right and if I'm truly seeking God, I can walk in Christian perfection. And guess what? You can too! We may never win another blue ribbon the rest of our lives, but we can still be winners. Who says nobody's perfect? If we're in love with God, we are!

———————— MOM TO MASTER ————————

*Father, help me to attain Christian*
*perfection every day of my life. Amen.*

# April 5

*You need to persevere so that when you have done the will of God, you will receive what he has promised.*

HEBREWS 10:36

Tae Bo. Pilates. Curves. Yep, I've tried them all (and I'm still trying most of them) to achieve that perfect body. You know—the bodies we had before pregnancy? I look at pictures of myself from my early twenties, and I'm amazed. You could actually see my abdominal muscles! Those were the days.

As a determined woman in my midthirties, I decided to regain my youthful figure. So I started exercising more than usual. I traded in my nightly power walk for an intense hour-long Winsor pilates workout. Once I was able to walk again, I added a thirty-minute resistance workout to my weekly routine. After three months, I found that I'd hurt myself in places I didn't even know existed! But I made progress. And I learned some things along the way.

Striving for perfection is a painful process no matter if you're trying to achieve the perfect body or the perfect walk with God. Perfection is a myth, really. We are made perfect through Christ Jesus—not through working it as hard as we can. If we keep our eyes on Jesus, He will cause us to succeed.

## MOM TO MASTER

*Father, help me not to get overwhelmed with the desire to be perfect. I want You to perfect me. Amen.*

# April 6

*"I have loved you with an everlasting love."*
JEREMIAH 31:3

I absolutely loved the quirky things about my kids. I loved the way Abby laughed uncontrollably at movies. I loved the way Allyson liked wearing clothes that matched mine. I loved the way they only liked purple grape juice because white grape juice just didn't make sense. I loved the way they fell asleep in the car—even if it was only a ten-minute drive to Walmart! I loved those little things about my girls because they are my precious children.

Do you know that God feels the same way about you and your quirky habits? He loves you—everything about you—period! Isn't that good to know?

So many people feel they have to become perfect before God will ever accept them, but that's simply not true. It's a lie that the devil likes to whisper in our ears to keep us from having a relationship with God. The truth is this: God loves us just the way we are! We don't have to be perfect. When we make Jesus the Lord over our lives, He gives us a clean slate. When the Father looks down at us, all He sees is Jesus inside of us, and Jesus is pure perfection.

———————— MOM TO MASTER ————————

*Father, help me to appreciate and celebrate*
*the quirkiness of my kids the same way*
*You love and celebrate me. Amen.*

# April 7

*In the same way, the Spirit helps us in our weakness.*
ROMANS 8:26

There's a great line from a movie that says, "You have to pass a test to get a driver's license, but they'll let anyone be a parent."

Of course, that line was said in jest, but it's actually true. Sometimes I feel like I received way more training to get behind the wheel than I did to raise two precious little girls. I had driver's education in high school. My father let me practice parallel parking in his car. I had lots of help, and I needed lots of help.

But when it came time to have my children, there was no mandatory parenting class. If it hadn't been for my mother and sister, I would've really been in trouble. I didn't know the first thing about sterilizing bottles. I had no clue how to work the Diaper Genie. I was hoping a genie would come out and do the forty-two loads of laundry awaiting me. I felt pretty inadequate to fill the "mommy shoes."

I discovered that I had to quit focusing on my inabilities as a mother and begin focusing on my abilities. God had chosen me to be a mom, and if He had chosen me, I knew that He had equipped me. He has equipped you too!

—————— MOM TO MASTER ——————

*Father, thank You for equipping me
to be a good mother. Amen.*

# April 8

*Each one should test their own actions. Then they can take pride in themselves alone, without comparing themselves to someone else.*

GALATIANS 6:4

If there were an award for "World's Most Creative Mom," my buddy Angie would win hands-down. She doesn't just call the bakery at Walmart to reserve a birthday cake. Are you kidding? She creates her own masterpiece! One year she made a barnyard scene cake, using snack cakes for the silo. Another year she made these adorable bug cupcakes, playing on the theme of *A Bug's Life.*

Angie is very creative and very fun. If I were a kid, I'd want her to be my mom. As you can imagine, Angie's creativity is hard to match. I used to feel like a big nerd compared to her. I'd worry that my children would end up on *Oprah,* telling the world that their mother never loved them enough to bake a barnyard cake.

One day while I was wishing I were more creative in the kitchen, the Lord convicted me. The gist of His message was simply, *"Get over it!"* God wanted me to know that He had given me special abilities that He hadn't given anyone else. Once I grasped that concept, I no longer felt nerdy. I still order Walmart cakes for my children, but I do so with great joy!

———————— MOM TO MASTER ————————

*Father, help me to be the best mom that I can be. Amen.*

# April 9

*For we are God's handiwork, created in Christ Jesus to do
good works, which God prepared in advance for us to do.*
EPHESIANS 2:10

I've always loved this scripture. Did you know that the word
*handiwork* indicates an ongoing process? So if we are God's
handiwork, we are God's ongoing project. In other words, He
isn't finished with us yet! Isn't that good news? I am so glad! I'd
hate to think that I was as good as I was going to get.

So if you are feeling less than adequate today, thinking that
you are a terrible mother and wife and Christian—cheer up! God
is not through with you yet! In fact, He is working on you right
now—even as you're reading this devotional. He knew that we'd
all make big mistakes, but this scripture says that He created us
in Christ Jesus to do good works. He's prepared the road for us.
He's been planning our steps long before we arrived here, so
don't worry!

We may not be where we want to be today, but as long as
we're further along than we were yesterday, we're making progress. We're on the right road. After all, we're God's handiwork,
and He only turns out good stuff!

———————— MOM TO MASTER ————————

*Thank You, God, for working on me,
perfecting me from glory to glory. Amen.*

# April 10

*"Before I formed you in the womb I knew you,*
*before you were born I set you apart."*

JEREMIAH 1:5

While I was pregnant, I read a book titled *What to Expect When You're Expecting* and learned the exact week that my baby would be able to hear sounds outside the womb. That's when I began reading stories to my belly. I even put headphones around my large middle section and let the baby listen to inspirational music. Jeff and I talked to my tummy, saying silly things like, "Hey, little girl! Can't wait to see you!"

Looking back, we were completely captivated by the entire experience. We felt as though we knew our daughters before they were ever born. After all, we'd been "interacting" with my belly for months—talking to it, reading to it, singing to it. I bet you did the same thing. Isn't it amazing how much you loved the baby you were carrying even though you'd never actually met that little person?

Having gone through that experience has given me a new appreciation for Jeremiah 1:5. To think that God knew me before I was ever born—wow! One translation says that God knew me and approved me. So if you are struggling with a poor self-image today, snap out of it! You've been approved by almighty God!

———————— MOM TO MASTER ————————

*Lord, thank You for approving me before*
*I was even born. Amen.*

# April 11

"I'm fat!" Abby said, stepping off the bathroom scales.

"Wonder where she's heard that before?" Jeff asked, raising his eyebrows at me.

Yes, I've been known to be a slave to the scales. And, yes, Abby has heard me say that before. Well, I'm not fat, and neither is she. But it seemed that my negative body image had been passed down to my ten-year-old daughter. With bulimia and anorexia affecting so many girls and women today, I realized the seriousness of Abby's statement.

I took Abby's face in my hands, and I said, "You are not fat. You are the perfect size, and even if you weren't, that wouldn't change how special you are to me, your daddy, and your heavenly Father."

She smiled and took off to play with her sister.

Our words are powerful. They have an effect—either good or bad. That encounter with Abby made me reevaluate my words. I repented, and I asked God to uproot those negative seeds that I'd unintentionally planted in Abby's heart and mind. Then I thanked God for His love and for His protection of my children.

If your mouth has been spewing words that aren't uplifting or godly, ask God to uproot those bad seeds. He knows our hearts, and He is a merciful God.

—— MOM TO MASTER ——

*Thank You, God, for protecting my children from wrong thinking. Amen.*

# April 12

*A heart at peace gives life to the body.*
PROVERBS 14:30

Are you at peace with the person God made you to be?

If you don't have peace within yourself, you'll never have peace with other people. God could send you another mom to be the friend you've been praying for, but if you're not at peace with yourself, that relationship won't work. You have to be happy with who God made you to be first before you can experience healthy relationships.

If you're focused on your imperfections and are constantly wishing you were someone else, you're allowing the devil to steal your peace and replace it with wrong thinking. Don't get caught in that trap. That's a miserable way to live. Learn to celebrate the person God made you to be.

The devil will try to convince you that you're a weak worm of the dust. He'll try to get you thinking wrong about yourself. But you need to declare out loud, "I am a child of the Most High King, and He thinks I'm great."

You may not be happy with every aspect of yourself, but you need to be happy about the basic person God created you to be. When you start practicing that mind-set, your peace will return. And that's a great way to live!

———————— MOM TO MASTER ————————

*Lord, I pray that Your peace overtakes me today.*
*Change my wrong thinking. Amen.*

# April 13

*Be strong and take heart, all you who hope in the Lord.*
PSALM 31:24

Do you ever just wake up and think, *Forget it! I'm not even going to try anymore!*? I sometimes do—especially if the scale says I've gained a pound or two and I've truly been trying to eat better. Or if my house is a total wreck and I have spent several hours the day before cleaning and "de-cluttering" it. Or if my work-load is massive and every editor is breathing down my neck at the same time. That's when I hit overload and basically shut down. That's when you'll find me in the fetal position, under the bed, with chocolate in hand.

A better way to handle those days when stress and feelings of inadequacy try to overtake us is to run to Jesus. Some people forget that Jesus is Lord over every part of our lives—even the stressful parts. Tell yourself, "My hope is in the Lord. I don't have to have everything figured out. He has already gone before me, ensuring my victory." Now, rejoice! Be strong! Take heart! And, sure, have a piece of chocolate if it makes you feel better!

——————— MOM TO MASTER ———————

*Father, I am feeling stressed out and inadequate today.*
*Help me to handle every part of my life with Your loving*
*touch and Your infinite wisdom. I love You. Amen.*

# April 14

*Therefore, if anyone is in Christ, the new creation has come:*
*The old has gone, the new is here!*

2 CORINTHIANS 5:17

My sister, Martie, is a genius at her craft. She is a professional interior designer, and her eye for detail is unbelievable! She can take most any room and make it lovely. It's pretty amazing, really. Using the same furniture, the same pillows, and the same accessories, she can arrange them in such a way that the entire room is transformed into something beautiful.

With just a tweak here and a new seating area over there, voilà! My living room looks great! Who would have dreamed it could look so wonderful? And I didn't even have to get new furniture to get a "new look."

Well, let me introduce you to another Master of Design— the Almighty Himself! God is so masterful that He can take our old lives, and with a tweak here and a tweak there, He can transform us into beautiful creatures. Our once old and ugly hearts are revived, rejuvenated, and transformed by the Master's touch. So if you're in need of a heart transformation today, go to the Master Designer. He has a new look just waiting for you!

———————— MOM TO MASTER ————————

*Father, I am in need of a makeover. Please mold me and make me*
*into the beautiful creature You've called me to be. Amen.*

# April 15

*Finally, brothers and sisters, whatever is true, whatever is noble,*
*whatever is right, whatever is pure, whatever is lovely,*
*whatever is admirable—if anything is excellent or*
*praiseworthy—think about such things.*

PHILIPPIANS 4:8

"Don't go there, girlfriend!"

I have a friend who always says that to me when I am heading toward the self-pity pit. Funny as that expression sounds, it packs a lot of wisdom. If we can stop ourselves before we start wallowing in that self-pity pit, we'll be a lot better off in the long run. See, once you get down in that pit, it's hard to claw your way back out.

For me, all it takes is dwelling on something negative for a few minutes. I'll start to think about the fight I had with my daughters that morning, and the next thing I know, I am looking up from the center of that yucky pit.

I believe that's why the Bible tells us to think on good and lovely things. God knew that if we thought on the other stuff for very long, we'd wind up in that old, yucky pit. So if you're in that pit today, reach up! God is reaching out to you, ready to help you out. Think on Him—not on your past failures.

—————— MOM TO MASTER ——————

*Lord, help me to spend time thinking on good*
*and lovely things—not my past failures. Amen.*

# April 16

*I will praise you as long as I live.*
PSALM 63:4

Have you ever watched a college cheerleading squad? Their motions are perfectly timed, in sync, on beat, and very sharp. If one member is behind a half a count, you'll be able to tell. Even minor flaws and mistakes are greatly magnified when the rest of the team is so good.

Do you ever feel like that cheerleader who is a half step behind the entire routine? Me too. Sometimes it seems that all of the moms I know have it all together, and I'm kicking with the wrong leg. The devil loves to point out our shortcomings and whisper things like, "Hey, you are the worst mother ever. If you were a better mom, your children would be doing better in school."

See, the devil knows what buttons to push in order to make you feel the very worst, but don't let him have access to your buttons. When you start to compare yourself with another mother, stop yourself. Right then, begin thanking God for giving you the wisdom and strength to be the best mom you can be. When you respond to the devil's button pushing with praise for the Father, you will send the devil packing.

———————— MOM TO MASTER ————————

*Father, help me to be the best mom I can be. Help me to stop comparing myself with others. I praise You. Amen.*

# April 17

*"God does not show favoritism."*
ACTS 10:34

Did you ever see the movie *The Princess Diaries* starring Julie Andrews and Anne Hathaway? It's a wonderful story of an "ugly duckling" who is turned into a "lovely swan." We loved the movie so much that we also purchased the soundtrack, which features a song called "What Makes You Different." I love this song by the Backstreet Boys. The chorus says, "What makes you different makes you beautiful to me."

Isn't that cool? As moms, wouldn't it be great if we could communicate that message to our kids on a daily basis? I want Allyson to know that her cute little beauty-mark-of-a-mole above her lip not only makes her different but also makes her beautiful. And more importantly, I want my girls to know that God adores their differences and that He thinks they are beautiful.

I wish I'd learned that truth early on. As an adult, it's harder to accept God's unconditional love and approval. Some days I look at all of my shortcomings, and I wonder how anyone could love me. On those days, it's hard to feel beautiful. Yet, in my quiet time, I can hear God singing softly in my ear, *"What makes you different makes you beautiful to Me. . . ."* Let God sing to you today.

——————————— MOM TO MASTER ———————————

*Thank You, Father, for Your unconditional
love and acceptance. Amen.*

# April 18

*But whoever looks intently into the perfect law that gives freedom,*
*and continues in it. . .they will be blessed in what they do.*
JAMES 1:25

My niece Mandy and I always tease each other, saying, "You *so* want to be me." Of course, that comment must be followed with a smirk and a head toss for the full effect. While we're just having fun, there are some days when I'd rather be anyone but me. Ever been there? How about when you're fifteen minutes late for your child's parent-teacher conference? Or how about when you forget to send out your daughter's birthday invitations? Yes, I've done both of those dastardly deeds. Guilty!

Isn't it good to know that God doesn't expect us to be perfect? He understands that we are going to drop the ball once in a while. We're human! He knows that because He created us. You're allowed to make mistakes. Whew! Good thing, eh?

As I get older, I have learned to relax a bit more. Or, as they say here in Texas, "I've learned to let stuff roll off of me like water off a duck's back." (Okay, so I'm not exactly sure what that expression means, but it's a good visual, isn't it?)

So relax. If you make a parenting mistake, God has you covered. Look to His Word for wisdom and guidance. We should all "*so* want to be like Him."

---
## MOM TO MASTER
---

*Lord, thank You for loving me even though*
*I am not, nor ever will be, perfect. Amen.*

## April 19

*When they measure themselves by themselves and
compare themselves with themselves, they are not wise.*

2 CORINTHIANS 10:12

Our assignment was to make a poster encouraging parents to join the PTA. Sounds easy enough, right? Well, this easy task turned into an all-day fiasco. Once I was informed that each class would have its own poster, I got nervous. That meant that our poster needed to be extraordinarily good because it would be compared to all of the other PTA posters. This poster for Abby's fifth-grade class became more than a task—it became a mission!

Using our newly purchased art supplies, Abby and I began creating a very peppy poster. The theme was "Join the Team!" so we cut out pictures of sports figures and glued them all over the blank poster board. Then we wrote the words "Join the Team!" and decorated each letter with glitter. I was quite proud of our creation—until I saw all of the other posters.

They were masterpieces! Our best hadn't been good enough. Suddenly, I was sad for Abby because her mommy was such a poor artist. But she wasn't one bit disappointed! In fact, she thought our poster was the best. You see, it's all in the perspective. Ask God to give you back your childlike perspective today.

——————— MOM TO MASTER ———————

*Lord, help me to be satisfied with my best.
Please give me a childlike perspective. Amen.*

# April 20

*. . .fixing our eyes on Jesus, the pioneer and perfecter of faith.*

HEBREWS 12:2

We were planning a bridal shower at my house for a dear friend of mine. Her maid of honor asked that we all wear pink—Camille's main wedding color. I thought that was a lovely idea; however, I look like Ronald McDonald in pink! My hair has a lot of gold in it—and, yes, a bit of red—and pink is one color that makes my hair look brassy. When I wear pink (which is hardly ever), my husband and kids call me the "Heat Miser." (Remember the Heat Miser cartoon villain from *The Year without a Santa Claus?*)

As I whined about wearing pink, my ten-year-old daughter, Abby, spoke something I'll never forget.

"Don't worry about what you'll look like," she said. "All eyes will be on Camille anyway. It's her party."

Wow, what insight from a ten-year-old!

She was right. I was so focused on looking presentable that I'd lost sight of the whole reason we were having the shower—to honor Camille.

Many times I become so self-absorbed that I lose sight of the real mission. Do you do that too? The Word tells us to fix our eyes on Jesus. If you have your eyes on Him, you'll remain focused on the mission—not on yourself. Where are your eyes today?

——————— MOM TO MASTER ———————

*Lord, help me to keep my eyes on You. Amen.*

# April 21

*I can do all this through him who gives me strength.*
PHILIPPIANS 4:13

I have big dreams—so big that I'd be embarrassed to share them with anyone. Sometimes I'll write about my dreams in my journal, and later when I read over them, I even embarrass myself. I get that whole attitude of, "Who do you think you are? You could never accomplish those things."

That "Negative Nellie" voice rears her ugly head from time to time, and I have to silence her with the Word of God because it says I can do *all* things through Christ who gives me strength. It's not me—it's Him! God in me can accomplish things even bigger than I could ever dream.

God in you can do "big, huge" things too—as my daughter Allyson likes to say. So get your big, huge faith on, and go after those dreams! Maybe you've always wanted to write a children's book or teach a women's Bible study. Chances are, God placed those dreams in your heart, so He will help you accomplish them.

Isn't that great news? God has caused you to dream big dreams, so you can expect Him to help you *big-time*! You have big dreams and a big God—that's a powerful combination!

———————————— MOM TO MASTER ————————————

*Father, I know that You are the author of my dreams,*
*so I am asking You to assist me as I pursue them. Amen.*

# April 22

*But thanks be to God!*
*He gives us the victory through our Lord Jesus Christ.*
1 CORINTHIANS 15:57

It's been one of those days. You know the kind I mean—when no matter what you do, you end up frustrated. It's on those days when perfection seems an eternity away. It's on those days when I'm sure I'll never measure up. It's on those days when I have to stop and crawl into my heavenly Father's lap and let Him reassure me.

He reminds me that I am an overcomer through Him. He tells me that I am the apple of His eye. He whispers, *"You can do all things through Me."* Suddenly, I am restored, revived, revved up, and ready to go.

You know, we need to do the same thing for our kids. There are many days when my children come dragging in from school—lower than a snake's belly. I can tell that they've encountered some "yucky stuff" that day. That's when we as moms can speak life into them—just as our heavenly Father does for us. We can restore, revive, and rev them up and send them back out ready to go.

So get yourself reenergized so that you'll be ready to give to your children. Remember, you are victorious through Jesus. Shout your victory today!

—— MOM TO MASTER ——

*Thank You, Father, for loving me when I fall*
*way short of perfection. I love You. Amen.*

# April 23

*Do you not know that in a race all the runners run,*
*but only one gets the prize? Run in such a way as to get the prize.*
1 CORINTHIANS 9:24

I used to run track. Okay, it's been *many* years since I ran competitively, but I remember what it was like to race toward that finish line, giving it everything I had. I didn't always win, but I sure gave it my all. Our track coach never expected any more than our best performance. He was happy with us if we ran our hardest, even if we didn't win first place.

You know what? God feels the same way. He doesn't expect you to be the best in every situation. He just expects you to do your best every time. If you go for the gold and only bring home a silver, that's okay.

Like the Bible says, press toward the mark. Run a good race. Step out in faith. Then, even if you don't get the prize, you'll be able to hear God whisper, *"Well done, My good and faithful servant,"* because you gave it your all.

So lace up those spiritual track shoes and get back in the race. The finish line awaits!

——————— MOM TO MASTER ———————

*Thank You, Father, for giving me Your approval even when I don't*
*win the race. Help me to always give it my all. I love You. Amen.*

# April 24

*To all perfection I see a limit,*
*but your commands are boundless.*
PSALM 119:96

You know the problem with trying to be perfect? You always end up disappointed in yourself and others. During the seasons of my life when I've been on the "Polly Perfectionist" kick, I've noticed that's when I become more critical of myself and others. When I get in that perfectionist mode, I not only find fault with everything I do, but also with everything that others do. As you might imagine, I don't have a lot of friends who want to hang out with me when I have on my Polly Perfectionist hat.

Bottom line—no one is perfect. No matter how hard we try, we'll never achieve perfection until we get to heaven. That doesn't mean we shouldn't strive to be and do our best, but it does mean we should give ourselves and others a break. Take your eyes off of your shortcomings, stop finding fault with others, and look to God.

Rest in the Lord and meditate on His perfection. After all, He is the only Perfect One. He doesn't expect perfection from you, so you shouldn't expect it from others. If you're in that Polly Perfectionist mode, ask God to help you accept yourself as human and move on.

---

## MOM TO MASTER

*Father, help me to strive for perfection*
*but accept when I fall short. Amen.*

# April 25

*We all stumble in many ways. Anyone who is never at fault in what they say is perfect.*

JAMES 3:2

I'm so thankful that God chooses to use imperfect people to accomplish His will on this earth. Take Moses, for example. He killed an Egyptian for mistreating an Israelite and later got so angry that God's people were worshipping a golden calf, that he smashed the Ten Commandments—yikes! Or what about Peter? He cut off a guy's ear and denied that he ever knew Jesus—not once. . .but three times! Wow! Isn't it good to know that even Moses and Peter messed up once in a while? Somehow, I find that comforting.

Okay, so I haven't cut off anybody's ear lately, but I have bitten off a few heads. And while I haven't smashed any commandments recently, I've broken a few of them. My husband and children would be the first to tell you that I'm not perfect. But I am a work in progress. Just like Moses and Peter, we are all attaining from glory to glory. And thank the Lord that He uses imperfect people just like us. He knows our limitations, and He still loves us. So if you're having a "commandment-smashing, ear-cutting-off" kind of day, don't worry. God can still use you!

———————— MOM TO MASTER ————————

*Thank You, Lord, for using me—even though I am less than perfect. Amen.*

# April 26

*But he said to me, "My grace is sufficient for you, for my power is made perfect in weakness." Therefore I will boast all the more gladly about my weaknesses, so that Christ's power may rest on me.*

2 CORINTHIANS 12:9

Nobody likes to admit weaknesses, but hey, we have all got them. The good news is this—God can work with weakness. In fact, His Word tells us that His power is made perfect in our weakness. Pretty cool, eh? So why is it so difficult to admit we have weaknesses?

I hate to admit that I have weaknesses—especially with my children. I like to appear perfect and "superhero-like." I want Abby and Allyson to think they have the coolest mom in the world—a mom who loves God, loves them, and can still skateboard with the best of them. But over the years, I'm pretty sure my daughters have figured out that Mom has some weaknesses—definitely! The cat is out of the bag, so to speak.

And I'm okay with that. If we let our children see our shortcomings, they'll feel better about their own weaknesses. So quit trying to disguise your weaknesses or make excuses for them. Just admit you have them and let God's power be made perfect in them.

—————— MOM TO MASTER ——————

*Father, thank You for working through my weaknesses. Amen.*

# April 27

*Every good and perfect gift is from above,*
*coming down from the Father of the heavenly lights,*
*who does not change like shifting shadows.*

JAMES 1:17

When Abby and Allyson were born, I wrote in their baby books "My Gifts from Up Above." That's exactly how I felt about each one of my daughters. As I looked down into their faces, I couldn't believe how blessed we were. I bet you felt the same when you had your children. Whether you gave birth to them or adopted them, they were the best gifts you'd ever received, weren't they?

I remember thinking, "They are so perfect, and I didn't do anything to deserve these precious children. God just gave them to me. He loves me that much!"

God is like that. He just loves to give gifts to us—that's what daddies do.

So even on the days when your little darlings are less than perfect and you're thinking, *I thought that scripture said the Father only sends good and perfect gifts*—rejoice! You are blessed. Send up praise to the Father for your children, your spouse, your home, your extended family, your friends. God loves sending blessings our way—especially when we appreciate the ones He has already sent.

—— MOM TO MASTER ——

*Father, thank You for every gift You've sent my way. I am especially thankful for my children. I appreciate You. Amen.*

# April 28

*There is no fear in love. But perfect love drives out fear.*
1 JOHN 4:18

Okay, so I've accepted the fact that I'll never be perfect. But it's good to know that God's perfect love is available to me and that His love drives out fear. You know, as moms, we encounter a lot of fears concerning our children. We fear they won't develop properly when they are growing inside of us. We fear we'll do something wrong as parents. We fear they aren't learning like other children. We fear we aren't spending enough time with them. . .and on and on and on.

But Romans 8:15 tells us that we did not receive a spirit that makes us slaves to fear; rather, we received the Spirit of son-ship. That entitles us to the right to cry out to God as our Abba Father. He wants us to run to Him when we're fearful. He wants to cast that fear right out of our hearts.

So if you're struggling with fears of inadequacy, or if you're worried about your children to the point that your stomach is in knots—run to God! Let Him replace your fear with His perfect love. Now that's a deal you can't refuse!

—————— MOM TO MASTER ——————

*Father, thank You for Your perfect love.*
*I will not fear for You are my God. Amen.*

# April 29

*Clothe yourselves with. . .patience.*
COLOSSIANS 3:12

Have you ever noticed that everybody seems to have an opinion concerning how you should raise your children? Oh yeah—even the woman at the dry cleaners said I should take away my daughters' pacifiers before long, because if I didn't, their teeth would rot. That was an interesting tidbit of information I hadn't counted on when dropping off my "Dry Clean Only" laundry.

Many times you'll receive parenting advice from your own mother or your mother-in-law—whether you ask for it or not. They feel it's their duty to impart their nuggets of knowledge. If you're like me, you sometimes tire of endless advice. You've read the parenting books. You are prayerfully parenting your kids. Admit it, there are times when you want to yell, "Back off! They're my kids, and I'm doing the best I can do!"

But before you verbally attack your mom the next time she criticizes the type of detergent you're using on your baby's garments, pray. Ask God to help you receive everyone's input with graciousness and gratitude. You certainly don't have to follow their advice, but grin sweetly as they relay their theory of potty training. Someday you'll be the one dishing out advice. It's true, you know. We do become our mothers!

——————— MOM TO MASTER ———————

*Father, help me to receive advice
with grace and gratitude. Amen.*

# April 30

*"As for God, his way is perfect: The Lord's word is flawless;*
*he shields all who take refuge in him."*

2 SAMUEL 22:31

"It's my way or the highway!" I heard my voice shout to Abby as she stormed out of the room.

We were having a rather spirited discussion about her disobedience. I let her know that she would follow the rules of the house, or she would spend a lot of time grounded to her room—period! At age ten, Abby wasn't too keen on the whole "grounded for life" scene. So my declaration of "It's my way or the highway!" seemed quite effective.

While it's a catchy phrase, it's not very correct in God's eyes. It's not my goal to parent my children my way, because my way is rarely the right one. My instincts are often wrong, and I'm way too emotional to make good, solid decisions every time. God's way is *way* more effective. Funny, though, how I sometimes forget that until I've already tried it my way and fallen flat on my face. Ever been there?

So if you're trying to handle everything on your own today—don't! Give it to God. Ask for His divine intervention. His way is best. After all, He is the Way!

———————— MOM TO MASTER ————————

*Lord, I want to do things Your way—*
*all the time. I love You. Amen.*

# May 1

*You should praise the LORD for his love and for
the wonderful things he does for all of us.*

PSALM 107:21 CEV

Don't you just love to give gifts to your children? Isn't it exciting to surprise them with something they've really been longing for—like a new bike or a trip to an amusement park? It is so much fun to see their eyes light up and their enthusiastic smiles and giggles commence. I love to bless my children. When Abby and Allyson give me big hugs and squeal "Thank you," my heart melts. I can hardly wait until the next time I can do something nice for them.

You know, God is the same way. He loves to bless His children. He loves to surprise us with the desires of our hearts. He delights in sending us unexpected gifts and blessings. But He also expects us to acknowledge His blessings. He expects us to have grateful hearts. So make sure the next time the Father sends down a blessing, you immediately stop and thank Him for His wonderful gift. Go ahead. Tell Him right now just how thankful you are today. He does so much for all of us. He is worthy to be praised!

--- MOM TO MASTER ---

*Thank You, Lord, for all that You do for me.
I appreciate You, and I am so thankful for
the many blessings in my life. Amen.*

# May 2

*Give thanks to the LORD, for he is good;*
*his love endures forever.*

PSALM 107:1

Have you ever heard the expression, "You'd better thank your lucky stars!" People say it all the time. In fact, you may have even said it a time or two. Or how about, "Well, thank goodness!" Funny how sayings slip into our speech without us really giving them much thought. But we really should be more careful with our speech—especially when we're dishing out thanks.

When something good happens to you, don't thank your lucky stars or goodness—they didn't have anything to do with it! Thank your loving heavenly Father who lavishly blesses us every day. Get into the habit of immediately recognizing the Lord for His goodness right when it happens. If I get a parking spot up front at Walmart, I say, "Thank You, Lord, for holding that spot just for me." Make thanking God a habit, and you'll find that you have many reasons to praise Him. It puts you in an attitude of gratitude, and that's a great place to be!

———— MOM TO MASTER ————

*Thank You, Lord, for everything that You do for*
*me each day. Help me to be better at recognizing*
*every blessing You send my way. Amen.*

# May 3

*Great peace have those who love your law,*
*and nothing can make them stumble.*
PSALM 119:165

Did you know that God's Word contains approximately seven thousand promises in its pages? It has promises to cover any circumstance or problem you'll ever encounter. If you're ill and need God's healing touch, the Word says, "By his wounds you have been healed" (1 Peter 2:24). If you're struggling financially, the Bible says, "My God will meet all your needs according to the riches of his glory in Christ Jesus" (Philippians 4:19). If your teenagers are rebelling against you and God, the Word says, "But from everlasting to everlasting the LORD's love is with those who fear him, and his righteousness with their children's children" (Psalm 103:17).

No matter what is going on in your life today, God has you covered. If you can find a promise in His Word, you have something solid to stand on and build your faith on. Aren't you thankful for that today? God's Word has all of the answers, and we have access to those answers twenty-four hours a day. We live in a country that enjoys religious freedom, so we can even read His promises in public. Praise God for His promises today.

-------- MOM TO MASTER --------

*Thank You, Lord, for Your Word. I praise You for*
*the many promises contained in its pages. Amen.*

# May 4

*And do not forget to do good and to share with others,
for with such sacrifices God is pleased.*
HEBREWS 13:16

Remember that '80s song "What Have You Done for Me Lately" by Janet Jackson? While I like that song (you're humming it right now, aren't you?), I do not like that attitude—especially when I get it from my children. One time I carted home several new outfits from Limited Too, my daughters' favorite store. They were ecstatic—for about twenty minutes.

Later that evening when I wouldn't drop everything and run them into town for a McDonald's fix, I heard one of my angels say, "You never do anything for us." I wanted to flush their new outfits down the toilet! But I didn't. Instead, I shut my bedroom door and brooded. During that time, the Holy Spirit revealed to me that I sometimes act that same way with God. He will give me a huge blessing, and I'll rejoice for a while, but two days later, I am whining around about how God has forgotten me simply because something didn't work out exactly as I'd desired.

Do you do the same thing? If so, repent and ask God to rid you of your "What Have You Done for Me Lately?" 'tude.

---------------------- MOM TO MASTER ----------------------

*Thank You, Lord, for all You do for me.
Help me to never forget Your goodness. Amen.*

# May 5

*I urge, then, first of all, that petitions, prayers,*
*intercession and thanksgiving be made for all people—*
*for kings and all those in authority, that we may live peaceful*
*and quiet lives in all godliness and holiness.*

1 TIMOTHY 2:1–2

Ever since the United States experienced the tragedy of September 11, 2001, I've looked at life a little differently. I think we all have. September 11 made us realize that we're not promised tomorrow, so we'd better be thankful for today.

It's made me more thankful for every minute of every day. It's made me hug my children more often. It's made me call my husband just to say I love him. It's made me share my faith a little more aggressively. It's made me reprioritize my life. And it's made me appreciate the freedom and privileges that come from being an American.

Are you thankful today for your rights as an American? Then join with me and commit to praying regularly for our leaders and our military personnel who defend and protect this country. Let's thank God for His covering over this nation and praise Him that we can worship Him without fear. And let's encourage our kids to do the same. With prayer and praise, we give the devil a one-two patriotic punch!

—————————— MOM TO MASTER ——————————

*Lord, I pray for my nation today, and I thank You for allowing me to live in a country that was founded on Christian beliefs. Amen.*

# May 6

*"But seek first his kingdom and his righteousness,
and all these things will be given to you as well."*
MATTHEW 6:33

Do your kids ever get the "gimme syndrome"? You know, the "gimme this and gimme that" phase. We've lived through a few of those in our house. Of course, there are the "terrible twos" when everything is "mine!" And then the tweens seem to bring out the "gimmes" in a more expensive way. Instead of "Gimme that sucker," it's "Gimme that go-kart." (I always feared the teen years would give birth to "Gimme that Corvette!")

No matter the season, the "gimme syndrome" is bad. You see, "gimmes" always lead to more "gimmes." The Bible might say it like this: "Gimmes beget gimmes." Once you fulfill the first "gimme requests," there are always more to follow. It's continual!

But if we seek God first, all of our wants and "gimmes" will be fulfilled. We need to keep our "gimmes" under control and focus our energies on seeking God. If we breed little "gimme" kids, they'll carry that mentality over into their relationship with God. Their prayers will be filled with, "Hi, God. Gimme this and gimme that. Amen." Ask God to get the "gimmes" out of your household today. That's one request He'll be happy to fulfill!

――――――― MOM TO MASTER ―――――――

*Lord, I pray that You remove the "gimme"
attitude from my household. I love You. Amen.*

# May 7

*One who has unreliable friends soon comes to ruin,*
*but there is a friend who sticks closer than a brother.*
PROVERBS 18:24

Sometimes being a mom is a lonely gig. Before my children were born, I was quite the social butterfly, fluttering my way to social event after social event. After Abby and Ally came along, I was lucky to get a shower by noon. So I lost contact with a lot of those social friends—the ones you only see at events. And even some of my dearest buddies from college sort of ditched me once I was a mom. After all, they were still single and living a totally different life. That left me with a few mommy friends I'd met through my MOPS (Mothers of Preschoolers) group and our church. I wasn't very close with any of them, and there wasn't much time for building close relationships with two toddlers in the house. So I cried out to God for a friend. That's when I heard that still, small voice say, *"I'm your Friend."*

Wow. I'd totally forgotten that I had a friend in Jesus—even though I'd sung that hymn a thousand times in my life. So if you're feeling isolated and friendless today—look up. You have a friend in Him. I'm thankful for His friendship today.

—————————— MOM TO MASTER ——————————

*Lord, thank You for being my best Friend. Amen.*

# May 8

*. . .that my heart may sing your praises and not be silent.*
*LORD my God, I will praise you forever.*

PSALM 30:12

We teach our kids to say "please" and "thank you," and that's a good thing. Manners are very important; however, I often wonder if we're just teaching our kids to go through the motions without the proper motivation. In other words, do they just say "thank you" because they know they're supposed to, or are they really thankful?

If I do nothing else right, I want to raise my girls to be thankful, appreciative children. Of course, I'd like them to truly mean their "thank you" responses in day-to-day life. But more than anything, I want them to be thankful to our Lord Jesus Christ for His many blessings.

I think the best way to teach our kids to have thankful hearts toward our heavenly Father is by example. If they see us—their moms—praising God and acknowledging His goodness in everyday life, they'll follow our lead. So take time to teach not only the manner part of "thank you," but also the heart part of "thank you." Let's enter His gates with thanksgiving in our hearts every day! He is worthy of our praise, and our children need to know that. So go on, get your praise on!

---

## MOM TO MASTER

*Lord, thank You for being my heavenly Father.*
*I praise You today! Amen.*

# May 9

*They were also to stand every morning
to thank and praise the Lord.*
1 Chronicles 23:30

I've never been much of a morning person. This was especially true when I was a child. I'd wait until the absolute last possible moment to get out of bed. But my morning "wake-up call" began at 6 a.m. every weekday, courtesy of my mother, Marion, who *is* a morning person.

She didn't just knock on the door and say, "Time to get up." Oh no—she was far too joyful for that. My mother had an entire musical extravaganza worked out. She'd begin with her rendition of "This is the day that the Lord has made. We will rejoice and be glad in it." All of this singing was accompanied by very loud handclapping, and if that didn't do the trick, she would flip the lights on and off in time to her singing.

As you might have guessed, I proudly carry on this tradition. I even sing the same song, accompanied by loud handclaps and my own light show. And my kids moan and groan, much the same way I did. Nevertheless, we begin each day praising God and thanking Him for another day—some of us a little more than others! We're starting the day on the right note—why not join in the fun?

—————— MOM TO MASTER ——————

*Lord, thank You for another day to praise You. Amen.*

# May 10

*Give praise to the LORD, proclaim his name;*
*make known among the nations what he has done.*

1 CHRONICLES 16:8

Did you know there are several places in the Bible where we are instructed to tell what God has done for us? In other words, when God blesses us, we need to shout it from the rooftops. My kids are really good about this.

One time Abby could hardly wait to tell everyone how God had blessed her with tickets and backstage passes to the Newsboys concert in Dallas. She had prayed that God would enable her to go because she'd never been to a concert, and miraculously, God came through *big-time*! It was pretty amazing. The Lord "just happened" to have one of the band members come to one of my book signings. And my daughters "just happened" to be with me, and he "just happened" to give us tickets and backstage passes. Isn't it spectacular the lengths that God will go to in order to bless His children?

So go ahead and testify about God's goodness in your life. Encourage your children to share their praise reports too. In fact, you might even schedule a special time each week for family praise reports. It could be fun, and God will love it!

—————— MOM TO MASTER ——————

*Lord, You are so good to us, and I want to shout*
*Your goodness from the rooftops! Amen.*

# May 11

*Praise the Lord. Give thanks to the Lord,*
*for he is good; his love endures forever.*
PSALM 106:1

When my girls were really little, I used to listen to them pray at night. They thanked God for everything under the sun—grasshoppers, popcorn, mud pies, Oreo cookies, puppies, swimming pools, kittens, chocolate bars, ballet classes—everything! In fact, one of Allyson's prayers actually inspired my board book, *Why I Love You, God.* She totally cracked me up, thanking God for the littlest of things—even lollipops!

But you know, besides being cute, our children's prayers should be a model for our grown-up prayers. When they count their blessings, they *really* count their blessings. Many times, as adults, we rush through our evening prayers without really thanking God for anything specific. We just send up a generic prayer and hope for the best. If we come to the Lord like little children, as the Word says, we are sure to get it right. So follow your children's lead. Thank the Lord and *really* count your blessings!

——————— MOM TO MASTER ———————

*Lord, I want to thank You for all of the blessings in my life—*
*Your unconditional love, my children, my mate, my extended*
*family, sunny days, springtime flowers, my pets, my church,*
*my friends, Doris Day movies—everything! Amen.*

# May 12

*You are my God, and I will praise you;*
*you are my God, and I will exalt you.*

PSALM 118:28

When I think about my earthly father, I always smile. My dad is the kind of dad who dotes on his children. My sister teases that she's his favorite, and I tease back that I am, but in all honesty, he makes both of us feel like the favorite child. And if you asked my brother, he'd say *he* was Dad's favorite! That's just how my dad is, and that's exactly how God is too. He is a doting Dad. He loves us so much. In fact, He adores us!

But I don't love my dad because he is good to me or even because he makes me feel like I'm his favorite. I love my dad simply because he is Dad. You know, we should love our heavenly Father for that very same reason—not for what He can give us or do for us—but simply because He is our Father. That's what Psalm 118:28 says to me: "You are my God, and I will praise you." Tell Him today how much you love Him—just for being Him.

—————— MOM TO MASTER ——————

*Father, I want to praise You today just for being You.*
*I am so thankful You are my heavenly Father. Amen.*

# May 13

*Let us come before him with thanksgiving*
*and extol him with music and song.*

PSALM 95:2

When I think of attacking someone in battle, I think of a "sneak attack." I envision a great army in camouflage, quietly approaching the enemy at night when all are asleep. If I were going to plan an attack, that's probably how I'd do it. But you know what? God didn't plan attacks like that. Over and over again in the Old Testament, God sent "the praise and worship team" ahead of the troops, singing and playing music unto the Lord. You can bet they weren't sneaking up on anyone, not with all the singing and shouting going on up front.

Obviously, God was trying to communicate something to us—praise and worship are very important! There are days when I don't feel much like praising God. You know the days I'm talking about, right? Like when your child's teacher calls to tell you that your child is failing math. Or when your boss tells you the company is downsizing and you're being let go. Those are not joyous times; however, we are supposed to praise God in spite of the circumstances. Why? Because when we praise Him—especially in the bad times—we ensure our victory. If you're in need of a victory today, praise the Lord!

───────── MOM TO MASTER ─────────

*Father, I praise You today in spite of*
*the bad stuff in my life. Amen.*

# May 14

*Let the message of Christ dwell among you richly as you teach and admonish one another with all wisdom through psalms, hymns, and songs from the Spirit, singing to God with gratitude in your hearts.*

COLOSSIANS 3:16

The phrase "with gratitude in your heart" appears over and over again in the scriptures. You know what that says to me? It says, "Hey, Michelle. Just thanking God isn't enough. Your heart has to be filled with gratitude." You may fool your family and friends with your false gratitude or pitiful praise, but God looks on the heart. He sees what's really in there.

I found myself doing this with my kids too. Abby or Allyson would draw me a picture and hand it to me (usually when I was right in the middle of something hugely important), and I would say, "Thanks, honey. That's really nice." Hardly giving it a glance, I'd slap it up on the fridge. Ever been there? See, we should not only have a heart filled with gratitude when we praise God, but also when we thank our family. Kids are perceptive. They may not be able to see your heart, but they sense when you're just going through the motions.

So do a heart check today. Is your heart full of gratitude? If not, get a refill. God has gratitude with your name on it. Just ask Him.

—— MOM TO MASTER ——

*Father, I praise You with my whole heart today.*
*I love You and appreciate You. Amen.*

# May 15

She was one of Abby's friends, but this little girl bugged me. I love kids. I even write children's books! But she was a challenge. One afternoon I took Abby and her little friend shopping. While in the Bible bookstore, I purchased a cute cross bracelet for each of them. Abby hugged and thanked me. But the little friend didn't even say thanks! She just slipped on the bracelet and went on her merry way.

I kept thinking, *If she were my daughter, I would be disciplining her right now.* But you know what? It wasn't my place to discipline her. My job was simply to show her the love of Jesus. See, God expects us to show grace and mercy to others the same way He shows grace and mercy to us. I know there have been times when God has sent down a blessing and I've "slipped it on" and gone on my merry way. How about you? If you've been less than grateful lately, repent and spend some time thanking God for His goodness today.

## MOM TO MASTER

*Father, help me to always have a grateful spirit.*
*Help me to be an example for You. Amen.*

# May 16

*"But be sure to fear the L*ORD *and serve him faithfully with all your heart; consider what great things he has done for you."*
1 SAMUEL 12:24

Ever heard that catchy little praise and worship chorus that says, "Look what the Lord has done."? It's one of my all-time favorites. I love the tune, of course, but I especially like the words, "Look what the Lord has done!" I like to keep a journal so I can look back and see what God has done.

I have a little notebook (pretty ratty looking at this point) that I call my *Prayer and Praise Journal,* and I record various requests and prayer concerns inside. Then, when God answers my prayers, I go back and check them off, recording the details of God's miraculous interventions. It's exciting to look back and see what the Lord has done.

I encourage you to begin keeping a prayer and praise journal if you don't already. Maybe you can create a family prayer and praise journal so the kids can participate too. Incorporate the journal into your family devotion time. You'll be surprised how often God comes through in a big way. We just tend to forget unless we've recorded it somewhere. So celebrate God and look what He has done!

—————————— MOM TO MASTER ——————————

*Father, thank You for Your faithfulness.*
*I am amazed at all You've done in my life. Amen.*

# May 17

One time our pastor posed this question to us: "If you were told you only had a week left to live, what would you do?"

Wow. I hadn't ever thought about that before. Of course, I'd want to spend every second with my family, giving them love and hugs. I wouldn't let the daily stresses of life get to me. I'd focus on the positives. And I think I'd spend a lot of time thanking the people in my life for the love they've always shown me. I'd want them to know how much their love had meant in my life before I headed to heaven.

As I was contemplating these things, our pastor said, "So why wait? Go ahead and do those things now. You don't need a negative diagnosis to act on those things, do you?"

Well, I guess not. My pastor was right. We can show our love, give hugs, and display our gratitude today. We don't have to wait for a terrible health crisis to shake us up. So go ahead. Live today like it's your last, because someday it will be.

——————— MOM TO MASTER ———————

*Father, I want to thank You for another day of life.*
*I love You. Amen.*

# May 18

*Consider it pure joy, my brothers and sisters,
whenever you face trials of many kinds.*
JAMES 1:2

I recently visited a website that made me feel a bit guilty for all the times I've complained about everyday stuff. Its headline said, THINGS TO BE THANKFUL FOR:

The taxes I pay—because it means that I'm employed.

The clothes that fit snugly—because it means I have enough to eat.

The mounds of laundry—because it means I have clothes to wear.

Okay, be honest. Have you ever been thankful for taxes, extra weight, or loads of laundry? Me neither. But it is an interesting concept. It does make you think, doesn't it? We should be looking for reasons to be thankful—even in the stuff that would not ordinarily fill our hearts with gratitude.

And we should impart that same attitude to our kids. They'll be much happier children if they'll take that stance in life. So when your daughter doesn't get invited to the big party, she can be thankful she has a mom who will take her to the movies instead. Or when your son doesn't make the football team, he can be thankful he has more free time to practice his guitar. It's really about looking for that silver lining in every gray cloud. Find that silver lining today.

——————— MOM TO MASTER ———————

*Lord, I praise You for the good and
not-so-good things in my life. Amen.*

# May 19

*We were not looking for praise from people,
not from you or anyone else.*

1 THESSALONIANS 2:6

In fiction writing, your characters always have to have a motivation for their actions. If your reader doesn't understand that motivation, the characters' actions seem contrived and unnatural. Motivation is key.

In life, motivation is key too. I found this out the hard way. You see, I have always been a people pleaser. I'm the one who will volunteer to bake seventeen pies for the annual bake sale, simply because I want the PTA members to like me and think I'm a really devoted mother. Maybe you're a people pleaser too.

Being a people pleaser is not only exhausting but also very pointless. First of all, you'll never be able to please everyone. And second, if you're doing things for people just to gain their adoration and approval, your motivation is wrong.

Think of it like this—would you still be serving in that way if you weren't going to be recognized or appreciated for your actions? If your answer is yes, then your motivation is right. But if you are doing things simply to gain praise, your motivation might be off. Even if no one ever recognizes your good deeds, take heart—God knows. He's keeping track. And He thinks you're great!

——————— MOM TO MASTER ———————

*Lord, help me to keep my motivation pure
when serving You and others. Amen.*

# May 20

*Be kind and compassionate to one another.*
EPHESIANS 4:32

Do you know that some people never hear a "thank you"?

You'll be able to spot these folks. They are usually the grouchy ones. I encountered one the other day at a shoe store. She was checking me out (with a scowl on her face, I might add) when I noticed that she had charged me full price for my shoes. So I said, "Miss, according to that sign over there, these shoes are on sale for 30 percent off."

She looked at the sign, then the shoes, then the sign again, and said, "These aren't the same shoes."

"I think they are," I said, "because I checked the SKU number against the advertisement."

She huffed and puffed and slammed the shoes down on the counter. Then she stomped over to the sale area and did her own investigation. After a few minutes, she came back, still scowling, and said, "You're right. They are on sale. I'll have to redo the whole transaction."

It was obvious she was having a hard day. So I made it my mission to encourage her. I thanked her for redoing my receipt. I praised her for her efficiency. We ended up having a nice conversation. She even smiled. Make it your mission to appreciate someone today. Start with your kids!

— MOM TO MASTER —

*Lord, help me to seize every opportunity*
*to bless others.*

# May 21

*A friend loves at all times.*

<br />PROVERBS 17:17

Did you ever watch the old sitcom *The Golden Girls*? I still catch the reruns sometimes. I love that show, and I especially like the theme song "Thank You for Being a Friend" by Andrew Gold. The lyrics still make me smile: "Thank you for being a friend. Traveled down the road and back again. Your heart is true; you're a pal and a confidant."

Who wouldn't want a friend who fits that description? Good friends are hard to find and even harder to keep. That's why we should be very thankful for our friends. As moms, we're so busy being moms that we rarely take time for our friends. But we need friends. If you haven't taken time lately to tell your friends how much you appreciate them, why not tell them today? Drop a card or place a call. Send a bouquet of flowers. Bake her some cookies. Schedule a lunch date with her.

While you're at it, tell your children how much you value their friendship too. As my girls get older, I realize how blessed I am to have their friendship. They are my best shopping buddies! Go ahead, reach out to a friend today.

——————— MOM TO MASTER ———————

*Lord, thank You for my friends. Help me to be a better friend to those special people You've put in my life. I love You. Amen.*

# May 22

*I will proclaim the name of the LORD.*
*Oh, praise the greatness of our God!*

DEUTERONOMY 32:3

Have you ever heard the expression, "Praise and be raised, or complain and remain"? Now that's a phrase that really packs a punch! It means if you complain about your current circumstances, you'll remain there a lot longer than if you'd just praise the Lord in spite of it all.

Sure, that's easy to say, but it's not so easy to do. I don't know about you, but praising God during difficult times is the last thing I want to do. I'd rather retreat to my bedroom with a box of Junior Mints and sulk awhile. But sulking won't change things any more than complaining will.

By praising God during the dark times, we're telling God that we trust Him—even though we can't see the daylight. Anyone can trust God and praise Him on the mountaintop, but only those who really know God's faithfulness can praise Him in the valley. And it's during those valley times that we truly feel God's tender mercy and experience extreme spiritual growth. So praise God today—even if you don't feel like it. Through your praise, you open the door for God to work in your life.

———————— MOM TO MASTER ————————

*Lord, I praise You in spite of the difficulties*
*in my life. Help me to resist complaining*
*and praise You instead. Amen.*

# May 23

*"How long will this wicked community grumble against me?
I have heard the complaints of these grumbling Israelites."*
NUMBERS 14:27

Have you ever read about the children of Israel's forty-year journey to the Promised Land? In actuality, that journey should've only taken them about forty days. As it turned out, they were their own worst enemy. God had just rescued them from slavery, caused the Egyptians to give them clothes and riches, parted the Red Sea so that they could walk across, provided manna from heaven for food, and yet they still complained! In fact, they whined about the manna God had been faithfully sending down every morning. They wanted something different. They were basically saying, "Hey, could You send down some waffles? We're really bored with the whole manna thing."

Unfortunately, we occasionally have that whole Israelite attitude at our house. I'll make meat loaf with potatoes and carrots, and Abby will whine, "Why'd you make meat loaf? You know I don't like meat loaf."

Or I'll buy wheat bread and Allyson will say, "I only like white bread. I'm not eating that!" Can you relate?

Complaining is not only aggravating to us; it's also aggravating to God. So don't let Connie and Connor Complainer exist in your house. Let's keep teaching gratitude. Our kids will finally get it, or they'll have to stay in their rooms for forty years!

— MOM TO MASTER —

*Lord, help me to teach my kids to be praisers,
not complainers. Amen.*

# May 24

*"Now, our God, we give you thanks,
and praise your glorious name."*

1 Chronicles 29:13

Just the other day I was rounding up the dust bunnies from underneath our bed, when I found something special. It was a letter I'd written to my cousin Judy but never mailed. The letter was five years old! Apparently, it had fallen out of my old address book. As I read my words, I had to smile. I told of all the wonderful things that God had done in our lives over the past six months. He had healed Jeff from a terrible infection. He had opened up the door for me to write for a Christian magazine. He had caused our house to sell for full asking price—so many praises!

As I finished reading the letter, I knew why I had never mailed it. God wanted me to find it five years later. The words of that letter caused me to reflect on that time in our lives—a time when we didn't have very much. I wasn't working full-time, and we were living from paycheck to paycheck. Still, God always provided.

I spent the rest of that afternoon reflecting on the faithfulness of God. Why not take some time today and remember the times God has come through for you? It's a trip down memory lane worth taking!

— MOM TO MASTER —

*Lord, thank You for always coming
through for me. I love You. Amen.*

# May 25

*You should praise the LORD for his love and for
the wonderful things he does for all of us.*

PSALM 107:21 CEV

"Thank You, Lord, for saving my soul. Thank You, Lord, for making me whole. Oh, thank You, Lord, for giving to me—Thy great salvation so rich and free." Those are the words to a little chorus that I always sang in children's church growing up. Do you know what I remember most about that little song? It's how Ivan Hunter, a wonderful man who led our worship time, looked when he sang it. His face almost glowed. Even as a kid, I knew that Ivan was singing about something he truly believed in and cherished.

Ivan took every opportunity to thank the Lord. He'd testify to anyone who would listen—whether it was the garbage man or the mayor. Well, Ivan went to heaven a few years ago, but his memory lives on. And we're doing all that we can to carry on the testifying tradition. On more than one occasion, I've heard Abby tell her friends about something that God has done for her. And Ally often reminds me of the blessings in my life—especially if I'm in "one of those moods." Jeff does the same. You see, it's good to be bold for Jesus. Make testifying a habit in your household.

———— MOM TO MASTER ————

*Lord, help me to be bold for You. I praise You. Amen.*

# May 26

*Then Jesus looked up and said, "Father,*
*I thank you that you have heard me."*
John 11:41

I totally understand why Jesus wants us to come to Him like little children. When kids pray, they have no doubt that God hears their requests and will answer them. That's how we all ought to pray.

I used to send up a *Wheel of Fortune* prayer. I'd petition the Lord, and then I'd "spin the wheel of prayer," hoping I'd land on the right one that would really touch God's ears and cause Him to act on my behalf. Silly, isn't it? Maybe you've done the same thing.

But since I discovered this verse in John, I haven't been sending up *Wheel of Fortune* prayers anymore. Instead, I petition the Lord and thank God for hearing my prayers. I figure if Jesus thought it was a good idea to thank God for hearing His prayers, it's probably a good idea for me too. Plus, I really am thankful that He hears my prayers. Sometimes God is the only One who will listen to me. (If Cartoon Network is on, forget about it—my kids totally tune me out!) So go ahead—talk to God. Tell Him your dreams, setbacks, and heartaches. Pray in faith, and thank Him for hearing you. It will make all the difference.

------ MOM TO MASTER ------

*Lord, I want to thank You for hearing my prayers.*
*You are an awesome God. Amen.*

# May 27

*. . .because of the surpassing grace God has given you.*
*Thanks be to God for his indescribable gift!*
2 CORINTHIANS 9:14–15

*Grace.* We say grace. We name baby girls Grace. But do we really understand how wonderful God's grace is in our lives? I wouldn't want to live one second without it operating in my life. Grace is defined as God's unmerited favor. In other words, we didn't earn it. We certainly didn't deserve it, but God gave us His grace anyway. How great is that?

And where you find grace, you almost always find mercy alongside it. Whew! That's good news, isn't it? People who lived under the law didn't have the luxury of grace. When they broke even the teensy-weensiest rule, they were in a lot of trouble. I'm so thankful for God's grace, because I mess up on a regular basis. But when I do mess up, I can run to Him. I don't have to hide, because when I repent, He gives me grace. He says, "That's okay, Michelle, you'll do better next time."

In the same manner that God shows us grace, we should show our children grace. They aren't perfect. They are going to mess up once in a while. But if we show them grace, they'll run to us when they get into trouble. They won't hide from us.

——————— MOM TO MASTER ———————

*Father, I praise You for the gift of grace. Amen.*

# May 28

*May the God of hope fill you with all joy and
peace as you trust in him, so that you may overflow
with hope by the power of the Holy Spirit.*

ROMANS 15:13

One of my favorite praise and worship CDs is *Thank You, Lord,
for the Holy Ghost* by Keith Moore. When I first bought this
CD, I began singing the words, "Thank You, Lord, for the Holy
Ghost," but in actuality, I hadn't ever really thanked God for His
gift of the Holy Spirit.

The Holy Spirit truly is a gift. The Word of God calls the
Holy Spirit our Comforter. As a mom, there are days when I
definitely need comfort. Do you ever have those "feel sorry for
yourself" kind of days? On those days, I feel unworthy. I feel
like a failure as a mother. I feel unlovely. At times I don't even
know what to pray. But that's when I turn to the Holy Spirit. He
comforts me. He helps me know what to pray. He leads me to
scriptures in the Word that pertain to my exact circumstances.
He gives me a pick-me-up greater than any B-12 shot could ever
offer! The Holy Spirit will do the same for you. So if you haven't
ever thanked God for the Holy Spirit, why not do so today?

———————————— MOM TO MASTER ————————————

*Father, thank You for the gift of the Holy Spirit. Amen.*

# May 29

*"Now, our God, we give you thanks,
and praise your glorious name."*

1 CHRONICLES 29:13

*Muchas gracias!* Okay, that's about the only phrase I remember from my college Spanish classes. No matter what the language, "thank you" is pleasing to the Father. Praising His holy name should be second nature for us. Do you know the Bible says the angels continually praise the Lord? I always picture them face down before His throne, praising Him 24-7. That's a pretty good gig, don't you think?

Since I've become a more avid praiser, I now understand why God seeks our praise. It's not that He is on some ego trip. He certainly doesn't need our praise. He knows that praising Him and having a thankful heart changes us on the inside. If you're praising, you can't be complaining. If you're praising, you're opening up what I like to call "the blessing highway." While a negative spirit and complaining attitude puts up road-blocks on that superhighway, a thankful heart clears the road!

So praise Him today—in every language you can think of! He is worthy of our praise! Get your kids involved. Think of lots of reasons to give thanks. Maybe have each child learn to praise God in a different language. Make it fun, and make a joyful noise!

—————— MOM TO MASTER ——————

*Father, I give You all of the praise
and honor today. You are worthy! Amen.*

# May 30

*He blesses the home of the righteous.*
PROVERBS 3:33

I love to give my children things they adore. I think that's why I love Christmas shopping so much. I Christmas shop all year long. If I see something I know Abby or Allyson will adore, I'll buy it and store it away for the holidays. However, I'm always tempted to give those Christmas presents to the girls right away. In fact, a lot of times, that's exactly what I do. I can't stand it. I just have to give them their gifts early! I bet you do the same thing. We're moms. It's our nature to give to our kids. We can't help ourselves!

As much as we love to give our kids the desires of their hearts, it pales in comparison to how much our heavenly Father enjoys blessing us. Where do you think that desire to give to our children comes from? God.

He is the best present giver. He can hardly wait to give you that new set of wing chairs that you've been longing for. He wants you to have that Walt Disney World vacation. He loves to see us enjoying the blessings He sends our way. So enjoy your blessings today. By doing that, you're blessing the Father.

—————————— MOM TO MASTER ——————————

*Father, I appreciate all of the special gifts You give to me.*
*Thanks for loving me so much. Amen.*

# May 31

*Whoever is kind to the poor lends to the LORD, and*
*he will reward them for what they have done.*
<small>PROVERBS 19:17</small>

Have you ever seen those commercials on TV that show the boys and girls overseas who don't have anything to eat? I can hardly watch them. It's heartbreaking to see the poverty and hopelessness that they encounter daily. Upon the prompting of my children, we currently support a little girl overseas named Carmen. The girls love to write letters to Carmen and send her snapshots of our family and pets. They also love to send her presents. While we're not allowed to ship anything too bulky, we can send small tokens now and then.

We like picking out paper dolls for her, and we've been told she loves them. Most children in the United States wouldn't think paper dolls were too exciting, but if you've never had anything, a paper doll would seem really cool. You'd probably be truly grateful for a paper doll.

That's the kind of attitude I want to have—a "paper doll thankfulness." I want to be grateful for even the smallest gesture or gift. I want my heavenly Father to know that I'm thankful whether He sends down a paper doll or a Cadillac Escalade. I want the same grateful attitude for my children. Let's teach our kids that kind of thankfulness.

——————— MOM TO MASTER ———————

*Father, I praise You today for the big and*
*little blessings in my life. Amen.*

# June 1

*Then the LORD answered me and said: "Write the vision and make it plain on tablets, that he may run who reads it."*
HABAKKUK 2:2 NKJV

Have you ever heard the expression, "Run with the vision"? Like many expressions, this one is based on a scripture. It's sort of the sound bite version of Habakkuk 2:2. This is one of my favorites. In fact, for the longest time I had it taped to my computer so that I would see it every day and be reminded of "the vision."

While my vision or dream may be different from yours, in order to see our visions come full circle, we have to do the same thing—keep the vision before us! That means meditating on scriptures that pertain to our vision, praying over our vision, talking about our vision with those of like-minded faith, and believing God to bring our visions to pass.

If you've lost your dream, ask God to restore it in you. He has placed dreams and visions on the inside of every one of us. Your dream may be dormant, but it's there. Ask God to reawaken it today. Then write your vision in your journal so you'll never forget it again.

——————— MOM TO MASTER ———————

*Thank You, Lord, for placing that special vision in my heart. Help me to keep it before my eyes. I trust You to make it come to pass as I follow You. Amen.*

# June 2

*I can do all this through him who gives me strength.*
PHILIPPIANS 4:13

For a long time, I didn't think it was okay to have other dreams besides being a mom. I thought it was selfish to want more. But those thoughts were not right thinking. I discovered that God had placed those dreams and desires inside of me. He is the One who caused me to dream in the first place, so why should I feel guilty?

Maybe you've always desired to write children's books, but you thought it was just a crazy whim. If you're passionate about it—if writing books for children burns in your heart—it's more than a whim. It's probably part of God's plan for your life. Ask Him to show you His plan today. He may not show you all of it (because it would totally overwhelm you to see the entire plan), but He will show you enough to take the initial steps toward the fulfillment of your dream. Isn't that exciting?

Being a mom is the greatest gig we'll ever have, but God doesn't want us to limit ourselves. He can use us—even in the midst of motherhood. Nothing is too big for Him, and nothing is impossible with Him. So dream on and get with it!

———— MOM TO MASTER ————

*Lord, help me to follow You down the road
that leads to my dream. Amen.*

# June 3

*"If you believe, you will receive whatever you ask for in prayer."*
MATTHEW 21:22

So I was watching TV a few years back. I was already familiar with the Crocodile Hunter, but I had no idea we also had snake wranglers. I couldn't help but watch as these two people used a big stick and a bag to capture a brown, poisonous snake in Australia—scary!

Can you imagine waking up and saying, "You know, I'd like to chase and capture poisonous snakes for a living someday"? Obviously, these folks who deal with dangerous and deadly animals enjoy what they do. If you watched Steve Irwin, the Crocodile Hunter, you know he loved it. He truly walked in his dream—as odd as that dream is to most of us.

That's what I love about our heavenly Father. He gives each of us unique dreams, and then He equips us to accomplish those dreams if we'll only believe. There is no dream too silly, scary, adventurous, or extreme for our God. It gives Him great joy to see us pursuing the ambitions He has placed within us. He can't wait to see you walking in your dream—even if that dream is chasing crocs in the outback!

## MOM TO MASTER

*Lord, thank You for placing unique dreams
in my heart. Help me to follow after them
without any fear or hesitation. Amen.*

# June 4

*Where there is no vision, the people perish.*
PROVERBS 29:18 KJV

I've seen it happen with people who retire early in life. They lose their drive. They lose their vision. They lose their reason for getting up in the morning. But you don't have to be of retirement age to lose your vision. I've also seen young mothers lose their hope and drive. The devil loves to discourage us and steal our hope.

No matter where we are in life—a mother of a newborn or a mom whose last child just graduated high school—we need to have a goal, a dream, a vision. If we don't, the Word says we'll perish. I don't think it means we'll perish physically, but we'll die spiritually. That's why it's so important to find out God's plan. Do you know God's plan for your life?

If not, ask God to show you His vision for your life. Seek His plan, and once you discover it, write it down and keep it before you. Thank Him for that vision every day. Keep the vision close to your heart, and only share that vision with people you can trust. Your vision is something to be treasured and celebrated.

——————— MOM TO MASTER ———————

*Lord, help me never to lose my vision or my drive.*
*I want to move forward with You. Amen.*

# June 5

*Teach me to do your will, for you are my God.*
PSALM 143:10

"A dream is a wish your heart makes. . . ." Remember those lyrics from the theme song in the Disney movie *Cinderella*? I've always loved that movie. I was so excited when my daughters were over Barney and old enough to appreciate Cinderella. And I've always loved those lyrics. There's a lot of truth in those words.

A dream isn't just a thought your mind comes up with on its own. Instead, it's a vision your heart comes up with before it ever reaches your brain. You see, the real dreams in our lives are birthed in our spirit—deep down inside of us. Dreams are more than passing fancies. They are more than whimsical mind wanderings. They are much more. They are of God.

If you haven't let your heart make any dreams lately, ask God to show you the dreams He has for you. He hasn't forgotten about them, and neither should you. Get excited about your dreams. Be thankful that God finishes the things He authors. He authored your dreams, so you know He's going to bring them to pass. Go ahead and dream. Dream big!

## ——— MOM TO MASTER ———

*Lord, reawaken the dreams on the inside of me—*
*the ones that You placed there. I love You. Amen.*

# June 6

*A heart at peace gives life to the body, but envy rots the bones.*
PROVERBS 14:30

Have your dreams ever ripped at the seams? Mine have.

There have been times when I've wondered if God even cared about my dreams, wishes, goals, or desires. I'd look around and see good things happening for everyone else, and I'd wonder if God had forgotten about me. I'd get the whole "What about me?" mentality. Ever been there? It's an unpleasant place to be. That "What about me?" mentality eventually leads to jealousy, envy, bitterness, and hopelessness. So if you're on that road, hurry to the nearest exit!

If you can't be happy for your friend when she finally gets to move into her dream home, God will never be able to bless you with your dream house. If you can't do the dance of joy with your sister when she wins an all-expense-paid cruise, God will never be able to bless your family with a dream vacation. In the midst of everybody else's dreams coming true, we have to keep our hearts right. If we don't, we'll never get to walk in ours. Keep your eyes on the Master, and He will make your dreams come true too. Don't worry when you see others getting blessed. God has more than enough blessings to go around.

——————— MOM TO MASTER ———————

*Lord, help me to be happy when others realize their dreams,
because I know my dreams will come true too. Amen.*

# June 7

*But those who hope in the LORD will renew their strength.*

ISAIAH 40:31

"Any contractions today?"

"Not yet," I mumbled. "Maybe I'll try running up and down the stairs a few times."

I ran the stairs. I walked around the block. I took castor oil. I did everything I could think of to start my labor, but that baby wasn't budging. She didn't care that I was seven days overdue. She didn't care that I was really anxious to have her. She wasn't coming out until she was good and ready. When she finally decided to make her descent, we welcomed Abby Leigh Adams into the world. She was perfect and right on time in God's eyes.

Waiting. That's one of the toughest things we have to do as our dreams percolate inside of us. Have you ever noticed that God's timing doesn't always seem to be our timing? And it doesn't matter how much we cry out to Him, He won't bring about our dreams until it's the right time. It doesn't matter if you spiritually run the stairs or walk around the block, your dream won't be birthed until God says it's time. So if you're pregnant with a dream, and you're tired of waiting—hold on. Your promise is on its way!

———————————— MOM TO MASTER ————————————

*Lord, thank You for my dream. Help me to wait patiently and faithfully until it is birthed. Amen.*

# June 8

*Now faith is confidence in what we hope for
and assurance about what we do not see.*

HEBREWS 11:1

At ten years of age, Abby was an aspiring writer always coming up with stories. So like her mom, she liked to carry a notebook with her. That way, if she came up with a great idea, she could jot it down before she forgot it. One day in a store I found a royal blue notebook with the words "Dare to Dream" written in silver across the cover. I had to buy it! It spoke to me. What a great message for Abby—and what a great message for all of us!

*Dare to dream.*

You know, dreaming is a bit daring. It requires mentally sticking your neck out. Dreaming big dreams requires taking big steps of faith. It's not always a comfortable place to be, but it's definitely an exciting one. It's what I like to call living on the edge.

God likes those who dare to dream. Remember Peter? He was the only one who dared to dream and stepped out of the boat. He was doing great too—until he took his eyes off of Jesus. But here's the good news. When Peter started to sink, Jesus rescued him. He'll do the same for us. So get out of the boat and dare to dream!

———————— MOM TO MASTER ————————

*Lord, help me to be daring when it comes to
the dreams You put inside me. Amen.*

# June 9

*"Do not give dogs what is sacred; do not throw your pearls to pigs.
If you do, they may trample them under their feet,
and turn and tear you to pieces."*

<small>MATTHEW 7:6</small>

Have you ever heard the expression "Don't cast your pearls before pigs"? My mama used to give me that advice when I'd share my dreams with a friend at school, only to be teased. Later I found myself sharing that same wisdom with my girls.

You see, not everyone is going to embrace our dreams and celebrate our victories with us. It's true! Even your Christian friends may not want to hear what God has placed in your heart—especially if it's bigger than the things they have in their hearts. Unfortunately, the green-eyed monster lives in some Christians too.

So be careful whom you choose to let in your inner circle. Don't share your dreams with just anyone. Your dreams are too precious to waste on the dogs and pigs. Only share your dreams with your family and close Christian friends—the ones who will be happy for you and celebrate with you. If you don't have anyone like that in your life, pray that God will send you someone you can trust. And remember, you can always trust Him.

———————————— MOM TO MASTER ————————————

*Thank You, Lord, for giving me such precious dreams.
Help me to be careful when sharing them with others
that I don't confide in the wrong people. Amen.*

# June 10

*God gives some people wealth, possessions and honor,*
*so that they lack nothing their hearts desire.*
ECCLESIASTES 6:2

Did you know there is actually an association designated for the study of dreams? There are many people who have devoted their lives to interpreting and discovering the meanings of various dreams and images. Wild, huh?

If you're like me, you're probably thinking, *Don't you actually have to go to sleep for an extended period of time to have dreams?* If you're in that "mother of newborns or toddlers" stage, you're probably not racking up a lot of REM time. Hang in there—those dark circles do have silver linings!

Too much pizza or something we've watched on TV can trigger the dreams we have at night, but the dreams that beat deep within our hearts come from a different source—God! We don't need any association or expert to interpret their meaning for us. God is the originator of those dreams, so just ask Him. He has all of the answers, and He is willing to share His wisdom with you. So meditate on the dreams that live within you, and always remember who placed them in your heart. He wouldn't have placed them there if He wasn't going to make sure those dreams came true.

—————— MOM TO MASTER ——————

*Thank You, Lord, for the dreams you've placed inside*
*of me. Please reveal them to me so that I can*
*understand them more fully. Amen.*

# June 11

*I can do all this through him who gives me strength.*
PHILIPPIANS 4:13

"What do you want to be when you grow up?" I asked my daughter Ally when she was only four.

She thought for a moment and then she answered matter-of-factly, "A movie star."

"Great," I responded. "Then you can pay for Mommy's and Daddy's retirement condo in Florida."

Children know how to dream big. Do you know why? Because no one has told them yet that they can't dream big. I love that about kids. They don't have that inner voice going that says, *You can't be a movie star. You're not good enough. You're not pretty enough. You'll never be able to accomplish your dream.* No, they believe they can do anything. And you know what? They're right! God's Word says that we can do all things through Christ who gives us strength. *All* means all, right?

That's why Jesus said we should have childlike faith. We should be able to believe *big* when it comes to the dreams and ambitions that God has placed within us. God wouldn't have placed them there if He weren't going to help us achieve them. So learn from your kids. Get back that childlike faith, and start believing.

—————————— MOM TO MASTER ——————————

*Lord, help me to believe You like my children believe You.*
*Help me to dream big like they do. I love You. Amen.*

# June 12

*"If you have anything to say that will help the people, please say it."*
ACTS 13:15 CEV

Dream squashers. They seem to be everywhere. Recently, I taught at a Christian Writers' Conference where I sat on a magazine panel with editors of prestigious publications and other professional writers. As the questions came in from the audience, the panel members unleashed their dream squasher personalities. One by one, they told these people who longed to be writers that they wouldn't be able to make a living as writers. "The competition is stiff." "Magazines don't pay very much per story." "Don't quit your day jobs!"

I wanted to stand up on the middle of the table and say, "It's not true! You can make it! If I can make a living as a professional writer, so can you! God is no respecter of persons. What He did for me, He will do for you!"

I did say a bit to ward off the dream squashers, and you wouldn't believe how many people came up and thanked me. Wow! That experience really opened my eyes. People are hungry for encouragement. They are tired of the dream squashers.

If you are surrounded by dream squashers, let me encourage you today. God believes in you. Ignore the dream squashers. In truth, they are afraid to believe, and they resent you for stepping out in faith. Pray for them, but avoid them at all costs.

───────── MOM TO MASTER ─────────

*Lord, help me never to be a dream squasher. Amen.*

# June 13

*My guilt has overwhelmed me like a burden too heavy to bear.*
PSALM 38:4

Have you taken any guilt trips lately? Oh yeah, I've been on a few. One time I had to miss my daughters' Honor Choir performance because of a business commitment. It hurt my heart not to be there. Sure it's captured on video, but I can't get that live performance back—it's gone forever! Even now as I tell you about it, I feel guilty.

Sometimes living out our dreams comes with a price. As a writer, I occasionally have to travel to promote my books. I'm not gone very often, but when I miss something as important as an Honor Choir concert, I begin questioning my commitment as a mom. Then I start wondering if I am even a good mom. If I let my mind stay there very long, I begin wondering if I should give up writing altogether.

Then God reminds me that He is in control of my life. He has already ordered my steps. He knew that I'd have to miss that Honor Choir performance, and He enabled my husband to go and videotape it for me. So if you've been on a guilt trip lately, unpack now! Guilt doesn't come from God, so don't go there! Thank God for the good things in your life.

—————————— MOM TO MASTER ——————————

*Lord, help me to avoid those intense feelings of guilt. I give them to You right now. Amen.*

# June 14

*"Again, truly I tell you that if two of you on earth
agree about anything they ask for, it will be
done for them by my Father in heaven."*
MATTHEW 18:19

I have a niece who collects these cute little chubby angelic figurines called Dreamsicles. Maybe you collect them too. I have a couple in my daughters' rooms. You know what I like about these little figurines? I like their name—Dreamsicles. So much of today's merchandise that represents dreamers takes on a New Age feel. That's not the case with these little guys. My niece likes them because they are little reminders that say, "Hey, believe in your dream! Dare to dream! Don't give up!"

Who doesn't need to be reminded to do those things? Even if you don't have Dreamsicles throughout your home, you need to remind yourself to dream. Let your mind dwell on your dreams. See yourself walking in your dreams. Share your dreams with your children and allow them to share their dreams with you. Remind each other of your dreams and encourage one another. Then, as a family, you can pray over those dreams every night. Finally, when those dreams begin to manifest, you can celebrate together as a family. When a family gets its faith on, look out! Those dreams are just around the corner.

## MOM TO MASTER

*Thank You, Lord, for my dreams.
Help me to follow after them and to encourage
my kids in their dreams too. Amen.*

# June 15

*Now to Him who is able to do far more abundantly beyond all that we ask or think, according to the power that works within us. . .*

EPHESIANS 3:20 NASB

When I was a little girl growing up in Indiana, I was the classic daydreamer. I'd sit in class, look out the window, and dream of being anywhere but in Mrs. Webster's room. I couldn't wait to grow up and have a life that didn't include homework. Now that I'm all grown up, I still daydream. I've traded homework for housework, but basically I feel like that same little girl on the inside.

I still have hopes and dreams that I think about on a daily basis. I still believe that God is going to do big things for me. And now, decades after I was in Mrs. Webster's fourth-grade class, I know that God is capable of doing the impossible in my life. He has proven Himself to me time and time again.

Has God proven Himself to you? Do you have confidence that He is able to do above all that we could ever ask or think? Now, I don't know about you, but I can ask and think of a lot of stuff, so that verse totally excites me. It should totally excite you too. If you've never seen the power of God in your life, ask Him to show Himself strong to you today. He will. He's just been waiting for you to ask.

— MOM TO MASTER —

*Father, I believe You will do above all
I could ever ask or think, and I thank You
for working in my life. Amen.*

# June 16

*"You may ask me for anything in my name, and I will do it."*
JOHN 14:14

Have you ever seen a shooting star whiz past in the night sky and whispered to your children, "Hurry, make a wish!" We love to look into the night sky and see who can spot the first shooting star. It's lots of fun—especially if you're out in the country where the sky is so awesome, away from the city lights.

But you know, the last time we saw a shooting star and I said that to my girls, I heard that still, small voice whisper something to me. He said, *"You don't need a shooting star to make a wish. You can ask Me for anything."* Wow! That was quite a revelation. I guess I'd always known that I could ask my heavenly Father for anything—big or small—but I'd never thought of it in quite that way.

We need to quit wishing on shooting stars and make our requests known to God. Tell your dreams to the Father. Let Him know your innermost desires. Wishing never got anyone anywhere, but prayer changes things for the better. Faith-filled prayers will change your situation. So go ahead. Pray about your dreams today—you don't even have to wait on a shooting star.

—————————— MOM TO MASTER ——————————

*Father, I am asking You to accomplish _____
in my life. I believe You can bring it from
a wish to a reality. Amen.*

# June 17

*This is the confidence we have in approaching God:*
*that if we ask anything according to his will, he hears us.*
1 JOHN 5:14

When my girls were really young, they used to ask me the funniest stuff. They thought Mommy could do anything! Once, Abby asked if I could touch the stars. I guess to her three-year-old pint-sized body, my five-foot-three-inch frame seemed pretty tall. In her eyes, I *could* touch the stars. She believed in me.

That's how our heavenly Father wants us to feel about Him. He wants us to look up to Him in total amazement and trust and ask, "Father, can You touch the stars?" But unlike me, He can answer yes because He can do anything—He *made* the stars!

Sometimes when I think about the future and how I fit into His plan for my life, I think, *I can't do that! I don't have what it takes.* And I'm right—I don't, but He does. We just have to know Him. Do you know Him?

If you don't know Him, ask Jesus to be your Lord and Savior today. All you have to do is tell Him you're sorry for your sins and ask Him to take over every part of your life. The One who can touch the stars wants to live in your heart. . .so go ahead, ask Him.

— MOM TO MASTER —

*Lord, please take over every part of my life.*
*I love You. Amen.*

# June 18

*Joseph had a dream, and when he told it to his brothers,*
*they hated him all the more.*

GENESIS 37:5

Some dreams are just not meant to be shared. Take Joseph's dreams, for example. Remember when he told his brothers about his dreams? They were less than thrilled to learn that little bro had dreamed they would someday bow down to him. I can only imagine what my older brother and big sister would have said if I'd told them that God had given me a dream of them bowing down to me. I would probably not be alive to write this devotional!

You see, there are some dreams you're just supposed to keep to yourself. Not everyone is going to want to celebrate with you. That's why keeping a journal is such a good idea. When you want to share your dreams with others but you're pretty sure God wants you to keep them just between the two of you—write them in your journal! It's a way of recording the very things that God has placed in your heart. Then, when they come to pass, you can go back and reread what God revealed to you months earlier and celebrate with your close friends and family.

—————————— MOM TO MASTER ——————————

*Lord, thank You for the dreams You've given me.*
*Help me to know when it's the right time to share*
*and when it's not appropriate. I love You. Amen.*

# June 19

*"Have faith in God," Jesus answered.*

MARK 11:22

My pastor once preached about getting a new faith attitude. Here are the questions he used to challenge us:

Are you maintaining, or are you in hot pursuit?

Are you holding the fort, or are you taking new ground?

Are you dry-docked, or are you launching out into the deep?

Are you settled into the status quo, or are you reaching up to the next level?

Are you throwing in the towel, or are you going in for the next round?

Are you retreating, or are you advancing?

Are you circling the wagons, or are you leading the charge?

Are you chasing after your dreams, or are you running them down?

Wow! I want to be so full of faith that I am running down my dreams—not just chasing after them. But that kind of faith only comes from the Lord. Visualizing and meditating on our destinies isn't enough. We have to meditate on God's Word and spend time in prayer before we'll have the kind of courage it takes to launch out. If you'll spend time with God, He'll enable you to answer those questions with aggressive faith.

———————— MOM TO MASTER ————————

*Lord, help me to run down my dreams. Help me to be aggressive and determined when it comes to my faith. I love You. Amen.*

# June 20

*Finally, brothers and sisters, whatever is true, whatever is noble,
whatever is right, whatever is pure, whatever is lovely,
whatever is admirable—if anything is excellent
or praiseworthy—think about such things.*

PHILIPPIANS 4:8

Have you ever talked yourself out of a blessing? It's called thinking too much about the wrong things. I am guilty of it. God will place something in my heart, and by the time it reaches my head, I've already thought of ten reasons why it won't work.

When my girls were just toddlers, my sister taught a Bible study at our church in Bedford, Indiana. It was so great. My sister would dig things out of the Word that really ministered to the ladies. But God called my sister and her husband to another city to serve as pastors, leaving the Bible study without a leader. My cousin Aimee said she believed God was calling me to step up to the plate, but I was much more comfortable watching from the sidelines. Secretly, I'd also felt the Lord's leading to fill my sister's shoes, but I was scared. I hadn't been to Bible school. I was just a mom, and sometimes I wasn't even very good at that!

Finally, I agreed to do it, and God met me. He enabled me to teach things I didn't even know. See, He didn't call me because I knew a lot. He called me because I knew Him. What is God calling you to do today? Be obedient. He isn't looking for pros; He is looking for willing hearts.

—————— MOM TO MASTER ——————

*Lord, help me to be obedient the first time You call. Amen.*

# June 21

*The tongue also is a fire, a world of evil among the parts of the body. It corrupts the whole body, sets the whole course of one's life on fire, and is itself set on fire by hell.*

Over the course of Abby's and Ally's elementary years, I served on every PTA committee known to man. From talent shows to school carnivals, the girls were quick to volunteer dear old Mom. Running an elementary talent show was certainly not a childhood dream of mine, but I accepted that task because there was a need.

That talent show experience was quite difficult, but I certainly learned some things about working with people. Looking back, it was great preparation for serving on the faculty for writers' conferences, because whenever you get around a bunch of writers, you're going to encounter some egos.

Having battled with stage mothers during the talent show, I was much more prepared when I received cutting comments from other writers at these conferences. So when a fellow faculty member said to me, "I'm sorry, you're not allowed to dine in here. This is for faculty only," I was able to smile sweetly and say, "Well, that's good because I'm a faculty member." Had God not helped me train my tongue during the talent show ordeal, I might've throttled this "guardian of the faculty dinner door" and repented later.

So don't despise small beginnings. Do whatever you're called to do now to the best of your ability. Just consider it preparation work for your dream—it'll be worth it!

## ——— MOM TO MASTER ———

*Lord, help me to be the very best I can be today. Amen.*

# June 22

*"For I know the plans I have for you," declares the* LORD,
*"plans to prosper you and not to harm you,*
*plans to give you hope and a future."*

JEREMIAH 29:11

Once I told Allyson that when she was only eight weeks old, growing inside of my belly, the doctors thought I would miscarry. In fact, they sent me home to wait for "the inevitable." I had been bleeding quite heavily, and the prognosis was not good. But God is the Great Physician, amen? He stepped in where medicine stopped, and I was able to carry Allyson almost full term. She came just three weeks early—perfect in every way.

After hearing this story, Ally looked up at me with her big blue eyes and said, "I'm pretty special, aren't I, Mom?"

I smiled and said, "Yep, you sure are. God must have a very special plan for you, my dear."

No one will ever be able to convince Allyson that God doesn't have big plans for her, because she knows it in her knower. We all need to grasp that revelation today. We need to know that God thinks we're special and that He has awesome plans for our lives. Even if your life has been difficult up to now, that doesn't change the facts—God has a special plan for you. Grab hold of that today. Meditate on it. Begin to thank God for His plan, and then watch as He unfolds it.

——————— MOM TO MASTER ———————

*Lord, thank You for the plans You have for me.*
*Help me to walk in them. Amen.*

# June 23

*I gave you milk, not solid food, for you were not yet ready for it.*
*Indeed, you are still not ready.*
1 CORINTHIANS 3:2

Do you know that God doesn't dangle carrots just to tease us? No, if God dangles a carrot in front of us, He plans on giving it to us. He would be an unjust God if He placed a dream in our hearts with no intention of helping us achieve that dream. We serve a just and loving heavenly Father. He doesn't like to withhold stuff from us, but sometimes He has to—because we're not ready.

When our kids were babies, they couldn't wait to grow up. They wanted to do all the stuff the big kids were doing, right? But as parents, we had to protect them from the "big kid stuff" because they weren't yet big kids. I remember Abby wanting to climb the monkey bars at the park so badly. She would stand at the bottom, reach her arms toward the top of the bars, and cry. Her little lip would quiver and my heart would break. But I couldn't let her climb those bars—she wasn't big enough. She didn't know enough.

It's the same way with God. If you haven't yet realized your dream, it's not that God has forgotten you—you just may not be ready yet. If we'll just hang in there, we'll be on the big kid monkey bars before we know it!

————— MOM TO MASTER —————

*Lord, help me to be patient as*
*I wait for my dream to come true. Amen.*

# June 24

*Let us draw near to God with a sincere heart
and with the full assurance that faith brings.*
HEBREWS 10:22

If you're the mom of boys, you may have sat through hours of Little League games. How many times have you heard the coach yell, "Keep your eye on the ball"? Probably hundreds.

You know, that's pretty good advice for us too. If we'll just keep our eyes on the ball—our dreams—we'll stay focused and determined. But if we're looking in the stands at everybody else's fulfilled dreams, we'll never achieve the level of success God has for us.

I've always loved the scene from the movie *Runaway Bride*, where Maggie (Julia Roberts) is trying to stay focused on walking down the aisle instead of bolting like she usually does, and her "sports nut" of a fiancé says, "Come on, honey, be the ball." That too is good advice. If we can train our minds and hearts to stay so focused on God's plan for us, we'll finally become that plan. We'll enjoy the things that God has had planned for us since the beginning of time.

So keep your eye on the ball. Be the ball! Go forward with God, and before you know it, you'll be doing the chicken dance in the end zone. (Go ahead and spike the nearest football—you know you want to!)

—————————— MOM TO MASTER ——————————

*Lord, help me to keep my focus
on You and Your plans. Amen.*

# June 25

*The Spirit you received does not make you slaves,*
*so that you live in fear again; rather, the Spirit you*
*received brought about your adoption to sonship.*

ROMANS 8:15

Are you afraid that you won't ever accomplish your dreams? Do you worry that you're not good enough or smart enough or talented enough to do the things that God has placed in your heart? I think we all face those issues of self-doubt and fear. But we can't allow fear to dwell in our lives. Fear is lethal to our joy level. It's lethal to our self-esteem. And it's lethal to our walk with God.

Think of it this way—where fear begins, failure starts. So if you're allowing fear to rule your mind, you're not allowing yourself the opportunity to succeed. Fear is the opposite of faith, so you can't be in fear and in faith at the same time. You have to choose. So choose faith!

Stop the fear tape that's playing in your head. Ask God to fill you with so much faith that there won't be room for any fear. Don't let the devil stop God from using you. Don't let the devil stop you from walking in your dreams. This is your time, and his time is up.

——————— MOM TO MASTER ———————

*Lord, fill me with faith. I give You my fears. Amen.*

# June 26

*"If you believe, you will receive whatever you ask for in prayer."*
MATTHEW 21:22

I love to read children's stories that end in ". . .and they all lived happily ever after." Yeah, right! If only it were that easy, eh? In reality, our homes aren't always so happy. A good marriage takes work. A happy home takes work. But both are possible.

We must base our marriages and our families on the Word of God. That's the only way we'll ever have "heaven on earth" in our homes. That's the only way we'll ever experience the "happily ever after." Find scriptures in the Word that apply to your family situations and stand on those.

Begin praying for your husband and your children today. I don't mean just a quick, "Bless my husband and my kids," line in your morning prayer. I mean really commit some time to praying for them. You don't have to know exactly what to pray. The Holy Spirit will help you. The point is this—happily ever after *is* possible. Through prayer and Word time, you can live the dream of heaven on earth in your home. Now, that's a dream worth having and standing for!

———————— MOM TO MASTER ————————

*Lord, thank You for my spouse and my children.*
*Help me to be the wife and mother You've made me to be.*
*Please increase the happiness in my home. Amen.*

# June 27

Children have the best imaginations. Once, when my husband and I worked at our daughters' school carnival, we ran the "first aid" booth where we treated fake wounds with gauze, adding fake blood and fake hospital bands. It was a big hit! But the funnest part was listening to the stories each child came up with concerning the fake wounds. One little boy told his friend, "See this? It's a shark bite." Another said he was injured outrunning a wild pack of donkeys. I think that one was my favorite!

Listening to the kids share wild and outrageous stories all day made me realize why it's so easy for them to dream big dreams. They have the most amazing imaginations. It's nothing for them to dream big dreams. God doesn't have to work through all of that doubt and unbelief like He does with us. As we get older, we lose much of that ability to imagine and dream. We become cynical, loaded down with baggage.

We can learn from our kids. If we will dream without limitations like our children, God will be able to do big things with us. So go ahead. Let your mind become like a child, and dream.

─────────── MOM TO MASTER ───────────

*Lord, thank You that my children have such vivid imaginations. Help me to learn from them. Amen.*

# June 28

*Great is the LORD, and most worthy of praise.*
PSALM 48:1

Are you grateful when God opens the doors to your dreams? Do you immediately recognize that He is the door opener, or do you credit your success to good luck, chance, or your own skill? Sometimes when God answers our prayers and promotes us to the places we'd only dreamed about, we forget to thank Him.

Whenever my children forget to thank me for something major I've done for them, I'm disappointed and occasionally hurt, but I still love them. God feels the same way. He doesn't stop loving us because we neglect to thank Him, but He certainly deserves our praise and adoration. So be sure you take every opportunity to praise Him when He answers a prayer, opens a door, or gives you divine insight.

God longs to hear us praise His name. So look for opportunities to praise Him. When you get an unexpected promotion at work, immediately praise the Lord. If you inherit some money from a relative you didn't even know existed, thank the Lord. If you get a scholarship to return to school to finish your degree, thank the Lord. He is the opener of the doors to your dreams, and He deserves our praise.

——————— MOM TO MASTER ———————

*Lord, I praise You for being the deliverer of my dreams.
You are awesome, and I love You. Amen.*

# June 29

*The fear of the LORD leads to life:*
*then one rests content, untouched by trouble.*

PROVERBS 19:23

Have you ever heard the expression, "Be happy where you are on the way to where you're going"? If you're always looking to the future with longing, you'll miss the good stuff going on right now. You have to find the right balance.

My daughters do this from time to time. When they were younger, they'd get so many presents for Christmas that they couldn't enjoy the ones they'd already opened because they were so focused on opening the next gift. They would hardly look at the roller skates they'd just received before they were on to the next package. It wasn't until all of the presents were unwrapped that they could actually enjoy the blessing load they'd been given.

Have you been guilty of that too? Are you looking for the next present to unwrap instead of enjoying the blessing load all around you? It's easy to do—especially if you're in the diaper, teething, can't-get-back-into-your-prepregnancy-clothes stage. Some days it's hard to find the "gift" in all of it, but look closely. There are gifts all around. Enjoy this wonderful motherhood journey. Don't miss a minute of it. Every moment should be treasured. You have to enjoy today before you'll ever really appreciate tomorrow.

——————— MOM TO MASTER ———————

*Lord, help me to enjoy every minute*
*of this journey. Amen.*

# June 30

*The Master said, "Martha, dear Martha, you're fussing far too much and getting yourself worked up over nothing. One thing only is essential, and Mary has chosen it."*
LUKE 10:41–42 MSG

In the midst of carpools, cheer practice, gymnastics practice, Honor Choir, church youth group, and homework, my girls have little time to "chill" these days. They are so busy, I doubt they even have time to daydream. We'd have to schedule a daydream on Tuesdays between 4:00 and 4:15 p.m. for that to take place.

It's easy to see that today's kids are too busy for their own good, but what about us? Who do you think they learned it from? In addition to driving them to and from practices, we have our own activities and commitments. There's not much time to dream or meditate on the things God has placed in our hearts either.

But we need to *make* time. It is vitally important to our spiritual health. Take time to read over your journal notes, meditate on a scripture or two, talk to God about your dreams, or thank Him for His goodness. I can't go a day without that time, and neither should you. Our kids also need that time, so let's encourage one another to take time for God. He's worth it.

—————————— MOM TO MASTER ——————————

*Father, help me to meditate on Your goodness every day. And help me to teach my children that You are worth their time. Amen.*

# July 1

*Trust in G<small>OD</small>. Lean on your God!*
I<small>SAIAH</small> 50:10 <small>MSG</small>

Do you remember that song "Lean on Me" by Al Green? I think Club Nouveau remade it back in the '80s. I love the words to that song. I've always thought of it as rather inspirational in nature. Do you remember the words? "Lean on me when you're not strong. I'll be your friend. I'll help you carry on." (You're singing along right now, aren't you?)

If there's anything moms need, it's someone to lean on from time to time. Can I get an amen, sister? When the dishwasher is broken, the car is in the shop, the kids are sick, and your bank account is empty and payday is a week away, you need somebody to lean on.

I'm so thankful that we have God to lean on during difficult times. Even if our husbands or our children or our friends don't understand our feelings and even if there's no one else around to lean on, we always have God. He promises in His Word never to leave us nor forsake us. We can lean on Him, and He's happy to let us. So if you're having a lousy day, a lousy week, or even a lousy year, God understands, and He loves you. Go ahead—lean on Him. He will be your Friend.

———————— MOM TO MASTER ————————

*Thank You, Lord, that I can lean on You.*
*Thanks for always being there for me. Amen.*

# July 2

*Cast all your anxiety on him because he cares for you.*
1 PETER 5:7

When my friend had a stillborn baby, we were all devastated. I remember when I got the call. I was stunned. None of us knew what to say or do. There were no explanations. And there were no words to comfort her. The only comfort for her pain came from *the* Word—God's Word. The Lord was there for my friend and her family during this horribly painful time, and that's what pulled them through.

Maybe you've lost a child, or maybe your child has run away from home. I can't pretend to know exactly what you're going through, but God knows. Whatever pain you're experiencing, God is there for you. He loves you, and He cares about your loss. He hurts when you hurt. He longs to comfort you. All you have to do is ask.

While I'll never understand why my wonderful friend lost her baby, I've come to understand one essential thing—God is there for us when we're hurting. He will never leave us. So cast your cares on Him. He really does care for you—more than you'll ever know.

————————— MOM TO MASTER —————————

*Lord, I give my hurt and sense of loss to You today. Thank You for being there for me—no matter what. I love You. Amen.*

# July 3

*LORD, hear my prayer, listen to my cry for mercy;*
*in your faithfulness and righteousness come to my relief.*

PSALM 143:1

"I hate you!" Abby screamed, followed by an intense door slam.

"Well I'm not too crazy about you right now either!" I yelled back, stomping down the hallway toward my bedroom.

That kind of lethal word exchange will instantly turn any day into a bad one. And yes, it's happened at our house before. In fact, it happened not long ago when I wouldn't let Abby go over to a friend's house until her closet was in order. Abby lost her temper, and I lost mine. Ever been there?

There are days when I wonder if I'm cut out for this motherhood role, especially the days when my children yell, "I hate you!" That will bring on the self-doubt in a big way. On those days, I want to eat a big bag of M&Ms and drink a two-liter of diet soda. But that only leads to guilt and extra treadmill time. So I've learned a better route—give it to God. He has all the solutions. He cares about you. He wants to comfort you. And you'll feel better. Plus, prayer is calorie-free. Partake today!

—————— MOM TO MASTER ——————

*Lord, help me not to take offense when my children say*
*ugly things to me. I give my hurt to You. Amen.*

# July 4

*"If my people, who are called by my name, will humble themselves and pray and seek my face and turn from their wicked ways, then I will hear from heaven, and I will forgive their sin and will heal their land."*

2 CHRONICLES 7:14

Backyard barbecues. Family picnics. Patriotic parades. Red, white, and blue snow cones. Fireworks at the park. Ahhhh. . .I love the Fourth of July. But I love this day for many more reasons than the ones I just listed. I love it because, as Americans, we celebrate our freedoms on this day.

Every time I hear that song by Lee Greenwood that says, "I'm proud to be an American," I'm moved to tears. Every time I sing our national anthem at a ball game, I get chills. I am so thankful to live in the United States. I'm so thankful to be able to raise my children here—in the land of the free, home of the brave. We enjoy so many liberties here.

Let's take this moment to thank God for America, and let's pray for our leaders and the men and women who defend this country. Encourage your children to pray along with you. Make it a habit to pray for America and those who lead this mighty land—not just today, but every day. Happy Fourth of July!

————— MOM TO MASTER —————

*Thank You, Lord, for America. I pray for the leaders and the military personnel today. Lead them and protect them. Amen.*

# July 5

*"For your Maker is your husband—the L*ORD *Almighty is his name—the Holy One of Israel is your Redeemer; he is called the God of all the earth."*

ISAIAH 54:5

I have a very good friend who is a single mother. She is an amazing woman. She works long hours to pay the bills, and she still finds time to read stories to her little girl. She attends most every school event, and she does it all with a smile on her face. I am in awe of my friend.

When I compliment her, she always says the same thing: "You just do what you have to do." And to be honest, there are days when she doesn't know if she can do it all. She worries about paying the bills on time. She wonders if she'll be able to buy her daughter those designer tennis shoes. She gets lonely. But she knows the most important thing—that God said He would be her Husband. She has learned to trust Him for everything in her life. That's how I want to be. I'm thankful for my friend, and I'm thankful for all that she is teaching me about trusting the Lord.

————————— MOM TO MASTER —————————

*Lord, please take care of all of the single moms in the world. Thank You for being there for all of us. Amen.*

# July 6

*"People look at the outward appearance,
but the LORD looks at the heart."*

1 SAMUEL 16:7

Every morning when I look in the mirror, I seem to have changed a bit. The more I study my face, the more little lines I see forming around my eyes. How did those get there? It wasn't as easy to look good in my thirties as it was in my twenties. Can I get an amen? I am now slathering every magic potion on my face and neck. Firming. Toning. Antiwrinkle. Antiblemish. Anti-aging. Antioxidants. You name them, I'm using them. Maybe you are too.

Well, here's the good news: Even if we can't turn back the hands of time, even if our faces have a few more lines than they did ten years ago, even though we're growing older—God still adores us. He loves us on our very worst day. He thinks we're special, not because of our outward appearance, but because of our heart condition. The Word says that man looks on the outward appearance while God looks on the heart. So go ahead and slather on those beauty creams, but make sure you spend time basking in God's presence through His Word and through prayer. That's the only true and lasting beauty treatment, so go for it!

—————— MOM TO MASTER ——————

*Lord, thank You for loving me just the way I am. Amen.*

# July 7

*"No weapon formed against you shall prosper."*
ISAIAH 54:17 NKJV

Do you remember the song "I Will Survive" by Gloria Gaynor? I bet you're singing it right now, aren't you? There are days when "I Will Survive" becomes my theme song. Do you know the days I'm talking about? I'm talking about the days when everything goes wrong—your son finds out he is failing four of his six classes; your daughter needs $850 for cheerleading dues and uniform fees; your husband gets the pink slip; the dog throws up on your new carpet; and your home hair-coloring job turned your coif a lovely shade of orange.

On those days, the fighter in me screams—I will survive! It's sort of like saying, "Go ahead, devil. Bring it on. I will survive!" Of course, I wouldn't have the courage or strength or will to go on if it weren't for my heavenly Father. He is the One whispering in my ear, *"It's okay. Don't worry about that. I've got you covered. You're coming out on top! Hang in there! Press forward!"*

If you don't have God as your cheerleader on those really challenging days, you'll probably be singing the blues instead of "I Will Survive." So go ahead. Ask God to help you today.

——————— MOM TO MASTER ———————

*Lord, I need Your help today. Thank You for being my biggest cheerleader—especially when I need an extra boost of encouragement. Amen.*

# July 8

*And the people, that is, the men of Israel, encouraged themselves.*
JUDGES 20:22 NKJV

Do you ever encourage yourself in the Lord? As moms, we encourage everybody else—our husbands, our children, our friends, our extended family, and our neighbors. But we rarely take time to encourage ourselves. Instead, we're overly critical of ourselves. We allow the devil to beat us up, telling us how awful we are. If we'll listen long enough, the devil will convince us that we're unworthy to be servants of God. He'll tell us that we're horrible parents and wives. He'll tell us that we're failures in life. The devil will serve us condemnation with a side of guilt as often as we'll let him. So tell him, *"No more!"*

We have to stop allowing the devil to deceive us. Don't dwell on his lies; meditate on God's Word. The Bible says that you are fully able to fulfill your destiny (Isaiah 54:17). It says that no weapon formed against you is going to prosper. It says that you can do everything through God's strength (Philippians 4:13). Stop focusing on what you can't do and start focusing on what you can do. Quit looking at how far you have to go, and start looking at how far you've already come. Encourage yourself in the Lord today! It's your turn.

———————— MOM TO MASTER ————————

*Thank You, Lord, for giving me the ability to fulfill
my destiny. Help me to stay encouraged. Amen.*

# July 9

*"If all you do is love the lovable, do you expect a bonus?*
*Anybody can do that."*
MATTHEW 5:46 MSG

Do you realize that we have golden opportunities to show love to others every single day? It's true! When that telemarketer interrupts your dinner and you're tempted to hang up right in that person's ear, don't do it. Show mercy and kindness. Or when you encounter rudeness when checking out at the grocery store, don't return rudeness with more rudeness. No, counter that evil with goodness.

Why? The Bible says we're supposed to do unto others as we would have them do unto us. If we'll discipline ourselves and show kindness when we want to react rudely, God will reward us. This is especially true when it comes to our children. Try it! The next time one of your kids gives you the "whatever" sign and blows you off for no reason, smile sweetly and say, "You are so precious to me. I love you." It won't be easy. Your flesh will want to scream, "Listen, kiddo, you'll not 'whatever me' and get away with it! I am your mother. So don't even go there with me!"

Make kindness a habit. You'll find that if you sow seeds of kindness, you'll reap a mighty harvest of kindness. Now that's the kind of crop I want in my life—how about you?

——————— MOM TO MASTER ———————

*Lord, help me to show love and kindness to*
*those who are unlovely and unkind. Amen.*

# July 10

*Gideon said to him, "Me, my master? How and with what could I ever save Israel? Look at me. My clan's the weakest in Manasseh and I'm the runt of the litter."*

JUDGES 6:15 MSG

Do you ever feel incapable of being a good mother? Are there days when you think, *God, are You sure I can do this?* If you ever feel inadequate, you're not alone. Women all over the world struggle with those same feelings of insecurity, self-doubt, and hopelessness. Even though you feel less than able to do all of the things on your plate, God sees you as more than able to do everything He has called you to do.

Even great leaders in the Bible felt inadequate at times. Remember what Moses said when God called him to tell Pharaoh to let the Israelites go? Moses said that he couldn't possibly do it. He told God that He had the wrong guy before finally agreeing to do it. And what about Gideon? When God called him to lead His people against Midian, he said, "I'm the weakest in Manasseh—the runt of the litter." Still, God addressed him as "You mighty man of valor." See, God didn't see Gideon as a weak worm of the dust. He saw Gideon as a mighty man of valor. God sees you as mighty and strong and capable too! Ask God to help you see yourself as He sees you.

—— MOM TO MASTER ——

*Lord, help me to see myself as You see me. I love You. Amen.*

# July 11

*"And I tell you that you are Peter, and on this rock I will build my church, and the gates of Hades will not overcome it."*
MATTHEW 16:18

Did you know that God loves to use ordinary people to do extraordinary things? Look at Peter. He was just a fisherman, but God called him "the rock upon which I'll build my church."

What about Mary? She was a teenager who wasn't yet married, but God chose her to give birth to Jesus. How about David? He was the little guy in the family. When his brothers went to war, he had to stay at home and watch over the sheep. Still, God called him to defeat the giant. Amazing, isn't it?

So if you're feeling like you're not cut out for this motherhood job, cheer up! God is using you to do extraordinary things for the kingdom of God. He wouldn't have entrusted you with your precious children if He didn't believe you could handle it. Of course, it's difficult some days. But hey, God is a big God—bigger than all of our doubts, transgressions, and faults. You don't have to be perfect. You just have to be available. Open your heart and let God restore your hope today. He has more extraordinary things in store for you!

—— MOM TO MASTER ——

*Lord, do the extraordinary in me
and through me today. Amen.*

# July 12

*For great is the LORD and most worthy of praise.*
1 CHRONICLES 16:25

One day I was in Walmart (my home away from home), and I noticed a mom struggling with her toddler son. He was doing the whole "I want that toy!" sobbing routine. I smiled to myself, remembering the many times I'd gone through the exact same situation with Abby and Allyson. I felt for her. I wanted to tell her, "It will be all right. Someday you'll look back on this episode and smile." But I was afraid if I shared those sentimental words of wisdom with her at that moment, she might bop me over the head with the bat her little boy had a death grip on!

We all encounter difficult parenting moments, but if we can keep things in perspective, we'll lead much more joyful lives. When Abby and Allyson used to throw those fits in public, I'd feel humiliated. I'd let the devil steal my joy for several days over one of those crying fits. Looking back, that was wasted time. I should've spent that time enjoying my kids, not beating myself up for their behavior. Don't let Satan steal your joy—no matter how ugly it gets. Just smile and praise the Lord for every parenting moment—good and bad.

───────────── MOM TO MASTER ─────────────

*Lord, thank You for every parenting moment—*
*even the difficult ones. Help me to keep my joy. Amen.*

## July 13

*And let us not grow weary while doing good,*
*for in due season we shall reap if we do not lose heart.*
GALATIANS 6:9 NKJV

Do you ever wonder if you're getting through to your children? There are times when I impart words of wisdom to Abby and Allyson, and I can actually see it bouncing off their little heads into the great beyond. That was especially true if I imparted while Cartoon Network or *Lizzie McGuire* was on TV.

Well, take heart! It turns out they actually do listen to us and internalize some of what we say. I saw evidence of that down the road. As we prepared to head over to the much anticipated elementary school carnival, Ally began crying. She had a horrible red rash all over her face and arms. She'd obviously had an allergic reaction to something. As I fumbled around for Dr. Yee's telephone number, Ally began praying over herself. Within five minutes, the red rash faded to a light pink. Within ten minutes, it was completely gone! Jeff, Abby, and I were amazed. I don't know if I was more amazed that God had healed her or that Ally had thought to ask Him to heal her. Both were miracles worth celebrating.

So don't grow weary in teaching your kids. Some of that wisdom is getting in there—I promise!

———————— MOM TO MASTER ————————

*Lord, help me to take advantage of every teaching*
*opportunity where my children are concerned. Amen.*

# July 14

*"Get wisdom! Get understanding! Do not forget,
nor turn away from the words of my mouth."*
PROVERBS 4:5 NKJV

When you're the mother of little ones, it seems that everyone feels entitled to pass on advice. As if this motherhood thing isn't hard enough, people from all walks of life feel the need to share their nuggets of wisdom with you.

When Abby was two, she still loved her pacifier. I couldn't get it away from her. She just had to have her "pacy." It apparently bothered others, because everywhere we went, people shared ways I could help Abby leave her pacifier behind. After about the eighth tidbit of wisdom concerning her pacifier addiction, I stopped listening. Sure, I'd smile sweetly, nod my head occasionally, and say thank you, but I was singing Barry Manilow tunes in my head.

None of the advice that had been passed on to me worked, by the way. You know what worked? Prayer. That's right, Jeff and I simply prayed for wisdom concerning the pacifier dilemma, and God gave us a "purge the pacy plan." Guess what? It worked. So when everyone is trying to tell you what to do, smile sweetly, nod, and sing "I Write the Songs" in your head, but go to God for answers. Advice can be cheap, but wisdom from God is priceless!

--- MOM TO MASTER ---

*Lord, help me to be gracious to those who offer advice,
but I am asking for Your wisdom in every situation. Amen.*

# July 15

*"Do not sorrow, for the joy of the Lord is your strength."*
NEHEMIAH 8:10 NKJV

Do you know a person who is a "gloom and doomer"? You know the type—the person who *never* has a good day. The person you never ask, "How are you?" because you'll be there listening to her misfortunes, bad luck, and illnesses for hours. Maybe you're a gloom and doom kind of gal. If you are, there's hope.

You don't have to live with a dark cloud over your head anymore. God is your way out of gloom and doom. He will help you make joyful living a way of life.

Determine today to become a positive person—not only for your sake but also for the sake of your kids. They pick up on our defeatist attitudes. They will become mini gloom and doomers if we allow that spirit of hopelessness and depression to invade our homes. So let's get all of the gloom and doom out of our lives once and for all. Get in the habit of saying these confessions every day: "I am well able to fulfill my destiny. God has made me an overcomer. No weapon formed against me is going to prosper. The joy of the Lord is my strength." Before long, that dark cloud that's been blocking the Son is sure to move out!

—————— MOM TO MASTER ——————

*Lord, help me to be a positive person. Amen.*

# July 16

*Whatever I have, wherever I am, I can make it through anything in the One who makes me who I am.*
PHILIPPIANS 4:13 MSG

Have you seen the reality show *Survivor*? If not, here's the skinny on it: Basically, they take a group of men and women and put them in a remote, difficult place where they have to "survive" the game. The last one who is not voted off wins the million dollars. I've often thought they should hold the next *Survivor* series in my house. See how many of them can do three loads of laundry a day, get the kids up and ready for school, pack lunches, write six deadline stories, work out, get ready, pick up the kids at school, taxi the kids to and from their after-school appointments, go grocery shopping, fix dinner, help with homework, spend time with God, return phone calls, and on and on and on! I'm exhausted just typing all of the things that we moms do every day. *Survivor*? Give me a break! After being a working mom, I'm ready for any of them.

I'll bet you are too! Keeping all of the balls in the air is tough. In fact, some days it seems practically impossible. But on those days, I look to God. He says I can do all things through Him, so I'm holding Him to that. You should do the same!

———— MOM TO MASTER ————

*Thank You, Lord, for giving me the strength and ability to tackle all challenges. Amen.*

# July 17

*"Ask and it will be given to you."*
MATTHEW 7:7

"Nobody knows the troubles I've seen. Nobody knows the sorrows. . . ." Remember that little chorus? You have to sing it in a real "bluesy" voice to get the full effect. It's funny to tease about singing the blues, but it's not so funny if you're actually in a blues state of mind.

After I had Abby, I went through a bit of that postpartum depression that you hear so much about these days. Maybe you experienced that terrible condition too. I remember breastfeeding Abby and sobbing at the same time, wondering why I was even crying. I remember trying to fasten my Levi's and crying as they lacked two inches from meeting. I remember feeling helpless, hopeless, and clueless. I hadn't the first idea how to be a mom. But thank the Lord, God did know. He had all the answers, and after I got around to asking for His help, I came out of that "blue funk."

If you're feeling down today, look up. God is there for you. He has all of the answers you need. And He is ready and willing to impart that wisdom to you. All you have to do is ask.

—————————— MOM TO MASTER ——————————

*Heavenly Father, please deliver me from this depression.*
*I want to walk in joy. Thank You for all of the*
*blessings in my life. Amen.*

# July 18

*For God is working in you, giving you the desire to obey him
and the power to do what pleases him.*

Philippians 2:13 NLT

Do you ever feel rebellious? My mother calls that a "mean streak." It seems my mean streak is a mile wide at times. Bottom line? I sometimes have a hard time being obedient. Maybe you have that same challenge. But here's the good news: Whether or not you realize it, God is at work on the inside of you. He is constantly fixing you so that you'll want to obey Him. He loves us so much that He is willing to work on us until our mean streaks are entirely gone. He will never give up on us! He doesn't dwell on our disobedience. He sees us through eyes of love. The more we understand that love, the more we'll want to walk in obedience. The more we embrace our Father's love, the more we'll want to please Him.

Here's more good news: God is doing that same work on the inside of our children. So when they want to disobey, He is willing to go that extra mile to help them *want* to obey. See, He loves our children even more than we do. As we become more obedient to God and His ways, we'll become better examples for our children. It's a win-win situation.

—— MOM TO MASTER ——

*Heavenly Father, thank You for helping
me become more obedient. Amen.*

# July 19

*Never forget your promises to me your servant,*
*for they are my only hope.*

PSALM 119:49 TLB

When something devastating happens to one of our children, it's hard to go on. We're mothers. We're programmed to hurt when they hurt. We'd do anything to take their pain for them. We want so badly to make everything all right for them, but sometimes that's not in our power. When your child has been arrested for drinking and driving, when your baby is diagnosed with cancer, when your mentally challenged child is being tormented at school—that's when it's time to run to the Word of God. When you need God the most, He is there for you. And you'll find Him in His Word.

When we were preparing to move from Indiana to Texas, I was concerned that Abby and Allyson would have trouble making friends in their new home. I worried they'd miss their grandparents and friends too much. I feared we were making a mistake. After crying for a while, I opened God's Word and began reading in Joshua.

Now, I'm not a big Old Testament gal, but on this day the Holy Spirit directed me to Joshua 1:9 (NIV). That's when I read these words: "Do not be afraid; do not be discouraged, for the LORD your God will be with you wherever you go."

God knew I needed reassurance that He would be with me during the move, and He would be with my daughters too. His Word comforted me. It will comfort you too. So go there today.

——————— MOM TO MASTER ———————

*Heavenly Father, thank You for Your Word. Amen.*

# July 20

*When I pray, you answer me and encourage me*
*by giving me the strength I need.*

PSALM 138:3 TLB

My daughters love to sing that song "Supergirl" that goes, "I'm Supergirl, and I'm here to save the world." As they were serenading me with those lyrics the other night, I thought to myself, *That should be my theme song!* Sometimes I try to be Supergirl, thinking it's my job to save the world, and that's when I really get myself in a mess.

Moms are fixers. While that determination and can-do attitude works in our favor much of the time, it can also work against us if we become too self-sufficient. If we rely on ourselves too much, we take God out of the equation. Of course, that leads to total chaos, confusion, and ultimate failure.

So c'mon, Supergirl, rip that *S* off of your shirt and put God back into the equation. He has the strength you need. He has the answers you need. He has it all! Second Corinthians 12:9 tells us that He is made perfect in our weakness, so it's okay if you're feeling stressed out and incapable of fulfilling the demands that are on you right now. Hey, you're in the perfect situation for God to do His best work.

─────────── MOM TO MASTER ───────────

*Lord, I realize that I try to do too much on my own, so I'm giving it all to You today. Please take control of every area of my life. Amen.*

# July 21

*"Oh, that we might know the Lord! Let us press on to know him.
He will respond to us as surely as the arrival of dawn
or the coming of rains in early spring."*
HOSEA 6:3 NLT

I'm not much of a morning person. I'm more of a night owl. But it seems that when I travel, most of my flights are very early morning. So about three or four times a year I actually get to see the sun rise. Wow, Texas has the most gorgeous sunrises! Because the land is so flat here in Fort Worth, you get a really spectacular view. God's handiwork is definitely apparent—makes me want to get up early more often!

Even though I rarely see the sun rise, I know that it always does. That's one thing you can depend on—no matter where you happen to be in the world—the sun always rises. That's why I like Hosea 6:3 so much. It says to me, "Hey, as long as the sun rises, the Lord is going to be there for you." Isn't that good news? That means no matter what you're going through right now, God is there for you, ready to respond to your needs.

So every time you see the sun up in the sky, let it be a reminder of God's promise to you. He is there—ready, willing, and able to intervene on your behalf.

--------- MOM TO MASTER ---------

*Lord, thank You for always being there for me. Amen.*

# July 22

*"But as for me and my family, we will serve the LORD."*
JOSHUA 24:15 NLT

Are your children serving the Lord? Have they made Jesus the Lord of their lives? If you have a wayward child, I know the heartache you must be experiencing. But remember this: it ain't over until the fat lady sings, and she hasn't even stood up! It may look like your child is rebelling against you and God, but keep praying. Keep believing. Find scriptures to stand on. Have faith that God is working behind the scenes to bring your child into the kingdom.

It may look hopeless right now, but God is our hope and glory. He loves your child more than you do. He is able to turn situations around without even getting up from His throne. So don't worry. Only believe. During this time of praying for your child's salvation, surround yourself with the Word of God. Listen to praise and worship music. Watch Christian TV. Read the Word. Read Christian books. Immerse yourself in God, and let Him build your faith.

Remember the story of the prodigal son in Luke 15? Not so. The father represents God, and he kept watch for the return of his son. But he hadn't. The son returned. Your child will return too. Don't give up. Stand your ground and wait for your miracle.

---

### MOM TO MASTER

*Lord, thank You for protecting my wayward child.
I praise You that my child is coming into
the kingdom. In Jesus' name. Amen.*

# July 23

*For I am the Lord, I change not.*
MALACHI 3:6 KJV

I couldn't believe it when Abby asked if she could borrow Jeff's ties. She said, "It's cool to wear men's ties. All the kids are doing it." I had to laugh! We wore men's ties in the '80s! If you're an '80s chick, you probably wore a tie or two in your time. (Not to mention parachute pants, leg warmers, and neon plastic bracelets.) Wow, the '80s were a fashion fiasco, eh?

At ten years of age, Abby thought her generation was the first to wear men's ties and plastic bracelets. I guess it's really true what they say: if you hold on to something long enough, it will eventually come back in style. . . . Wonder where I put those parachute pants?

Well, styles come and go. Fashion and hairstyles change from season to season and year to year. One moment your mullet is in style; the next minute it's out. In this ever-changing world, I'm so glad that Jesus never changes. The Word says He is the same yesterday, today, and forever. Hallelujah! A relationship with Jesus—that's the one thing we can give our kids that will never go out of style.

──────── MOM TO MASTER ────────

*Lord, thank You for being the same yesterday,*
*today, and forever. I love You. Amen.*

# July 24

*The disciples went and woke him up, shouting, "Master, Master, we're going to drown!" When Jesus woke up, he rebuked the wind and the raging waves. Suddenly the storm stopped and all was calm.*

LUKE 8:24 NLT

It never failed. With the first boom of thunder, Abby and Allyson were crawling into bed with us. As little girls, they were very afraid of storms. Even as older girls, when one of those Texas-sized thunderstorms makes its way across the Lone Star State, they would retreat to our bedroom. I can totally relate, because I was also afraid of storms when I was a little girl. I can remember pulling the covers over my head and praying, "God, please make the storm go away!"

Today I find myself praying that same prayer when the storms of life get too scary. When my father had a severe stroke and they called in the family to say our goodbyes, I prayed for God to stop the storm. And just when I thought I couldn't handle one more black cloud, God intervened. My dad pulled out of it and continues to amaze us all.

God will quiet the storms in your life too. He doesn't always calm the storms in the way we want or anticipate, but He will do it. All we have to do is have faith. So come on out from under the covers and call on the One who can calm the storms.

―――――――――― MOM TO MASTER ――――――――――

*Lord, thank You for settling the storms in my life. Amen.*

# July 25

*How can I know all the sins lurking in my heart?*
*Cleanse me from these hidden faults.*
Psalm 19:12 nlt

Allyson's walk-in closet was always a mess. At times I could not even get inside it. About once a month, we had to aggressively motivate her to clean out her cluttered closet. Of course, I had a hard time punishing her for her messy closet when mine didn't look much better. How are your closets?

What about your "life closet"? Got any skeletons in there? We all have a few skeletons in our closets—things we're ashamed of and hope nobody ever discovers. But isn't it great to know that Jesus loves us—skeletons and all? When Jesus comes into our lives, He totally cleans out our closets. In fact, He not only cleans them out, He totally remodels them. He replaces hopelessness with hope. He replaces fear with love. He gets rid of sickness and puts in healing.

We no longer have to be ashamed of the skeletons in our closet, because Jesus has already taken care of those. He has cleansed us from them. We are new creatures in Christ Jesus. So don't worry about those skeletons anymore. Jesus adores you, and He makes no bones about it!

—————— MOM TO MASTER ——————

*Lord, thank You for making me a new creature.*
*Thank You for getting rid of the skeletons in my closet. Amen.*

# July 26

*So let us come boldly to the throne of our gracious God.
There we will receive his mercy, and we will find
grace to help us when we need it most.*

HEBREWS 4:16 NLT

We had a system at our house. We kept a "good behavior chart" on the fridge, and that chart kept track of Abby's and Ally's good deeds and completion of assigned chores. Earning As on report cards is worth several check marks. But mouthy, disrespectful attitudes earn several X's, which cancel out the checkmarks. This system really works! When the girls wanted to get their ears pierced, we challenged them to earn twenty-five marks. It wasn't long before both of them had met their quota, and we were off to the mall for an ear-piercing celebration.

Aren't you glad that God doesn't have a checkmark system? We can never earn our way to heaven. We can't be good enough—no matter how hard we try. It's only by God's grace and mercy that we get in on all of His promises.

As a child, I thought I had to be good all the time in order for God to love me. That's a warped perception of God, isn't it? Let's make sure that our kids know that God loves them—even when they don't behave perfectly. Let's make sure they know that God isn't out to get them—He's out to love them.

--- MOM TO MASTER ---

*Thank You, Father, for loving me even
when I behave badly. Amen.*

# July 27

*Don't you realize that in a race everyone runs, but only one person gets the prize? So run to win! All athletes are disciplined in their training. They do it to win a prize that will fade away, but we do it for an eternal prize.*

1 CORINTHIANS 9:24–25 NLT

I have a neighbor who is preparing to run a marathon. We started out walking/jogging together. My attitude was, *Let's get this over with so I can get on with my day.* But her attitude was different. She began to love jogging. It wasn't long before I could no longer keep up with her. I would jog my two and a half miles, and then she would continue for another eight or ten miles.

She is serious about this new endeavor. She now subscribes to magazines about running. She has purchased several outfits specifically designed for long-distance runners. And she is only eating foods that go along with her training program. She doesn't just want to finish the race—she wants to win this race!

As moms, we need to approach life in much the same way. We are running the most important race there is—raising our children. And, yes, sometimes it seems like we're never going to cross that finish line. Sure, there are days when you'd rather trade in your running shoes for bunny slippers, but hang in there! Keep feeding on the Word of God—that's your training food. The finish line awaits!

--- MOM TO MASTER ---

*Lord, help me to finish this most important race. Amen.*

# July 28

*"There is no other god who can rescue like this!"*
DANIEL 3:29 NLT

Keith Moore sings a song that goes, "There is no God as big as mine. Too big of a problem you cannot find." I love that song. I sing it all the time just to remind myself that we serve a very big God—a God who is able to handle any problem.

Children have no problem with this concept. When Abby is upset over something and I say, "Don't worry about that. God is in control. He is way bigger than your problem," she's totally okay. She knows that God is a big God. But as we get older, we pick up doubt, unbelief, and other baggage. Sometimes, those things can hinder our faith. They can block our faith eyes from seeing that God is bigger than anything we could ever encounter.

I want to challenge you today to get a vision of the vastness of our God. If you keep a journal, I want you to write down all of the problems you're facing today. Maybe you're facing bankruptcy. Maybe your husband has asked for a divorce. Maybe your children are failing school. Whatever it is, write it down. Now write these words over the top of your problems: "My God is bigger than all of these things!"

We serve a big God!

——————— MOM TO MASTER ———————

*Lord, I praise You for being bigger*
*than all of my problems. Amen.*

# July 29

*And I sought for a man among them, that should
make up the hedge, and stand in the gap before me
for the land, that I should not destroy it: but I found none.*

Ezekiel 22:30 kjv

We all know that we need God, but have you ever thought that God might need us too? Sure, He is almighty God. Still, God needs His people. In fact, He needs people like you and me working for Him and accomplishing His goals here on earth. More than anything, He is looking for willing hearts to take the message of His Son around the world.

As moms, we can do that in our own neck of the woods. Our world might be our children's ball games, the grocery store, Walmart, the dry cleaners, our workplace, our neighborhood, or our children's school. We don't have to travel to Africa to evangelize. We can touch the people in our little corner of the world with His love.

Look for opportunities to share God with others. If you're at the grocery store and you notice that your checker is having a hard day, say, "How are you doing today?"

If she says, "Well, I'm not feeling very well," simply ask, "Do you mind if I pray for you? I'd be happy to do that while you're ringing up my items." I've never had anyone say no yet. They are grateful, and God is pleased.

## —— MOM TO MASTER ——

*Lord, help me to touch my world with Your love. Amen.*

## July 30

*Let them turn to the LORD that he may have mercy on them.*
*Yes, turn to our God, for he will forgive generously.*
ISAIAH 55:7 NLT

One thing about my children, they are pretty quick to repent. When Allyson was only four, she loved to play with my china. She wanted to have tea parties with her stuffed animals. Of course, her tea set wasn't fancy enough. She wanted to use my good stuff. (You know, the kind that stays in the china cabinet until Thanksgiving dinner!) I had already told her not to touch my fine china, but she just couldn't help herself. Unfortunately, her little hands weren't so careful. When I heard a crashing sound coming from the living room, I knew what she had done. She had dropped one of my saucers on the hard tile floor, and it was lying there in several pieces.

Before I could even round the corner, her tiny little voice was chanting, "I'm sorry. I'm sorry. I'm sorry. I'm sorry," just as fast as she could say it. I couldn't help but laugh. She knew the best way out of her disobedience was repentance, and she was right.

You know, we could all learn from our children when it comes to quick repentance. When we're disobedient to God, it's best to go right to Him and confess our sin and move on. He wants us to run to Him, not away from Him.

—————————— MOM TO MASTER ——————————

*Lord, thanks for being quick to forgive. Amen.*

# July 31

*Have you never heard? Have you never understood? The LORD is the everlasting God, the Creator of all the earth. He never grows weak or weary. No one can measure the depths of his understanding. He gives power to the weak and strength to the powerless.*
ISAIAH 40:28–29 NLT

It's almost back-to-school time, which always exhausted me. How about you? Every year at this time, kids and their moms go back-to-school shopping for clothes, school supplies, and other stuff. This, of course, is a several weeks process (several paychecks too!).

One year when we began this adventure, we could not find the right size manila paper. It seemed that we drove all over the Lone Star State in search of this paper. I even called my friends in other states to see if they could find it and ship it. We finally found the paper at Staples, forty-five minutes from our home. We were tired, but we were victorious!

Being a mom requires that we take on many tiring adventures, but being worn out doesn't have to go along with the job description. God tells us in the above scripture that He never tires and that He gives strength to the weak and worn out. So if you're feeling a bit overloaded and tired today, ask God to supercharge your engine. He even has enough strength to get us through this back-to-school season.

——————— MOM TO MASTER ———————

*Lord, thanks for giving me strength and energy. Amen.*

# August 1

Words can be lethal weapons. Did you know that? With our mouths, we can curse someone and do irreparable damage to that person. I was watching one of the daytime talk shows not long ago while I walked on the treadmill, and the title of the show was "You Ruined My Life." All of the guests who came onto that show shared heartbreaking stories of how someone had said horrible things to them, changing the entire course of their lives. Some of these guests had lived with the sting of these words for more than twenty years. Can you believe that?

The guests who were the most messed up had internalized damaging words from their parents. Wow. That show just put an exclamation mark at the end of what I already knew in my heart—we need to speak good things to our children! We should take every opportunity to tell our kids, "You can do it! You are well able to fulfill your destiny! You have what it takes! No weapon formed against you is going to prosper! I love you, and God loves you!" So use your words wisely. They hold the power of life and death.

--------- MOM TO MASTER ---------

*Lord, help me to speak only good*
*things to my children. Amen.*

# August 2

*The mouths of the righteous utter wisdom,*
*and their tongues speak what is just.*
PSALM 37:30

Do you ever feel like you have got a big *C* on your head, indicating your level of cluelessness? I am sure my *C* is visible from time to time. Growing up, I always thought that when I became a mom, I'd have all the answers. After all, my mom always had the answers. But I've discovered that being a mom doesn't necessarily come with the "answer key for life."

Many times I am clueless. Maybe you're clueless too. But thank the Lord, we don't have to remain clueless. Even if we don't have the answers, God does. And here's the best part—He is more than willing to share that wisdom with us so that we can pass it on to our children.

It's perfectly okay to admit ignorance when you don't know the answer to a question that your kiddos come up with—really. Just tell them, "I don't know, but I'll find out. God has all the answers, and He is willing to share them with me." It's good for our children to see us vulnerable once in a while. It's especially good for them to see us seeking God for His wisdom. So go ahead, wipe that *C* off your head and seek God.

————————— MOM TO MASTER —————————

*Lord, please fill me with Your wisdom so that*
*I can impart it to my children. Amen.*

# August 3

*[Love] doesn't fly off the handle.*
1 CORINTHIANS 13:5 MSG

How is your attitude today? Feeling kind of grouchy? Some mornings when I open my eyes, I just feel grouchy. It's as if the devil was waiting for me to get up so he could use my mouth to say ugly things. Ever been there? On those days, I have to force myself to walk in love. Let's face it. If you haven't been sleeping enough, or if you're under quite a bit of stress, or if you're feeling ill, it's easier to be a grouch.

But moms aren't supposed to be grouches! Haven't you ever seen *Leave It to Beaver* on TV Land? Mrs. Cleaver is always joyful. And how about that Carol Brady on *The Brady Bunch*? She is so sweet, it's sickening!

In reality, no mom can be perfect all the time. We all lose our tempers. We all complain. We all act ugly. We all get grouchy. But God knew that when He created us. He knew our flesh would win out once in a while. He sent Jesus to save us from our sins so we can repent for our grouchy attitudes and move forward in love. So get those grouchies off and let love control you today.

—————— MOM TO MASTER ——————

*Lord, flood me with Your love. Amen.*

# August 4

*Every word they speak is a land mine.*
PSALM 5:9 MSG

Have you ever wanted to say something so badly that you practically had to bite through your tongue not to say it?

Me too.

There's a great exchange in the movie *You've Got Mail* that stars Meg Ryan and Tom Hanks. In this clip, she is frustrated that she can't ever say the exact thing she wants to say at the moment of confrontation. On the other hand, Tom Hanks's character is able to say cutting comebacks without any hesitation. She emails him that she wishes she had that talent. He tells her that he wishes he could give her his talent because it's dangerous, stating that saying exactly what you think, exactly when you think it, leads to guilt and regret. Later in the film when she is able to say the most hurtful comments on cue, she realizes the truth in her friend's email. She felt badly for her hurtful words, but they had already been said.

That's the thing about spewing words without ever thinking about the consequences—you can't get those words back. They do damage immediately, and even when you say you're sorry, their sting remains. So think before you speak. Do whatever it takes to keep the cutting comments from escaping your mouth. You may have a sore tongue, but your heart will feel good!

―――――――――― MOM TO MASTER ――――――――――

*Lord, keep a rein on my mouth. Amen.*

# August 5

*He traveled through that area,*
*speaking many words of encouragement to the people.*
ACTS 20:2

I think all moms were born to be cheerleaders and vice versa. That's one of the only qualifications I actually had when I became a mom. I had been a cheerleader from elementary school through college. Many times our children don't need correction; they just need encouragement.

School is tough today. So much is expected from our children. Due to funding issues, schools really push the children to do well on the yearly assessment tests. After months of preparation for these all-important tests, the testing week finally arrives. One of Abby's friends actually suffered with an ulcer last year due to the stress. School is really difficult today. When you add in all of the extracurricular activities and other stuff, it's no wonder our children are stressed out!

So it's our job to encourage our little ones. We need to tell them they can do it! We need to tell them they are special. We need to find creative ways to encourage them. For instance, leave little notes of encouragement in their lunch boxes. They need our approval and affirmation, so let's be quick to offer it. Get out those pom-poms and become a super encourager!

———— MOM TO MASTER ————

*Father, help me to be an encourager for my family. Amen.*

# August 6

*Love never fails.*

1 CORINTHIANS 13:8

Do you know that some children grow up without ever hearing "I love you" said to them by their parents? It's true. Maybe you're one of the people who grew up without ever hearing those three important words. If you are, then I'm sure you know how hurtful and devastating it is to never feel loved.

I have a friend who grew up in a home like that—where love was never communicated—and she has struggled in that area. Her father used to say, "I don't have to say it. My actions show that I love you." While that might be true, we still need to hear the words. As wives, we need to hear those three words from our husbands. And as moms, we need to communicate our love to our children.

There are many ways we can say, "I love you." We can leave little love notes to our spouses and our children, sneaking them into briefcases and backpacks. We can verbally express our love every morning and every night. We can bake a big cookie cake and write, "I Love You!" on it. Be as creative as you want, just make sure you take time to express your love every day. Be an ambassador of love in your home.

—————————— MOM TO MASTER ——————————

*Father, help me to better express*
*my love to my family. Amen.*

# August 7

*"Therefore my heart is glad and my tongue rejoices."*
ACTS 2:26

When I was in fourth grade, I went to church camp at Camp Wildwood in southern Indiana. One of my most vivid memories of attending that camp was singing, "Rejoice in the Lord always, again I say rejoice," in a round on the bus. I've never forgotten that little chorus or the way I felt singing at the top of my lungs, surrounded by seventy other kids singing at the tops of their lungs. Let me tell you, we sang ourselves happy. It didn't matter that it was the hottest, stickiest, most humid day of the summer and we were riding on a bus without air-conditioning. We didn't care! We just praised the Lord anyway. Sometimes I still sing that little chorus just to encourage myself. Do you ever do that? If not, you're missing out!

Praising the Lord is one of the best things you can do to encourage yourself. It's hard to be worried or depressed when you're singing, "Rejoice in the Lord always." Even if you're feeling down when you begin singing, before long, your heart will be glad. This scripture says our tongues should rejoice, so let your tongue rejoice today. Let your kids see you rejoicing in the Lord, and before long, they'll join in. It's contagious!

———————— MOM TO MASTER ————————

*Father, I praise You for being who You are! Amen.*

# August 8

*"For the mouth speaks what the heart is full of."*
LUKE 6:45

"U-G-L-Y, you ain't got no alibi, you're ugly. Hey, hey, you're ugly. Whoo!" Did you ever do this cheer as a child? We used to say it to the opposing team when I was on the eighth-grade cheer squad. Nice, huh? And now this little chant has found its way into a song of the same name. (It's on the *Bring It On!* soundtrack.)

The kids love it. A group of girls recently performed this song in a local elementary talent show and brought the house down with laughter. It was really funny! One of the girls was dressed up like a big nerd, and the other cheerleaders chanted this song at her.

While that was funny in a talent show, it's not so funny on the playground or in the classroom. Unfortunately, children (tween girls especially) can be cruel to one another. They call each other fat, ugly, stupid, poor, and other terrible things such as "Loser!" As parents, we want our children to understand the power of their words and to choose them wisely. We want them to grow up to be kind and respectful of others' feelings. And they will if we continually remind them that saying ugly things indicates the presence of an ugly heart.

--- MOM TO MASTER ---

*Father, help me to teach my children the power of their words and the importance of being kind to others. Amen.*

# August 9

*"My lips will not say anything wicked,
and my tongue will not utter lies."*

JOB 27:4

"Ally, did you turn in your lunch money?"

"Yep," she answered, breezing past me in the hallway.

Fast forward to the next morning. As I'm cleaning out my daughter's closet, I discover the envelope with "Lunch Money" written on the outside. It had been ripped open, obviously to remove the money.

Can you say, "Busted"?

The school confirmed what I already knew—the lunch money had never made it to school. My little, clever, blond child had pocketed the cash. I confronted her when she arrived home from school that afternoon. She immediately began crying, asking for forgiveness for telling a huge lie. Of course we forgave her, but her lying resulted in punishment. She had to miss a party that weekend among other things.

It's easy to see that Ally's lie was wrong. But what about the little white lies that we encourage? You know, like when we ask our kids to tell the telemarketer that Mommy isn't at home right now. A lie is a lie is a lie. We need to be conscious of our words because our kids are paying attention. We're their role models. Let's make sure we're good ones.

——————— MOM TO MASTER ———————

*Lord, help me to be a good role model for my children,
and help us all to speak no deceit. Amen.*

# August 10

*May the LORD silence all flattering lips*
*and every boastful tongue.*

PSALM 12:3

Have you ever known anyone who always has to one-up you? If you had twins, she had triplets. If you had a thirty-four-hour labor and delivery, she had a forty-five-hour trauma. If you share that you've lost four pounds, she's lost seven. Ahhh! It can drive you crazy! It's even more maddening when that person one ups you on your children's accomplishments.

You say, "My daughter just learned to do a back handspring."

And she says, "Really? My daughter can do a round off back handspring back tuck."

It's enough to make you want to join in the one-ups game too, but don't go there. The Bible tells us in 1 Corinthians 13 that love does not boast. So if you join in the one-ups game, your love walk will become more of a love crawl. It's not worth it.

The next time that someone tries to one-up you, simply take a deep breath, smile sweetly, and move on. Give your frustration and irritation to God. He can give you a love for that person. He can help you see that person through His eyes of compassion, because someone who is always one-upping everyone else is a person with self-esteem issues. That person needs your prayers, not your anger. So take the high road and walk in love.

———————— MOM TO MASTER ————————

*Lord, help me to walk in love no matter what. Amen.*

# August 11

*"Go near and listen to all that the LORD our God says."*

DEUTERONOMY 5:27

Do you talk too much? Listening has become sort of a lost art form in today's society. We are a generation of people who simply love to hear ourselves talk. But you know, if we're constantly talking, we're missing out on a lot. This is especially true in our prayer lives.

When you pray, do you do all of the talking? From the time we're little children, we're taught to pray to God. We're taught to say the Lord's Prayer. We're taught to bring our praises and petitions unto Him. But very few of us are taught to wait upon the Lord and listen for His voice. It's a difficult thing, waiting and listening. It requires time on our part. It requires patience. It takes practice. God's voice doesn't come down from the sky and speak to us in a Charlton Heston–type voice. No, He speaks to us through that still, small voice—that inward knowing—the Holy Spirit. He also speaks to us through His Word.

So quit doing all of the talking and take time to listen to Almighty God! He has much wisdom to share with us if we'll only be quiet long enough to receive it.

———————— MOM TO MASTER ————————

*Lord, I want to hear Your voice.*
*Help me to listen better. Amen.*

# August 12

*Your boasting is not good.*
1 CORINTHIANS 5:6

Abby, at ten years old, had a very vivid imagination. In fact, I thought she might become a writer and an illustrator when she grew up. But all of that creativity sometimes found its way into her speech. Abby, like many children, had a tendency to exaggerate once in a while. When she and Daddy went fishing, she always had an exciting "fish tale" to tell.

While this is kind of cute in our kids, it's not quite so cute and harmless when *we* do it. At times when I've been backed into a corner, I've resorted to exaggeration to justify myself. Maybe you've done the same thing. A few years ago, a colleague of mine said something condescending to me in front of other writers and editors. So to defend myself, I exaggerated a bit on my financial situation. They were immediately impressed, and I was immediately depressed. I had exaggerated in self-defense, but no matter the reason, God isn't pleased when we stretch the truth—because "stretching the truth" simply means telling a lie.

If you have a tendency to exaggerate, ask God to help you. The Lord has helped me in this area. He reminded me that I don't have to prove myself to anyone. He is already pleased with me. He is pleased with you too!

——————— MOM TO MASTER ———————

*Lord, thank You for validating me with Your love.*
*Help me to stop exaggerating. Amen.*

# August 13

*"If you have any word of encouragement
for the people, come and give it."*

ACTS 13:15 NLT

"You go, girl!"

That has sort of become the expression of today's women, hasn't it? In the past, Helen Reddy's "I am woman, hear me roar" was the cry, but now it's simply an encouraging, "You go, girl!" We need to encourage each other. As moms, we should uplift one another in prayer, in word, and in deed.

I don't know what I would do without the gal pals in my life. There are days when I need to call and vent. There are times when I simply need my buddy to say, "You don't look fat." There are situations when I just need a hug and a simple, "You go, girl! You can do it!"

As moms, we are constantly speaking words of encouragement to our families. We're the cheerleaders! But we need a little cheering every so often too. That's why it's so important to surround yourself with positive people. Find friends who are women of faith, and be there for one another. Pray for one another. Love one another. And encourage each other with a "You go, girl!" now and then. We're all in this motherhood experience together, so let's cheer each other on to victory!

—————— MOM TO MASTER ——————

*Lord, thank You for the friends You've given me.
Help me to encourage them as You encourage me. Amen.*

# August 14

*His mouth is full of lies and threats;*
*trouble and evil are under his tongue.*

Psalm 10:7

There's always one in every crowd—the troublemaker. The one who constantly speaks evil, taking great pleasure in stirring up strife. There was a little girl at Abby's and Allyson's school who fit this description. She was constantly in the middle of some dispute. She made up lies about other children. She gossiped and divided friends. She was a busy girl!

Maybe your children have had bouts with this kind of kid. It's tough to just stand by as a mom and watch another child destroy our children's reputations. I know, I've been there. But stepping into the middle of the situation and taking charge on your child's behalf isn't the best way. I know because I've tried that too.

Do you know the best course of action? Prayer. Of course, that's the last thing you want to do when someone has hurt your child, but prayer is the only thing that will produce positive results. Pray that the troublemaker finds Jesus. Pray for wisdom to deal with the situation. And of course, pray for your child's protection. Confess together, "No weapon formed against me is going to prosper." The Word is powerful, and so is prayer. So hit your knees and use your tongue in the right way. Prayer changes things every time!

## MOM TO MASTER

*Lord, I pray for my children's protection, and I ask that this child*
*who is causing so much hurt will find You. Touch her, Lord. Amen.*

# August 15

*Beautiful words stir my heart. I will recite a lovely poem about the king, for my tongue is like the pen of a skillful poet.*
PSALM 45:1 NLT

Do you want your tongue to be like the pen of a skillful poet? That's a lofty goal but one that is totally within our reach if we let God fill our hearts with His love. You see, the Word says that out of the heart the mouth speaks. So if your heart is full of ugliness and trash, then your tongue will be writing ugly things.

As moms, we need to write very skillfully with our tongues because those "little poets" who call us Mom are taking notes all the time. They listen very carefully to everything we say—good or bad. We only have a short time to impact our kids for the kingdom of God, so we need to make every word count.

Sure, we're going to miss it sometimes. We're only human. But it should be our goal to be more like Jesus every day. If we become more Christlike, then our mouths will be like the pens of skillful poets, writing good things on the hearts of all we encounter.

—————————— MOM TO MASTER ——————————

*Heavenly Father, help me to use my words wisely. Fill my heart with Your love so that my mouth might be filled with Your words. Amen.*

# August 16

*Timely advice is lovely, like golden apples in a silver basket.*
PROVERBS 25:11 NLT

It's funny—as young children, we thought our moms knew everything. As teens, we thought they knew nothing. As adults, we realize we were right in the first place—they do know everything. Moms are full of wisdom; however, when I became a mom, I didn't feel so wise. In fact, I didn't know the first thing about being a mother. As I've matured, I've learned a little about being a mom—mostly from my mom. Her advice is priceless.

We can learn much from the godly women in our lives. Maybe your mom hasn't been there for you, but God has placed other women in your life—an aunt, a grandmother, a close family friend, or your pastor's wife. Cherish their words of wisdom. God has placed them in your life for a purpose.

Just think, some day your children will look to you for wisdom—it's true! The Word says that they will rise up and call you blessed. So make sure you have some wisdom to share. Treasure the advice that's been given to you, and more importantly, meditate on the Word of God. There's much wisdom waiting for you!

———————— MOM TO MASTER ————————

*Heavenly Father, thank You for those special women in my life. Help me to honor them and You. Amen.*

# August 17

*"Take to heart all the words of warning I have given you today.*
*Pass them on as a command to your children so they*
*will obey every word of these instructions."*

DEUTERONOMY 32:46 NLT

As parents, we have a mandate from the Lord to teach our children about God. We are to pass on our knowledge to our kids; however, that is difficult to do if we don't have any knowledge to pass on. Maybe you weren't raised in a Christian home. Maybe you are a new Christian. That's okay. God is great at giving crash courses in Christ. He longs to fill you full of His wisdom. He will enable you to memorize scriptures. He will teach you about His character. He will help you pray. Just ask Him!

Even if you've been a Christian for as long as you can remember, there's still more to learn. Have you ever read a scripture that you're very familiar with, but all of a sudden, it teaches you something totally new? That's the Lord teaching you. Isn't that exciting? God's Word is alive. It's there for you when you need it. It holds the answers you need. And it's never been more pertinent than it is right now.

Fall in love with God's Word. Listen to teaching tapes. Attend a Word-based church. Get wisdom so that you'll have wisdom to pass on to your kids.

———————— MOM TO MASTER ————————

*Lord, teach me so that I may teach my kids. Amen.*

# August 18

*In the morning, LORD, you hear my voice;*
*in the morning I lay my requests before you and wait expectantly.*
PSALM 5:3

How do you start your mornings? Do you roll out of bed, grumbling and grumpy? Or do you spring out of bed, praising the Lord with great expectation? If you're like me, you're not exactly chipper in the morning. But I'm learning to like those early hours a little better. Why? Because mornings are a great time to praise the Lord!

If you start your day giving praises to God, it's even more energizing than a shot of espresso. No matter how grumpy you feel, once you start praising God for His love and His goodness, you're bound to change your mood for the better. That's just the way it works!

So why not use your mouth for something worthwhile like praising the Lord? Begin each day thanking God. It will take some practice, but you'll get the hang of it. The Holy Spirit will help you. Praise God for the many blessings in your life. Praise Him for another day to be alive. Praise Him just because He is God and deserving of our praise. Let your children see you praising the Lord, and encourage them to join in. If you do, the mornings around your house will be a lot brighter.

——————————— MOM TO MASTER ———————————

*Lord, I praise You for who You are. Amen.*

# August 19

*My brothers and sisters, can a fig tree bear olives, or a grapevine bear figs? Neither can a salt spring produce fresh water.*

JAMES 3:12

We know from the Word of God that the tongue is hard to tame. Of course, I didn't need the Bible to tell me that fact. I am well aware that my mouth is hard to control. Maybe you have that same challenge. That's why this scripture really brings conviction to me. If you're praising the Lord in church and hollering at your children on the way home, this scripture probably hits home with you too.

We need to continually ask the Lord to put a watch on our mouths. We need to ask for His help so that we might be good examples for our children. If they hear us praising God one minute and hollering at them the next, they will be confused and disillusioned with the things of God.

James 3:9 says, "With the tongue we praise our Lord and Father, and with it we curse human beings, who have been made in God's likeness." We must be careful of our words because not only are our children listening, but God is also listening. And we'll be held accountable for our words—all of them.

—————— MOM TO MASTER ——————

*Lord, please put a watch on my mouth that I might speak only good things. Help me to be a good example for my children. I love You. Amen.*

# August 20

*"Whoever would love life and see good days must keep their tongue from evil and their lips from deceitful speech."*

1 PETER 3:10

When I was a little girl, I lied to my father just once. When he found out, I received a few licks across my backside, but that didn't hurt nearly as much as what my dad said to me. He looked me in the eyes and uttered, "There's nothing I dislike more than a lie. I am disappointed in you."

Whoa! I could handle anything except my dad being disappointed in me. Today, as a mom of two girls, I've been on the other side of that lying scenario a time or two. And I've discovered that I don't like being lied to any more than my father did.

It's not enough just to tell our children that lying is a sin. We need to take every opportunity to let them know that lying always has consequences. Once when I caught the girls in a lie, I told them that even if they got away with their lie and I never found out about it, God would always know. That got their attention. You see, they love God, and they didn't want to disappoint Him any more than I wanted to disappoint my earthly father. So strive for honesty in your house. God will be pleased, and that's no lie!

---
MOM TO MASTER
---

*Lord, help me to raise honest, godly children. Amen.*

# August 21

*Dear children, let us not love with words or speech but with actions and in truth.*

1 JOHN 3:18

Saying "I love you" to our children is very important. They need to hear those words on a daily basis. But we also need to *show* that we love our children. Have you ever really thought about the common expression "Actions speak louder than words"? There's a lot of truth to that saying.

While it's easy to say, "I love you," it's not so easy to show our love all the time. That's why another expression, "Talk is cheap," is used so often. As moms, we need to find ways to back up our "I love yous" every single day. In other words, walk the talk.

Make a conscious effort today to do something special for your children—something out of the ordinary. Leave them little love notes. Make them a special pancake breakfast and serve it by candlelight for added fun. Plan a family night out at one of their favorite places. Just find a unique way to show your kids how much you adore them. Ask God to help you in this area. He will. After all, the Bible says that God is love. He is the expert in showing love.

—————— MOM TO MASTER ——————

*Heavenly Father, help me to show Your love to my family on a daily basis. I love You. Amen.*

# August 22

*Do not be anxious about anything, but in every situation,*
*by prayer and petition, with thanksgiving,*
*present your requests to God.*

PHILIPPIANS 4:6

Do you pray for your children every day? I'll bet you do. Moms are prayer warriors. It's part of our job description. But are your prayers effective, or are you canceling them out? Are you praying for God to give your children wisdom to do better in school, thanking Him for His intervention, and then canceling out your prayers by talking about Junior's inability to learn? You see, we can't be double-minded people. The Word speaks to that fact in James 1:8: "Such a person is double-minded and unstable in all they do."

You see, a negative will always cancel out a positive. You can't pray about something and then talk against it, or your mouth has just canceled out your prayers. That's why you must only speak words of faith. Our words are power containers. They shape our world, good or bad. So be careful what you speak. Use your words to speak life to your children. Use your words to praise the Lord. Use your words to change your current situation. If you're in the habit of speaking negative things, just be still. It's better to be quiet than to speak against the Word. Get in the habit of speaking good things, and watch your world change!

## ——— MOM TO MASTER ———

*Heavenly Father, help me to speak only*
*words of faith. Amen.*

# August 23

*Nor should there be obscenity, foolish talk or coarse joking,*
*which are out of place, but rather thanksgiving.*

EPHESIANS 5:4

Does your mouth filter ever quit working? You know, the filter that keeps you from saying the things you're thinking? Mine goes out from time to time. That's when I suffer from "foot in mouth" disease. That happened to me not long ago when I asked a lady when her baby was due and she informed me that she wasn't pregnant. Ouch! Okay, from now on, unless a woman is wearing a BABY ON BOARD T-shirt, I'm never asking that question again!

Sometimes, we say things without thinking. We don't mean to say them; they just come out before we can retrieve them. Many times those words can be hurtful. So think before you speak. Run it through your Holy Spirit filter before uttering a single syllable. Ask the Lord to help you say only uplifting, encouraging, and wise words.

We need to help our children with this filtering process too. Kids are notorious for saying inappropriate things. We need to help them to be respectful of others—especially those who are different. Make sure your filter is turned on all the time, and help your children develop their filter too.

—————————— MOM TO MASTER ——————————

*Heavenly Father, help me to develop my Holy Spirit filter, and help*
*me to teach my children to watch their words too. Amen.*

# August 24

*"A good man brings good things out of the good stored up in his heart, and an evil man brings evil things out of the evil stored up in his heart. For the mouth speaks what the heart is full of."*

LUKE 6:45

Are you an angry person? In other words, do you have a short fuse? If you do, chances are your tongue betrays you all the time. Angry people typically retaliate with words—angry, hurtful words—at a moment's notice. They are quick to attack and slow to repent.

When we get angry, we often say things we don't mean. But according to Luke 6:45, we actually speak what is in our hearts. That's a scary thought, isn't it? Who knew all of that yucky stuff was stored up in our hearts? I once heard it explained like this: If you squeeze a tube of toothpaste toothpaste comes out. If you put pressure on a person who is full of ugliness and anger, ugly and angry words come out.

So here's the key: We need to store up more of God in our hearts so that when the pressure is on, godly words will flow out of us. In other words, when our true colors are revealed, they will be the colors of Christ. Go ahead, fill up on God!

―――――――――― MOM TO MASTER ――――――――――

*Heavenly Father, I want more of You and less of me.*
*Please take away the angry part of me. Amen.*

# August 25

*My people are ruined because they*
*don't know what's right or true.*

HOSEA 4:6 MSG

As moms, it's our awesome responsibility to tell our children about the things of God. That's what this verse communicates to me. If we don't tell them about salvation, they'll never know that Jesus died on the cross to save them from sin. If we don't tell them about His unconditional love, they won't run to Him in times of trouble. If we don't tell them about healing, they'll never know that God can heal their sicknesses. They need to know these important truths so that they won't perish for lack of knowledge.

Teaching our children God's Word and His ways are the two most important things we can give our kids, because if they have that knowledge, they have it all! As moms, we can't always be there for our children. But if we've equipped them with the Word of God, they will be all right without us.

It's like John Cougar Mellencamp says in one of his '80s tunes: "You've got to stand for something, or you're going to fall for anything." If our children stand on the Word of God, they won't be easily fooled or swayed. So take the time to teach your children the Word. It's the most important investment you'll ever make.

—————— MOM TO MASTER ——————

*Heavenly Father, help my children to love Your Word*
*and carry it with them always. Amen.*

# August 26

*"So shall My word be that goes forth from My mouth; it shall not return to Me void, but it shall accomplish what I please."*

ISAIAH 55:11 NKJV

I once heard Evangelist Kenneth Copeland say, "One word from God can change your life."

I wrote that phrase in my notebook and thought, *Wow, that is so true!*

It was certainly true for Lazarus when Jesus said, "Lazarus, come forth," and he got up and walked out of the tomb, grave clothes and all. It was also true for the little daughter of Jairus when Jesus said, "Little girl, arise," and she stood up after being dead.

The more I thought about it, the more I realized that if one word from God can change your life, then I should be speaking His words into my children at every opportunity. Of course, we can't shove it down their throats like we did those strained peas when they were babies, but we can spoon-feed them the Word—a little each day.

And if your children are acting resistant to the Word, don't push. Just let your life show His love, and eventually they'll listen to what you have to say. They'll finally come around. God promises that His Word will not return void, so keep speaking it. That Word will finally take root in their hearts and produce some radical results.

## ———————— MOM TO MASTER ————————

*Heavenly Father, help me to find creative ways to teach Your Word to my children. Amen.*

# August 27

*"Do to others as you would have them do to you."*

LUKE 6:31

Remember those telephone company TV commercials that featured the slogan "Reach out and touch someone"? I always loved those commercials. . .the ones that were real tearjerkers. While that slogan has come and gone, its meaning is still very relevant. We can reach out and touch someone with our words every single day.

My father, who has suffered several strokes, can't get out and minister like he used to do, so he shares the love of Jesus to telemarketers when they call his home. They call hoping to sell him something, and he ends up telling them about the free gift of eternal life. That's what I call really reaching out and touching someone!

Others in my church call the shut-ins and those in the area hospitals and nursing homes weekly—just to let them know that someone cares. Still others take time to call all of the first-time visitors to the church, giving them a personal welcome. Through their words, they are reaching out with the love of Jesus. Maybe you've been feeling like you'd like to serve the Lord in some capacity but you didn't feel qualified in any area. Well, you can use the telephone, right? Ask God if this might be a way that He can use you, and begin reaching out today!

——————————— MOM TO MASTER ———————————

*Lord, help me to use my words to reach out*
*to others with Your love. Amen.*

# August 28

*"I know, my God, that you test the heart
and are pleased with integrity."*
1 CHRONICLES 29:17

My dad often talks about a time when a handshake and a man's word were the only things needed to seal a deal. There was no need for contracts. Everybody operated on trust and integrity. Can you imagine if the world were still like that today? Giving someone your word should be enough, but integrity—even among Christians—is hard to come by these days. After you've been burned a few times, it's easy to become jaded and start questioning everyone's integrity.

As Christians, and as mothers, we should walk in integrity. Of course, we know it's wrong to lie. That's a given. But there are other ways that we compromise our integrity. For instance, if you tell friends that you'll meet them at 10 a.m. and you don't show up until 10:20, that's a lack of integrity. The Lord convicted me of this just the other day because as anyone who knows me will testify, I am notoriously late.

It's our goal to set good examples for our children, right? So let's determine today to be people of integrity in every area of our lives. Integrity is important to God, and it should be important to us.

———— MOM TO MASTER ————

*Lord, mold me into a person of integrity, and help me
to teach my children to walk in integrity too. Amen.*

# August 29

*He replied, "Because you have so little faith. Truly I tell you,
if you have faith as small as a mustard seed, you can say to this
mountain, 'Move from here to there,' and it will move.
Nothing will be impossible for you."*

MATTHEW 17:20

We don't have many mountains in Texas, but I once visited Colorado and was mesmerized by the magnificence of the Rockies. As I looked out over the landscape, this scripture came to mind. I love this verse. I love knowing that if I have faith—and not even a lot of it—nothing is impossible. Isn't that good news?

But I want you to notice something else about this verse. It says that we have to *say* to the mountain, "Move." It doesn't say that we have to think it or write it or wonder about it. Those little utterances that roll off of our tongues make all of the difference.

So don't just wish your life away—put some faith behind your words! If you want your kids to do better in school, begin praying that they have the mind of Christ. Speak it over them in the mornings. Teach them to make positive confessions over themselves. You've heard of the power of positive thinking, right? Well, the real power is in faith-filled words. Go ahead, fill the air with faith-filled words and watch God go to work.

--- MOM TO MASTER ---

*Lord, please fill my mouth with faith-filled words. Amen.*

# August 30

I love how God dealt with Moses. He was so kind and reassuring. Moses was full of self-doubt and unbelief. God told Moses what to say to Pharaoh, and Moses responded, "But what if he doesn't believe me?"

Later, after God gave Moses some additional instructions, Moses said, "But Lord, You know I am slow of speech. I can't do this."

But God said, "Moses, who made your mouth? Wasn't it Me, Moses?" Still, God reassured Moses and let Aaron help him.

Maybe you feel overwhelmed today. Maybe you feel like you're losing the battle where your tongue is concerned. Maybe you are unsure of yourself as a mom. Maybe you are a little like Moses—full of self-doubt and unbelief. You don't have to stay that way! Just as God reminded Moses, I am reminding you. God made your mouth. God made your mind. God made you exactly the way you are. He knew you in your mother's womb. He knew that you'd someday be a mother. In fact, He knows the number of hairs on your head. He has ordered your steps.

So don't dwell in doubt—walk in faith. In the same way that God did mighty works through Moses, He can do the same through you.

--- MOM TO MASTER ---

*Lord, I trust You. Teach me to trust You more. Amen.*

# August 31

*He is our father in the sight of God, in whom he*
*believed—the God who gives life to the dead and*
*calls into being things that were not.*

ROMANS 4:17

"That's a good boy, Miller," Allyson said, petting our new dachshund puppy's head. "You are such a good boy."

At the time, Miller wasn't such a good boy. In fact, he was
messing up my carpets on a daily basis. I wasn't sure he would
ever be housebroken. I loved him, but I didn't like what he was
doing to my house. Still, Allyson called Miller "a good boy." After
several months of calling Miller "a good boy," he became one!
Miller is the best dog we've ever had. He is loyal. He is smart.
He is sweet. And he is housebroken! I firmly believe that Allyson
had much to do with Miller's transformation. She believed in
him and called him good, and he became good.

This principle will work every time. Try it! Call things that
are not as though they were—just like Romans 4:17 says. You
know, God even changed Abram's name to Abraham because
Abraham means "the father of many nations" (Genesis 17).
Every time someone said, "Hey, Abraham," that person was
saying, "Hey, father of many nations." Call your children good
names. Speak good things over them. Fill your home with positive words. It will make a difference.

—————————— MOM TO MASTER ——————————

*Lord, help me to speak good things over my kids. Amen.*

# September 1

*The fear of the LORD is the beginning of knowledge,*
*but fools despise wisdom and instruction.*

PROVERBS 1:7

Nobody likes to hear the word *no*—especially our children! We had a rule at our house that simply stated, "No playtime until your homework is finished." Well, that wasn't always a popular rule. Maybe you have the same rule. If you do, I'll bet you occasionally get the same reaction I do—"Mom! Please! I don't have that much homework. I can finish it later. Let us ride our bikes now."

Yes, I made exceptions to the rule for special outings and parties, but the rule stood most of the time. We have to think "future minded" for our kids because they live in "the now." I knew that if they rode their bikes after school, they'd come in tired and grouchy and have no energy left to do their homework. And if they didn't complete their homework, they'd make bad grades. And if they made bad grades, they'd have to be grounded. It's a whole chain reaction of negative circumstances, which is why we came up with the "homework first rule" in the first place.

So don't be afraid to stand your ground. Don't cave in to the whining and begging. Your rules are for your children's own good—even if they don't see it that way.

―――――― MOM TO MASTER ――――――

*Lord, give me the wisdom to make good rules and the authority*
*to implement them and stick by them. Amen.*

# September 2

When Allyson was in preschool, she adored the Disney movie *Mulan.* Her favorite scene featured Mulan cutting off her long ponytail so she could fool everyone into thinking she was a boy. Ally thought that might be fun too so she cut off her long, blond ponytail and hid her hair throughout our home. When I discovered the beautiful blond ponytail in my kitchen trashcan, I immediately confronted Allyson with the evidence. Her response? "Miller did it." Now, I'm not saying our long-haired dachshund isn't a smart doggie, but I was pretty sure he hadn't learned to use the scissors!

Ally was playing the blame game. Rather than just repent and move on, she decided it would be much easier to blame poor old Miller. As I dealt with Ally, the Lord dealt with me, pointing out the times that I had blamed other people and bad circumstances for my behavior.

I find that many times as I discipline my children, the Lord takes those opportunities to teach and discipline me too. As it turns out, I struggle with many of the same challenges that my children do—imagine that? It pricks a bit when the Lord disciplines us, but we'll never mature if He doesn't correct. So embrace correction.

--------- MOM TO MASTER ---------

*Lord, help me to be quick to repent
when You correct. Amen.*

*My child, don't reject the LORD's discipline,*
*and don't be upset when he corrects you.*
PROVERBS 3:11 NLT

"Abby, you did number twelve wrong," I said, pointing to her homework.

"Did not!" she retaliated. "That's the way the teacher said to do it!"

"But it's wrong!" I explained.

"Is not," she argued.

Does this episode ever play out in your house?

Abby tended to become very defensive and discouraged when she was corrected. Unfortunately, I think she learned that from observing me. Let's face it—nobody enjoys correction. Even when correction comes wrapped in pretty words and encouraging insights, it still stings.

Maybe you also have difficulty receiving correction. It isn't much fun, but it's necessary if we ever want to mature and become more Christlike. This scripture encourages me, and I hope it will encourage you too. See, the Lord doesn't want us to be discouraged by His correction. He corrects us because He loves us. He knows all of our faults, and He wants us to get past them and grow up in Him. Don't argue with God or talk back to Him when He gently corrects you. Accept His criticism graciously and make the necessary adjustments. Just think, you're one step closer to being like Him!

———— MOM TO MASTER ————

*Lord, help me to accept God's correction with a good attitude. Amen.*

# September 4

*A refusal to correct is a refusal to love;*
*love your children by disciplining them.*
PROVERBS 13:24 MSG

Have you ever spent any time with children who have never been disciplined? You know the kind—the ones who run all over a restaurant, scream when they don't get their way, and show disrespect to everyone. On one occasion, we spent some time with one of these children. This little girl was unbelievable! She broke toys. She intentionally hurt animals. She back-talked to her parents. And she disobeyed every direction. I desperately wanted to discipline her, but it wasn't my place. It was her parents' place. Unfortunately, the parents didn't believe in discipline. They apparently read some book about allowing a child to develop his or her own boundaries.

The only parenting book that's truly needed is God's Word. Proverbs 13:24 tells us that we show love by disciplining our children. In fact, that verse clearly states that it is actually a refusal to love if we don't correct our children. So while Junior may not feel loved at the exact moment he is being punished, he is experiencing love.

Don't be fooled by the world's way of doing things. God's way is always the better choice. He knows a thing or two about parenting. After all, He is a parent. So ask Him for wisdom and guidance when it comes to disciplining your children. He has all the answers.

— MOM TO MASTER —

*Lord, teach me to be a better parent. Amen.*

# September 5

*Get the truth and never sell it; also get wisdom,*
*discipline, and good judgment.*
PROVERBS 23:23 NLT

I grew up with a friend who definitely qualified as "Miss Perfect." I was always getting her into trouble. Let's just say that in the "Lucy and Ethel" scenario, I was always Lucy, dragging her into situations she would never have ventured into alone.

Much to my annoyance, my friend would tell on herself if she had misbehaved. Then her mom would call my mom, and I'd be busted too. She just couldn't stand to be dishonest, so she'd tell her mom and seek discipline. Sometimes she would even suggest an appropriate punishment. It was amazing, really. Never once have my children come to me just begging to be punished. I might drop over from shock if that ever did happen! God probably feels the same way about us.

How often do you pray, "Lord, I am seeking Your discipline today. Bring it on." I can honestly say that I've never prayed those words. I bet you haven't, either. However, it might be a good idea to pray that prayer once in a while. If we'll be quick to repent and seek God's discipline, we can move on with Him. We won't have to go around that same mountain a hundred times. We'll learn the lesson and press on toward our dreams and victories. So go ahead—ask God to bring it on!

— MOM TO MASTER —

*Lord, help me to seek Your discipline more often. Amen.*

# September 6

*For this command is a lamp, this teaching is a light,
and correction and instruction are the way to life.*

PROVERBS 6:23

I guess I've never really thought of the corrections of discipline as a way of life, although looking back, I'd have to say I agree. I was sure that Abby would grow up thinking her name was "No, no" as many times as I said it to her during "the terrible twos." She was into everything! I had to tell her "No, no" to teach her safe from unsafe, right from wrong, and good from bad. I bet you had to do the same thing with your children.

Guess what? As our spiritual Father, God has to do the same with us. After all, we are His children. And I don't know about you, but my "terrible twos" went on a little more than two years in my spiritual development! There are some days when I revert to those terrible twos and throw a temper tantrum that's shameful. (C'mon, you do too. Admit it!) That's when our heavenly Father steps in and disciplines us as only He can.

The corrections of discipline should be a way of life for us—not just on the giving side but also on the receiving end. Through God's disciplining, we can become the best version of ourselves.

—————— MOM TO MASTER ——————

*Lord, thank You for Your discipline. Amen.*

# September 7

*A rod and a reprimand impart wisdom,*
*but a child left undisciplined disgraces its mother.*
PROVERBS 29:15

No matter where you stand on the spanking issue, this verse holds good meaning. You see, it's not so much about the spanking, it's about the wisdom that we impart when we discipline our children.

There are lots of differing opinions about how to discipline our children. Some experts say we should spank them with our hands. Others say we should spank, but only with a paddle. Still others say we should never spank, only punish by other means. It seems there is a new theory every year. So what is the answer?

God is the only true answer. You must seek His face and ask His direction. He will teach you how to discipline your kids. He loves them even more than you do. He won't lead you astray. Just trust Him. Don't get caught up asking lots of people how you should discipline your kids. If you ask a hundred people, you'll get a hundred different perspectives. They don't know any more than you do. Go to the Source. He will impart wisdom to you so that you can impart wisdom to your children. You see, discipline and wisdom go hand in hand.

—————————— MOM TO MASTER ——————————

*Lord, teach me the best way to*
*discipline my children. Amen.*

# September 8

*A fool spurns a parent's discipline,*
*but whoever heeds correction shows prudence.*
Proverbs 15:5

Did you know that parenting isn't a popularity contest? If it were, I would've lost a long time ago. How about you? No, as moms, we have to make some decisions that aren't very popular at times. We have to tell our children they can't go see some of the popular movies, even though all of their friends are going. We have to forbid them from attending certain parties, even though they don't understand why. It's all a part of what we do as moms.

It's the heartbreaking part of our job. I don't like having to say no to my girls. I want them to have fun. I want them to experience life. I want them to enjoy as much as possible. But I also want to protect them and nurture them and teach them in the ways of the Lord. And sometimes those wants contradict one another.

Yes, I want my kids to think I'm cool. Yes, I want them to think of me as a friend. But more than anything else, I want to raise my girls to love God and walk in His ways. If that means making some unpopular decisions, then that's okay by me. God still thinks we're special. We'll always be popular to God.

---

## MOM TO MASTER

*Lord, help me to stand my ground even when*
*it's not the popular thing to do. Amen.*

# September 9

*But the lovingkindness of the LORD*
*is from everlasting to everlasting.*
PSALM 103:17 NASB

Did you grow up in a strict household? Was your father harsh to you? Did you obey the rules of the house out of fear? Many people grow up in less than Brady Bunch–like households. Then, when they become parents, they sometimes carry on those negative parenting skills. If you fit this mold, don't despair. God can heal your hurts and help you parent with compassion and mercy. See, even though you might not have had a good role model growing up, God is the only role model you need. He's here for you right now.

I'm so thankful that He is gentle, forgiving, and merciful when He disciplines. He isn't harsh and scary. He makes His children want to run to Him, not away from Him. No matter how badly we mess up, He forgives and forgets.

So if you are struggling with being too harsh with your children, ask God to help you today. He will pour His unconditional love into you so that you can pour out that love on your children. You can break the cycle of cold, harsh parenting. You can become the kind of mother that God intended for you to be.

——————— MOM TO MASTER ———————

*Lord, fill me with Your love so that I can share Your love with my*
*children. Help me to be more compassionate and caring. Amen.*

# September 10

*For the LORD is good and his love endures forever;*
*his faithfulness continues through all generations.*

PSALM 100:5

God is so faithful. Can I get an "amen"? As a reporter for a daily newspaper, I was privileged to interview many wonderful people. Some of those stories stick with me today. I'll never forget interviewing a woman who was told she could never have children. She had a medical condition that prevented her from carrying a baby to term. Heartbroken, she cried out to God. She beseeched God for a miracle. This precious woman of God became pregnant and through an absolute miracle of God was able to give birth to a healthy baby girl. That little girl is in elementary school now—a living, breathing testimony to God's faithfulness.

God was faithful to her. No one will ever be able to convince her otherwise. She has experienced His faithfulness firsthand. Have you? Has God been there for you when no one else was around? Has He helped you make it through a difficult situation? Maybe you're in a tough place now and need His touch. Just reach out—He's right there.

No matter what your situation—He has the way out. If you're struggling with a disobedient child, He can help. If your marriage is falling apart, He can put it back together. If your children are in rebellion, God understands. He is able. He is willing. And He is faithful.

——————— MOM TO MASTER ———————

*Lord, thank You for being faithful. Amen.*

# September 11

*Do not boast about tomorrow,*
*for you do not know what a day may bring.*
PROVERBS 27:1

September 11 will forever mean something different since the tragedy that struck America in 2001. If 9/11 taught us anything as a country, it taught us to cherish our loved ones. As many found out that day, there's no promise of tomorrow. I've watched several news shows in which the family members of victims were interviewed, and almost every person said, "If only I'd had the chance to say good-bye. If only I could say, 'I love you,' just one more time. . ." Regrets lead down the road of guilt and condemnation. So don't go there.

Instead, take time today to pray for the families who lost loved ones on that tragic day. Take time to pray for our nation and its leaders. And take time to tell your family and friends just how much you love and appreciate them. Let God's love pour out of you and spill onto your children. Talk to your kids about the significance of 9/11/2001, and ask them to join with you in prayer. You might even make a donation to the American Red Cross or bake cookies for your local fire department. Whatever you do, make the most of every moment, because we're not promised tomorrow.

——————— MOM TO MASTER ———————

*Lord, help me not to take any day for granted.*
*I love You. Amen.*

# September 12

*If you are guided by the Spirit, you won't obey your selfish desires.*
GALATIANS 5:16 CEV

Did you know that we make approximately twenty-five hundred choices every single day of our lives? (No wonder I'm so exhausted at the end of the day!) So if you aren't happy with your current life, you're probably making lousy decisions. The only way to make good, solid decisions is to turn off your reasoning mechanism and allow the Holy Spirit to guide you. Discernment and reasoning can't operate at the same time. Our minds reason, but our spirits discern. I don't know about you, but I don't trust my mind. I'd much rather rely on the leading of the Holy Spirit to make decisions—especially when it comes to disciplining my children.

With so many conflicting opinions in the media, I get easily confused. I don't want to be a tyrant, but I don't want to be a wimp either. I want to raise good, godly kids, but I don't want to shove the Word down their throats.

There are no easy answers. What works for one parent-child relationship might not work for another. So don't reason and worry your life away. Instead, ask for God's leading to help you make the best possible decisions. He will help you in the area of disciplining your kids. He has all of the answers.

—————— MOM TO MASTER ——————

*Lord, I am asking for Your leading today.*
*Help me to do things Your way. Amen.*

# September 13

*"Before I formed you in the womb I knew [and approved of you as My chosen instrument]."*

JEREMIAH 1:5 AMP

Okay, I blew it again this week. In my efforts to be a good mother, teaching responsibility and other good morals to my girls, I went overboard. I actually went into the whole "Well, when I was your age. . ." Of course, that's an automatic disconnect for kids. As soon as you utter those words, their eyes glaze over.

Do you ever hear yourself saying something and think, *I've become my mother!* It's so funny, isn't it? One minute you're hip and cool, and the next parental moment, you're giving your rendition of "When I was a child, we had to walk through the snow, uphill both ways, barefoot to school. . . ."

On those days, when I feel like I'm losing this parental battle, it's nice to know that God has already approved me. Jeremiah 1:5 tells us that He knew us even before we were born and had already approved us. So no matter how badly we mess up, God still loves us and sees us as great parents. He always has His faith eyes in focus. Ask Him to help you get your faith eyes in focus too. See yourself as God sees you—approved!

—————— MOM TO MASTER ——————

*Lord, thank You for approving me and calling me to motherhood. I love You. Amen.*

# September 14

*The LORD disciplines those he loves,*
*as a father the son he delights in.*
PROVERBS 3:12

My father rarely spanked me when I was a little girl. I deserved spankings much more frequently than I actually received them, but Dad was merciful. One time I lied to my father and he found out, and that was it! I knew I was going to get it. Mother sent me to my room to await Dad's visitation. When he came home from work, he said just one thing before he spanked me: "Honey, I'm doing this because I love you." Then I got it—ouch!

Let me just share, I wasn't feeling the love at that exact moment. But it really was true. Dad disciplined me because he wanted me to learn respect and obedience—because he loved me. We do the same for our kids, don't we? We correct and punish them because we love them. We know that if we don't teach them and discipline them, our failure to do so will be detrimental to them in the long run.

God does the same thing for us. That's what this verse in Proverbs says to me—the Lord disciplines us because He loves us. He knows our potential, and if we'll let Him, He will mold us and make us into the moms He created us to be.

—————————— MOM TO MASTER ——————————

*Lord, thank You for Your discipline. I love You. Amen.*

## September 15

*Come, children, listen closely;*
*I'll give you a lesson in GOD worship.*
PSALM 34:11 MSG

If you could only teach your children ten things before you died, what would you share? Would you teach them to stand up for who they are in Christ Jesus? Would you teach them self-defense? Would you teach them good manners? Would you teach them to give to others? Would you teach them to treat others with respect? Would you teach them how to be a friend?

It's a tough call, isn't it? There are so many things we want to impart to our kids. We want to save them from making all of the stupid mistakes that we made. While we can't protect them from every mistake, we can put them on the road to success and happiness.

We can make the most of every opportunity to teach our kids about the nature of God—God the Healer, God the Provider, God the Savior, God the Deliverer, God the Great I Am! There are chances every day to share little lessons with our children. Ask the Lord to help you identify those opportunities so that you can take advantage of each one.

———————— MOM TO MASTER ————————

*Lord, help me to share Your love with my children each*
*day. And Lord, help me to take advantage of every*
*opportunity to teach my kids about You. Amen.*

# September 16

*Teach them to your children. Talk about them wherever you are, sitting at home or walking in the street; talk about them from the time you get up in the morning until you fall into bed at night.*

DEUTERONOMY 11:19 MSG

One time we were in a store where I overheard a conversation that really taught me something about parenting. A very attractive, professional-looking woman and her two preteen daughters were shopping together when they saw another girl they knew. She appeared to be in her teens. They visited briefly, and then the mother said to the teenager, "I just loved the muffins you served the other night at the party. Could I get that recipe from you?"

This flippant teen said, "No, I don't share that recipe. It's a family secret. I may try to sell them someday."

After the teen left, the mother leaned in close to her daughters and whispered, "Girls, that is a good example of being selfish. Her attitude was wrong, and God probably won't bless her muffin endeavors because of her selfish attitude."

This mom saw an opportunity to teach a lesson and embraced it. See, as moms, we need to seize the moment and teach our children lessons as opportunities arise. God will provide the perfect situations, but we have to be "tuned in" to Him in order to take advantage of these precious opportunities. Tune in today!

## MOM TO MASTER

*Lord, help me to teach my children Your ways. Amen.*

# September 17

*For lack of discipline they will die,*
*led astray by their own great folly.*
PROVERBS 5:23

Obviously, this verse in Proverbs lets us know that discipline is an important part of our job as parents. No, it's not fun. No, it's not popular. But it is very necessary. In fact, it's so necessary that if we don't correct our children and bring them up in the way of the Lord, they are sure to suffer.

None of us would intentionally hurt our kids. We love them. But sometimes we love them too much, meaning we don't discipline them for their wrong behavior. We let them get away with wrongdoing simply because we don't want to hurt their feelings or make a scene in front of their friends. But if we don't teach them right from wrong, they won't know how to make godly decisions. They'll make wrong choices, which will lead to heartache, ruin, and ultimately, destruction.

Our role is crucial. Ask the Lord to help you be firm yet loving as you discipline your kids. Ask Him for wisdom. You can do it. God has equipped you with everything you need to be a good parent.

——————— MOM TO MASTER ———————

*Lord, I need Your divine intervention—help me*
*to discipline my children so that they will follow*
*You all the days of their lives. Amen.*

# September 18

*"Declare what is to be."*

ISAIAH 45:21

If you are going to live a victorious life, you must speak positive words of faith and say what God says about your situation. So if your children are walking in rebellion today, you should speak what the Word says about your kids. Say, "As for me and my house, we will serve the Lord." If your children are struggling with their love walk and acting ugly all the time, you should declare, "Love is patient. Love is kind. My children will walk in God's love. My children will be patient and kind."

If you are unsure of your children's salvation, declare Psalm 103:17: "The LORD's love is with those who fear him, and his righteousness with their children's children."

Find scriptures to stand on—scriptures that fit your situation. Then speak them out! Encourage yourself in the Lord. Pray according to His Word. Those are the kind of prayers that get results. Don't allow yourself to talk negatively about your children. Don't talk the problem—talk the solution. Trust the Lord to do what He says in His Word. His Word never returns void. It will accomplish its purpose. Get ready for victory—it's on its way!

—————— MOM TO MASTER ——————

*Lord, lead me to the scriptures in Your Word that will help me stand in faith for the salvation of my children. Help me to stand strong. I love You. Amen.*

# September 19

*So do not throw away your confidence; it will be richly rewarded.*

HEBREWS 10:35

Are you focusing on the future, or are you having trouble seeing past the endless piles of dirty laundry that are in front of you right now? When today has so many worries, responsibilities, and obligations, it's difficult to be future minded. But we need to make a conscious effort. We need to let God stir up our faith. We need to start believing God for big things. We need to realize that even if the circumstances aren't so great today, God is bringing about a miracle in our future.

You see, no matter what you're dealing with today, God has a plan that will work things out better than you could ever imagine—if you'll just get your faith eyes in focus and become future minded. Ask God to help you change your focus.

The enemy doesn't want you to stand in faith for the fulfillment of your destiny. He doesn't want to see your children walking with God. He wants you to worry about all of the problems of today and forget about your future. Don't fall for the devil's plan. Focus on the future. See your children well and serving God. See your family happy and whole. See your dirty laundry washed, folded, and put away. Get a vision of victory today!

—— MOM TO MASTER ——

*Lord, help me get my faith eyes in focus
and looking toward the future. Amen.*

# September 20

*"This vision is for a future time. It describes the end, and it will be fulfilled. If it seems slow in coming, wait patiently, for it will surely take place. It will not be delayed."*

HABAKKUK 2:3 NLT

Have you ever heard the phrase "Rest and wait"? It's much easier said than done—especially when that waiting has to do with our children. Whether you're waiting for your kids to run back to God or simply waiting for them to be potty trained—resting and waiting is a good thing. Resting and waiting are meant to go hand in hand.

See, resting in God means trusting and not worrying. It means having so much of God on the inside of you that you can't do anything but rest. It's a place where you have absolutely no doubt that God is going to come through for you. It's a place where you no longer see the mountain; you only see a molehill. It's a place where all of us should dwell on a daily basis.

As moms, we need to rest and wait more than anyone else. If we're frazzled, we'll raise frazzled children. If we're impatient and worried, we'll raise impatient, worried children. So here's your assignment—rest and wait! You'll have to discipline your flesh to do it, but God will help you.

## —————— MOM TO MASTER ——————

*Lord, help me to learn to rest and wait on You. Amen.*

# September 21

*Therefore put on the full armor of God, so that when the day*
*of evil comes, you may be able to stand your ground,*
*and after you have done everything, to stand.*

EPHESIANS 6:13

We all face challenges in life. Some days we face more challenges than others. Let's face it, being a parent is a tough job. When you have children, there's no manual that comes with the job. Sure, there are lots of parenting books and magazines, but they all say conflicting things, giving opposing advice.

There's only one manual that covers it all. From disciplining your children to showing them unconditional love, the Word of God has you covered. Need an answer for a specific situation? Don't rely on secondhand information. Go to the Source. Read the Word and let it come alive to you.

Stand strong as you face challenges. Don't bow down to them. Remain faithful. Fight that good fight of faith. Keep feeding on the Word and standing firm. If you'll stay in faith, God will promote you. He loves to bless His children. Make yourself a good candidate for His supernatural blessing flow. Keep standing. I don't care how bad it might look right now, stand strong. Go to the Manual. Your answers and your promotion are on the way. Hallelujah!

--- MOM TO MASTER ---

*Father, help me to stand strong in*
*the face of difficulty. I love You. Amen.*

# September 22

*For this command is a lamp, this teaching is a light,
and correction and instruction are the way to life.*
PROVERBS 6:23

Have you seen those infomercials that feature the little stick-on lights? They are pretty cool. You simply take these round, flat lights and stick them wherever you need light. For instance, you can place them in your closet or post them down your driveway. I thought, *How neat! You can create a lighted pathway where there wasn't one before!*

Well, guess what? The Word of God is a lamp unto our feet and a light unto our paths, and you don't have to stick it any-where! All you have to do is read it and let God's promises and corrections fill you up.

Just think if we had an infomercial for the Word of God. Can you imagine? We could make claims like, "Guaranteed to produce results! Never gets old. Full of the wisdom of the ages! Works every time!" and they'd all be true! God's Word provides correction, keeping us on the straight and narrow path. It pro-vides healing, prosperity, joy, and wisdom through its many promises. It is all we need to accomplish anything in this life. No matter what you need today, go to the Word. Let the Word of God come alive for you today.

——————— MOM TO MASTER ———————

*Father, please light up my path today. Amen.*

# September 23

*Have mercy on me, O God, according to your unfailing love;*
*according to your great compassion blot out my transgressions.*
PSALM 51:1

Do your kids ever use "the puppy dog eyes" on you? Aren't those killers? As soon as they bring them out, my heart starts to melt. At that moment, no matter what they've done wrong, I am very forgiving. Of course, my children have learned this trick, so they use it often. Talk about manipulation! Ugh!

But you know, showing mercy to our children is a good thing. I don't mean that we should let them get away with horrible behavior, but we need to discipline in love and emulate our heavenly Father. Aren't you glad we serve a merciful God? He is never harsh to us when we repent. He doesn't say, "I'm sorry. You've just made one too many mistakes. I'm not going to forgive you this time." Instead, He lovingly whispers, *"That's okay. I love you, My child."*

I want to be as tender and forgiving with my children as the Father is with me. If we aren't tender with our kids, they won't run to us when they make mistakes; they'll run away from us. We need to discipline them and teach them the ways of God, but we need to do so with love and mercy.

———————————— MOM TO MASTER ————————————

*Father, help me to show mercy to my children*
*as You show mercy to me. Amen.*

# September 24

*It's the child he loves that he disciplines.*
HEBREWS 12:6 MSG

"You don't love me!"

Have you ever heard that response after disciplining your children? It's a difficult one to swallow. And it's a very inaccurate response. In fact, by disciplining our children, we're actually showing our love to them. Of course, no child is going to see it that way—especially in the heat of the moment. But it never hurts to explain our reasons for disciplining our children, even if it seems they aren't listening.

Before you spank your child or ground him or her from attending a party, take a deep breath, count to ten, and explain what the Word says about the situation. This is working at our house. It's amazing! While Abby and Allyson have no problem arguing with me, they won't argue with the Word of God. They can't. They know God's Word is always right. So if you can find a scripture that pertains to the situation at hand, you have all the ammunition you need to lovingly enforce discipline. It takes the pressure off of us and puts it on the Word, and God's Word can handle the pressure. Many times when I tell the girls what God's Word says about their behavior or the choices they've made, it opens up a wonderful conversation. True, the dialogue typically begins with "You don't love me," but it rarely ends that way. Go ahead! Try it.

--- MOM TO MASTER ---

*Father, help me use Your Word*
*to combat strife in my house. Amen.*

# September 25

Have you ever really thought about the definition of *obedience?* Not long ago, I heard a preacher say that obedience is doing what you're supposed to do the first time you're asked. I love that definition! Immediately, I thought of how often I repeat myself in hopes that my girls will actually pick up their rooms. I begin with a cheerful, "Before you can go outside and ride your bikes, I want you to clean your rooms." An hour later, the girls are plopped in front of the TV, mesmerized by Cartoon Network. So I say sternly, "I want you to turn off the TV and clean up your rooms right now." Thirty minutes later, as I walk past their rooms and see that they haven't been touched, I lose it and scream, "I want you to get in your rooms and stay in there until they are cleaned up! Do you understand me?"

We shouldn't have to ask our children numerous times in order to get their attention. We shouldn't have to get ugly with them in order to get obedience. Let's ask God to help us teach our children the true meaning of obedience today.

## MOM TO MASTER

*Father, help me teach my children the true meaning of obedience,*
*and help me to immediately obey You too. Amen.*

# September 26

*GOD is fair and just; He corrects the misdirected,
sends them in the right direction.*

PSALM 25:8 MSG

Do you ever get lost? I am the queen of getting lost. My friends refer to me as "directionally challenged." In my defense, Texas is difficult for the directionally challenged because you can never come back the same way you went. Reversing directions doesn't work in the Dallas–Fort Worth Metroplex. It's the most aggravating thing! So I spend most of my days aimlessly driving around, hoping to find a familiar street or shopping mall. Finally, when I've driven so much that I'm almost out of gas, I'll swallow my pride and call Jeff on my cell phone to ask for directions. With just a few corrections to my course, I'm once again headed in the right direction—toward home.

In the spiritual realm, God does the same thing with His children. He corrects our course, puts us back on the right road, and points us toward our heavenly home. Without His gentle correction, we might be headed in the wrong direction our entire lives. That's why the Word says that God corrects those He loves. If He didn't love us, He'd just let us wander around aimlessly. Taking correction is never an easy thing, but it's certainly a necessary one. So thank the Lord today for His divine correction and direction.

———————— MOM TO MASTER ————————

*Thank You, Lord, for Your correction. Amen.*

# September 27

*Don't be afraid to correct your young ones;*
*a spanking won't kill them.*
PROVERBS 23:13 MSG

My father only spanked me three times in my entire life. I prob-ably had it coming a lot more than that, but he was a merciful father. (Besides, Mom made up the difference!) I'll never forget when Dad spanked me that last time. He came into my room where I was waiting for him, and he said, "This is going to hurt me much more than it will hurt you." A few minutes later, my stinging backside and I weren't too sure about the validity of his previous statement.

In all honesty, it pained my father to spank me. He loved me, and he didn't want to cause me any hurt. However, he knew that if he didn't discipline me, I'd grow up to be a bratty kid. So he loved me enough to spank me. I feel the same way about my children. I wish I never had to discipline them. I wish they were perfect all the time. But since that's not the case, I have to take a disciplinarian stance from time to time. It's part of our job as mothers. We should never be afraid to discipline our children. We should be fearful if we don't.

—— MOM TO MASTER ——

*Lord, help me not to be afraid of*
*disciplining my children. Amen.*

# September 28

*"Not everyone who calls out to me, 'Lord! Lord!'*
*will enter the Kingdom of Heaven. Only those who*
*actually do the will of my Father in heaven will enter."*
MATTHEW 7:21 NLT

I was eavesdropping on my daughters and their friends one time, and I overheard the funniest conversation. One of the little girls said, "I obey my parents most of the time, but sometimes I just don't want to. I decide if the punishment is worth it, and then I go from there."

Wow! That was an eye opener for me. Obviously, obedience wasn't high on her priority list. Of course, I can understand that kind of thinking. I've acted the same way when it comes to serving God. You know—trying to get away with as much as possible, riding the fence. But this scripture in Matthew is pretty clear—obeying the Father should be high on our priority list. And it should be high on our children's priority list too.

Obeying our heavenly Father shouldn't be a difficult thing. If we truly love God, we should want to obey Him. If you're having trouble obeying God, spend some quality time with Him. Make Him your first love, and obedience will soon follow.

— MOM TO MASTER —

*Lord, help me to put You first and obey Your*
*commandments with a right attitude. Amen.*

# September 29

Part of training up our children is sharing the miracles of God with them. Of course, we know to teach them the many mighty works that God performed in the Bible. We should tell them of God's miraculous deliverance of His people out of Pharaoh's hand. We should share the story of David and Goliath. We should tell them about Jonah and the whale. But we should also tell them about the many mighty works that God has done personally in our families.

When I told Allyson how God had saved her life when she was only a few weeks old inside my tummy, her face lit up. She wanted to hear every detail. When I shared with Abby how God had protected us from a terrible car accident when she was only three, she hung on every word. Hearing those stories builds our children's faith, and it builds ours too.

Spend time playing "Remember when God worked that miracle in our lives?" You'll soon discover that your children will love that game more than any other. Go ahead, have fun reminiscing. Recall the mighty acts of God and build your faith in the process. It's a game where everybody wins!

## MOM TO MASTER

*Lord, help me to tell my children of
Your marvelous works. Amen.*

# September 30

*These older women must train the younger women*
*to love their husbands and their children.*
TITUS 2:4 NLT

It was my first night home from the hospital. Baby Abby was sleeping peacefully in my arms. She was so precious. But as I looked down into her little face, I panicked. I thought to myself, *I have no idea how to raise this little girl. I have a hard enough time just taking care of Jeff and myself and our dog!* I remember praying for God to send me help. That prayer was answered by way of my mother. She was (and still is) a constant source of encouragement, strength, wisdom, and laughter.

I've learned so much from my mother. Not only has she taught me about being a mom, but she's taught me how to be a better wife. When my father suffered three strokes over a year's time, I watched in amazement as my mother took care of Daddy. She was so strong and in control, yet so tender toward him. I thought, *Now that's the kind of wife I want to be.*

There is much to be learned from our elders, isn't there? That's why I love Titus 2:4 so much. Maybe your mom isn't a person you turn to for advice—and that's okay. God will send other wise women to be part of your life. Ask Him to do that for you today.

--- MOM TO MASTER ---

*Thank You, Lord, for placing wonderfully*
*wise women in my life. Amen.*

# October 1

*"Give, and it will be given to you: good measure,*
*pressed down, shaken together, and running over."*
LUKE 6:38 NKJV

Did you know that God wants you to be happy? He desires for you to live life to its fullest. It doesn't matter that you might be elbow deep in diapers and carpools right now—you can still enjoy life!

One of the main ways you can guarantee joy in your life is by living to give. You see, true happiness comes when we give of ourselves to others—our spouses, our children, our extended family, our church, our community, and our friends. As moms, we're sort of trained to be givers. We give up our careers, many times, to become full-time moms. We give up a full night's sleep to feed our babies. We give up sports cars for minivans and SUVs to accommodate our families. In fact, we'd give our lives for our children.

But sometimes our attitudes are less than joyful in all of our giving, right? Well, rejoice today. God promises to multiply back to you everything you give. When you step out in faith, you open a door for God to move on your behalf. It's the simple principle of sowing and reaping. And as mothers, we are super sowers. So get ready for a superhuge harvest!

———————— MOM TO MASTER ————————

*Lord, help me to live to give with the right attitude.*
*I love You. Amen.*

# October 2

*"In everything I did, I showed you that by this kind of hard work we must help the weak, remembering the words the Lord Jesus himself said: 'It is more blessed to give than to receive.' "*

ACTS 20:35

As we approached the holiday season, the "gimmes" were in full swing at our house. With the onset of autumn, my daughters started marking the catalogs, making their Christmas lists, and dropping subtle "Buy me this!" hints. Maybe you encounter the same thing at your house.

I often worried about spoiling my girls. After all, we bought them a lot and so did their grandparents on both sides. There were some Christmas mornings when they fell asleep before they could even open all of their gifts. That's why I was so blessed to see that their hearts are as big as their wish lists.

One time Abby and Allyson heard that a local ministry needed nice, gently used toys. Both girls sprang into action. By the end of the day, they had gathered seven bags worth of stuffed animals, board games, dress-up clothes, Barbie dolls, and more! As Abby was brushing a Barbie's hair, I asked, "Are you keeping her?"

She said, "No, I just wanted to make sure she looked nice when we dropped her off."

Now that's the right attitude! While my daughters love receiving, they also love giving. We should all give with such enthusiasm.

--- MOM TO MASTER ---

*Lord, help me to be a cheerful giver. Amen.*

# October 3

*"So when you give to the needy,
do not announce it with trumpets."*
MATTHEW 6:2

There we were—Abby, Allyson, and I—hiding out inside our SUV, just waiting for the right moment. We were on a stakeout. Our mission? To deliver several Christmas presents without the receiver of the gifts ever finding out who delivered them.

"Now!" Abby said. "She's leaving. We can put them in her office."

As we watched her car pull out of the school parking lot, the three of us quickly grabbed the wrapped gifts and headed inside the school. Like the wind, we breezed into this single mom's office, left the gifts, and exited without anyone knowing we'd ever been there. The card simply read, "Merry Christmas! Love, Jesus." That was such an exciting time for us—getting to surprise this precious woman with gifts for her and her daughter. We had the best time choosing each gift, wrapping each one with pretty paper and bows, and sneaking inside her office to deliver them.

That Christmas, the girls and I learned that it truly is better to give than to receive. The girls will never forget that experience, and neither will I. We should constantly look for opportunities to give unto others.

—————————— MOM TO MASTER ——————————

*Lord, help me to take advantage of every
opportunity to give unto others. Amen.*

# October 4

*Concentrate on doing your best for God,*
*work you won't be ashamed of.*
2 TIMOTHY 2:15 MSG

When it comes to being a mom, do you give it your all every day? Do you always do your best? Do you look for the easy way out, or do you go the extra mile? If you're like me, it just depends on the day. But according to this scripture in 2 Timothy, we're supposed to concentrate on doing our best day in and day out. It doesn't say that we should just do our best when we feel like it or when the mood strikes us.

You see, serving God isn't about feelings—it's about faith. It's about stepping out in faith and doing your best on a daily basis. You don't have to feel like you can do it. You don't even have to feel good about it. You just have to put forth your best effort.

Ask the Lord to help you do your best on His behalf. He can help you do your best in every area of life—housework, raising kids, buying groceries, teaching Sunday school, volunteering for the PTA, etc. He expects your best because, after all, God gave His best for us. He gave His only Son to die on the cross for our sins. Give God your best today!

———————————— MOM TO MASTER ————————————

*Lord, help me to always do my best for You. Amen.*

# October 5

*"You shall not give false testimony against your neighbor."*
EXODUS 20:16

It's a good thing to live to give—as long as you're not giving false testimony against your neighbor. I realize that "neighbors" here doesn't necessarily mean those who live in close proximity, but it certainly includes those folks too.

We've encountered a few neighborhood children who have chosen to give false testimony against Abby and Allyson, and those false testimonies were not very nice. In fact, they were downright cruel and, of course, not true. Maybe you've experienced the same situation in your neck of the woods.

As moms, it's tough just to stand by and let someone say hurtful untruths about our kids. I was so upset with those little boys who were making up stories. I wanted to call their mother and give her a piece of my mind. But the Holy Spirit instructed me to give something else—love. Ugh! That was the last thing I wanted to do. But I was obedient.

You see, the Lord gave me something special as we walked through that ordeal. He gave me peace. He gave me love. And He gave me the ability to comfort Abby and Allyson. Life really is about giving—good or bad. Let's make a decision to give only good things today.

———————— MOM TO MASTER ————————

*Lord, help me to give only good things.*
*Help me to be more like You. Amen.*

# October 6

*"I'll give him and his descendants the land he walked on because he was all for following GOD, heart and soul."*
DEUTERONOMY 1:36 MSG

Have you ever heard the expression "Let go and let God"? It's easier said than done. We sing songs in church about giving our all to God, such as "All to Jesus, I surrender," when all the while, we're holding something back. I'm guilty too. So many times I have gone before God and asked Him to take over every part of my life, and then later the Holy Spirit will point out an area of my heart that I didn't give to God.

It's silly, isn't it? I don't know why we'd ever want to hold out on God. He doesn't want us to give our all so that He can make us miserable. He wants us to give our all so that He can bless us beyond our wildest dreams. God isn't some big ogre in the sky, just waiting for us to give our all to Him so that He can control us like puppets. He simply wants us to give our all so that we can walk in the plan He has for us. So if you're struggling with giving your all today, ask God to help you. Go ahead—let go and let God. He will give you much more in return.

——————— MOM TO MASTER ———————

*Lord, I give my all to You today.*
*Help me to leave my life in Your hands. Amen.*

# October 7

*"Now I am giving him to the Lord,*
*and he will belong to the Lord his whole life."*
1 SAMUEL 1:28 NLT

Have you truly given your children to God? Sure, we all say those words when our babies go through the dedication service at church, but how many of us truly mean them? It's so easy to take back our kids. We trust God with everything in our lives, but when it comes to our children, *we* want to take care of them. We love them so much that we are afraid to give them to God. What if He calls them into the mission field in some unstable or war-torn country? What if He asks them to move across the country to begin a church? What if *His* plans for your child conflict with *your* dreams for your baby?

It's scary, isn't it? But it shouldn't be. As moms, we have to realize that God loves our children even more than we do. If He calls them into a war-torn country to serve Him, then that will be the place that holds happiness and peace for them. After all, being in the center of God's will is the safest place a person can be. So don't worry. Giving your kids to God is the best thing you can do for them.

———————————— MOM TO MASTER ————————————

*Lord, I give my children to You today. Amen.*

# October 8

*"Whoever wants to be first among you must be your slave."*
MATTHEW 20:27 MSG

Abby and Allyson both made Honor Choir one year. That, in itself, was a modern-day miracle, because no one else on either side of the family can carry a tune. It was fun to hear the girls warm up. They went through this whole *"mi, mi, mi, mi, mi"* routine. Well, that's okay if you're warming up your vocal chords, but if you're living with the *"me, me, me, me, me"* mentality, that's no good. If it's all about you, then it can't be all about Him.

Have you given yourself to God—totally and completely? I find that I have to do that daily. If I don't, I get way off track. I follow the path that benefits my wants, my desires, my needs, and I neglect to check with God on major decisions. (Not to mention, I become a real self-centered jerk. It's not pretty.) Ever been there?

If you're singing the "Me, Me, Me, Me, Me" chorus today, don't worry. We all sing that tune from time to time. Just ask God to put a new song in your heart—He will. As soon as you get your eyes back on Him, you can move forward in your Christian walk. God has a good plan for your life—don't mess it up singing the wrong song.

───────────── MOM TO MASTER ─────────────

*Lord, I give myself to You today and every day. Amen.*

# October 9

*"These people honor me with their lips,
but their hearts are far from me."*
MATTHEW 15:8 NLT

Do you give a good witness for Jesus? Do you have a HONK IF YOU LOVE JESUS bumper sticker on your minivan, yet you cut people off in traffic every chance you get? Do you wear WWJD jewelry, but you verbally attacked your kids in Walmart, totally humiliating them? Does your T-shirt say RADICALLY SAVED AND PROUD OF IT! yet you just acted ugly to the store clerk because she wouldn't honor one of your coupons? Of course, we aren't going to be perfect. There are going to be days when we completely miss it, but our "miss it" days should be far fewer than our "get it right" days.

You don't have to be wearing "witness wear" in order to be a witness. Whether you are aware of it or not, you are constantly witnessing to those around you—especially your children. They are like little sponges, soaking up everything you do and say. So do and say things in accordance with the Bible. Let God's light shine big in you. Let your mouth speak good things. Let your actions mirror the Father's actions. Walk the talk—no matter what. Ask God to help you.

——————— MOM TO MASTER ———————

*Lord, help me to be a good witness for You.
I love You. Amen.*

# October 10

*This is what the LORD says: "Stop at the crossroads and look around. Ask for the old, godly way, and walk in it. Travel its path, and you will find rest for your souls."*

JEREMIAH 6:16 NLT

Do you ever have days when you just want to scream, "Give me a break!"?

The laundry is piled high. The dishes are spilling out of the sink. There's a stack of newspapers in the kitchen that you haven't had time to read. Your toddler decided to express his creative side by coloring your dining room walls. And the puppy just shredded a roll of toilet paper throughout your house. Ahhh! Yes, on days like this we all want to scream, "Give me a break!"

While I can't whisk you away to a spa (although I think that's a great idea!), I can tell you how to get a break. And, no, it doesn't involve dropping off your children at the in-laws. Steal a few minutes today and retreat to the Word of God. If you're looking at that dusty old Bible sitting on your coffee table and wondering how an old book can give you rest, you've been missing out!

The Bible isn't just some ancient history book. It's alive! Just by reading it, you'll feel more energized and hopeful. You'll regain that vitality of life you had before having your children. God will restore you. Go ahead. Spend some time in His Word and find rest!

— MOM TO MASTER —

*Lord, help me to find time for Your Word. Amen.*

# October 11

*"Give praise to the LORD your God!"*
1 CHRONICLES 29:20 NLT

Have you ever worked with the preschoolers in your church? They are by far my most favorite group of people. Preschool children have no baggage or inhibitions. They are full of life and love and laughter. (I want to be like them when I grow up!) And they absolutely love to praise the Lord! They'll lift up their hands. They'll shout to the Lord. They'll do all of the hand motions to match the words of the songs. They'll spin around and jump and dance before the Lord. They are professional praisers and worshippers! When it comes to making a joyful noise before the Lord, these kids have got it going on!

I can just see the Father smiling as He looks upon their pure and precious praise and worship. We should take lessons from preschoolers in this department. We should never be embarrassed or ashamed to worship our Father. And we shouldn't have to wait until Sunday morning to praise Him. Make praising the Lord a part of your daily life. Ask your children to join with you. Make it a family affair! Pretty soon you'll be as proficient at giving God praise as the little ones.

―――――――――― MOM TO MASTER ――――――――――

*Lord, help me to praise You with the same*
*enthusiasm and vigor as little children. Amen.*

# October 12

*"Bring the whole tithe into the storehouse, that there may be food in my house. Test me in this," says the LORD Almighty, "and see if I will not throw open the floodgates of heaven and pour out so much blessing that there will not be room enough to store it."*

MALACHI 3:10

Are you teaching your children to tithe? This was an interesting aspect of learning at our house. When the girls were old enough to take on a few household chores, Jeff and I told them if they completed their tasks without a lot of griping, we would give them three dollars a week allowance. That three dollars seemed like a lot of money to a six-year-old and a seven-year-old.

Abby and Allyson could hardly wait until "pay day." Ally wanted to head straight for Walmart's toy section. Her money burned a hole in her pocket. (Unfortunately, I think she inherited that "shopping gene" from me!) Abby, however, wanted to save her money. She immediately placed those dollars in her piggy bank.

On the way to church one Sunday, Jeff explained to the girls that 10 percent of their money belonged to God. We helped them do the math, and both girls prepared their offering. Surprisingly, when the offering plate came around, they both put in way more than the required amount. And they were quite joyful about their giving! It seems they taught us more than we taught them.

——————— MOM TO MASTER ———————

*Lord, help me to be a cheerful giver. Amen.*

# October 13

*"The LORD turn his face toward you and give you peace."*
**NUMBERS 6:26**

Have you ever asked the Lord to give you peace? I don't think that's one of those things we typically ask for as moms. But peace is available to us.

I'm not talking about that kind of temporal peace that a nice, long, hot bath brings. (Although, I'm not opposed to that either!) I'm talking about the kind of peace that only the Father can give—the kind of peace that is present even in the midst of chaos. The Bible says it's a peace that surpasses all understanding. In other words, it's a kind of peace that people don't understand. It's hard to put into words.

I once interviewed a man and wife who understood this kind of peace. After having a premature baby who required three major surgeries during her first year of life, they got pregnant again. And again, the baby came early. This time the little baby only lived five and a half months. I asked them how they made it through that time, and they both said, "We had a supernatural peace." That's the kind of peace that I want to walk in every day—how about you? Let's ask God for it today.

———————— MOM TO MASTER ————————

*Lord, please give me Your supernatural peace today,
and help me to walk in that peace every day. Amen.*

# October 14

*He gives strength to the weary and
increases the power of the weak.*
ISAIAH 40:29

Do you ever feel like Mikey? That's Mikey from those old, old Life cereal commercials. I can still hear the older brother saying, "Give it to Mikey," as he pushed a bowl of Life in his little brother's direction. Sometimes I know just how Mikey feels, only in my case it's "Let's give it to Missy (my nickname)." I think I've been on every school committee you can be on—from room mom to talent show director to carnival co-coordinator—I've done it all.

My mother gets very agitated with me for agreeing to do all of these things. She'll ask, "Why don't you just say no?" It's a good question. I don't know why I don't say no. I guess I'm afraid of hurting someone's feelings, so instead I say yes and become very overwhelmed, overworked, and weary. Ever been there?

Well, I've got good news for you. Even if you can't say no like me, you don't have to feel weary anymore. God says in Isaiah 40:29 that He will give strength to the weary and power to the weak. I don't know about you, but I qualify! The next time you're feeling overworked and overwhelmed, just call on the Name of the Lord. Ask Him to give you strength. He will do it every time!

--- MOM TO MASTER ---

*Lord, please send down some strength and power today. Amen.*

# October 15

*"A new command I give you: Love one another.
As I have loved you, so you must love one another."*
JOHN 13:34

"C'mon, give me a little grin," Jeff and I would say in that goofy, new-parent voice.

We would say that to baby Abby over and over again just to see her cute little smile. Yes, we were annoying, but we were totally captivated by our firstborn. She was so amazing! If she yawned, we smiled. If she smiled, we laughed. If she made a mess in her pants, we called for Ma-maw. We gave Abby our undivided attention. We adored her!

After baby Allyson arrived, we gave Abby a little less attention because we had two little girls to amaze us. Just when we thought we couldn't love another human being as much as we loved Abby, we discovered that we could. We loved Ally with all of our hearts. God gave us more love to give our children. He literally increased our ability and capacity to love. I bet you experienced the same thing when you had your children.

It's like the song says, "Love is a funny thing." It is much more than an emotion—it's a state of being. And we should always be in love with the Father so that we can show His kind of love to our kids. Love your kids big today!

———————— MOM TO MASTER ————————

*Lord, help me to give Your kind of love
to my children. Amen.*

# October 16

*"For I know the plans I have for you," declares the LORD,*
*"plans to prosper you and not to harm you,*
*plans to give you hope and a future."*

JEREMIAH 29:11

Let's face it—life can throw you a curve once in a while. When Abby was just two, she went through a "biting phase." Just when we thought we had it whipped, she sunk her teeth into the nursery director's son at church one morning. I was called out of the service to retrieve my troublesome kid—and I felt like the worst mother ever! It's not like Hallmark makes a card that says, "Sorry my daughter bit your son on the arm." All I could do was smile, say I was sorry, and continue to discipline Abby for biting.

Eventually, Abby's biting phase passed, but the nursery director never seemed to care much for Abby or me after that one incident. I was elated when the woman relinquished her nursery director position the following year. Finally, Abby could return to the nursery, and I could attend services with the rest of the adults.

Isn't that life? You just can't plan for everything. But remember, while *you* can't plan for everything, God can. He has a plan for your life, so don't sweat the small stuff.

## MOM TO MASTER

*Lord, help me not to sweat the small stuff. Amen.*

# October 17

*For everyone born of God overcomes the world.*
*This is the victory that has overcome the world, even our faith.*

1 JOHN 5:4

Are you feeling discouraged today? Are you about ready to throw in the towel? Have you given motherhood all that you've got, and you still don't feel like you're winning the race? We've all been there. And when I start feeling like that, I used to grab a soda and a chocolate bar and comfort myself. I'd dwell in the land of "Poor Pitiful Pearl" for a while before I'd ever go to God. Somehow, feeding my face with chocolate made me feel better. (It cost me more miles on the treadmill though.) But now I've learned that feeding my faith works much better to pull me out of discouragement than feeding my face!

The Bible says that faith comes by hearing the Word of God. As you hear the Word and store it in your heart, your faith grows stronger. So listen to the Bible on tape while you do your housework or while you're on the treadmill. Then, the next time the enemy tries to make you feel worthless, discouraged, depressed, worried, or overwhelmed, you can put your faith to work by declaring the Word of God. Feed your faith, not your face. You'll feel much better!

—————— MOM TO MASTER ——————

*Lord, I am feeling discouraged today.*
*Please fill me up with more of You. Amen.*

# October 18

*I will refuse to look at anything vile and vulgar.*
PSALM 101:3 NLT

Have you ever heard a preacher say, "Give the devil no place in your life!" I always thought that was kind of an odd statement, because I would never *give* the devil a place in my life. But as it turns out, I was giving the devil a place in my life simply by allowing him in my thought life.

Did you know that what you think determines the direction and quality of your life? That's why the Bible tells us to think on things that are pure and lovely in Philippians 4:8. But in order to think on those things, we need to monitor what we allow into our hearts. That means we need to be careful about what we watch, read, and listen to. We need to fill our thoughts with the promises of God—promises of joy, peace, freedom, prosperity, and more!

We also need to monitor what we give our children to watch, read, and listen to. While spending the night at a friend's house, Abby recently saw a movie that she shouldn't have seen. Then she suffered with nightmares for weeks! Don't let fear and other negative material get into your children's hearts and minds. Be that filter for them. As a family, think on lovely things and give the devil no place in your home.

--------- MOM TO MASTER ---------

*Lord, help me to feed on Your Word and
only think on lovely things. Amen.*

# October 19

*For wherever there is jealousy and selfish ambition,*
*there you will find disorder and evil of every kind.*
JAMES 3:16 NLT

"Give it to me!" Abby shouted.

"*No,* it's my CD player!" Allyson rebutted.

"You are such a loser!"

"No, *you* are the loser!"

Ahh. . .the sounds of loving sisters. Yes, my girls love each other, but there are days when I have to see that love by faith. Do your children fight? Are there days when you're sure they'll never be friends? Well, take heart. There is hope.

God put your family together, and He knew what He was doing. So even though it may seem like the strife is there to stay, it's not. God is the answer. He can turn your kids into the best of friends in no time at all. Declare that your house is a household of faith. Declare that no weapon formed against your family will prosper. Declare that as for you and your house, you will serve the Lord.

Don't let strife take root in your home because you don't want to open up your household to every kind of evil as James 3:16 says. Instead, build your house on love. When your kids fight, nip it in the bud immediately. Pray for peace, and watch your family transform. You can have heaven on earth in your home. Start today!

––––––––––– MOM TO MASTER –––––––––––

*Lord, please help me to keep the strife out*
*of my household. I love You. Amen.*

# October 20

*"See, I am doing a new thing!*
*Now it springs up; do you not perceive it?"*
ISAIAH 43:19

Are you an espresso junkie? C'mon, you can tell me. You know how you feel after a shot of espresso? It's like, *Zing!* Talk about a pick-me-up! Well, I have something even better. How about giving yourself a shot of victory today?

Okay, here's your victory shot: "God is doing a new thing in your life right now!" Doesn't that do something for your heart? Isaiah 43:19 doesn't say that God is going to do a new thing in a year or two. It doesn't say that He is doing a new thing next month. It says He is doing a new thing now! So if you're in a faith rut, or if your kids are driving you crazy, or if you're fighting a weight problem, or if you're depressed—cheer up! God is doing a new thing for you. Isn't that good news?

God has a good plan for your life. He is working things out and lining things up for your life right now. He hasn't forgotten you. He wants you to develop a vision of victory so you can move forward and walk in the fullness of what He has for you. It's going to be so good—even better than espresso!

——————— MOM TO MASTER ———————

*Lord, thank You for doing a new thing*
*in my life today. Amen.*

# October 21

*"There's hope for your children."* God's Decree.
JEREMIAH 31:17 MSG

Are your children away from God right now? Are they in a state of rebellion? If they are, I know that you're heartbroken. And even if you're not in this situation, I bet you know someone who is. It's tough. When we've raised our children to know the things of God and they still rebel, we immediately start blaming ourselves. We wonder where we went wrong. We wonder what we could have done differently. Well, stop wondering and start praising the Lord!

You may not feel like praising the Lord right now, but that's exactly what you must do. You see, the Word says that your children will return to the Lord. The Word says there is hope for your children. The Word says that if you have the faith of a mustard seed, you can move mountains. So hey, bringing your children back to God is no biggie! God can do that in the twinkling of an eye!

But you must praise God for the victory even before it takes place. He has commanded that we live in victory, so that means no matter how bad it looks right now, you can be encouraged. We already know how it ends—we win! We walk in victory, side by side with our children. Praise the Lord today! Your victory is on its way!

———— MOM TO MASTER ————

*Lord, I praise You for my children's salvation. Amen.*

# October 22

*Gently encourage the stragglers, and reach out for the exhausted, pulling them to their feet. Be patient with each person, attentive to individual needs.*

1 THESSALONIANS 5:14 MSG

When I was a college cheerleader, we did the whole, "Give me a *G!* Give me an *O!*" You get the idea. Yes, that was "a few" years ago, and my cheerleading uniform is faded and in storage, but that encouraging spirit still remains. I'm still the resident cheerleader of our house. That's what moms do, right? Don't you feel like a cheerleader most of the time?

Our children (and our spouses too!) need our encouragement. They need to hear us say, "You can do it!" They need to hear us say, "You have got it going on!" They need our support and unconditional love on a daily basis. Of course, we cheerleaders need encouragement too. In order to have encouragement to dish out, we have to fill ourselves up again. We do that by praising the Lord, praying to God, reading His Word, and taking care of ourselves by getting enough rest. Don't let yourself get empty and rundown or you'll be the grouchiest cheerleader in the history of the sport! Now, go forth and "Give me a GO! GO! GO!"

――――――― MOM TO MASTER ―――――――

*Lord, help me to be a constant source of encouragement to my family. I praise You for my children's salvation. Amen.*

# October 23

*Let the Word of Christ—the Message—have the run of the house. Give it plenty of room in your lives.*
COLOSSIANS 3:16 MSG

Have you given the Word a prominent place in your life? This verse in Colossians says that we're supposed to give the Word plenty of room. That used to bother me. I'd think, *Doesn't God know how busy I am? How can He expect me to spend a lot of time in the Word and get all of this stuff done too?* But you know what I've discovered? If I make time for God, He makes time for me. In other words, if I spend time with the Father—no matter how busy I am—He makes sure that I accomplish all that is on my plate. He supernaturally increases my time.

I once heard a well-known minister say that she had decided to read the Gospels through five times in just a short amount of time. But it looked impossible! She had two little children. She and her husband had just moved into a new place, and there were boxes to unpack and closets to organize. In the natural, it seemed like an impossible goal. But do you know what? She not only met her goal but also was able to unpack every box, care for her children, and refinish a piece of furniture! Make time for God today. He will make time for you.

———————— MOM TO MASTER ————————

*Lord, help me to make more time for You. Amen.*

# October 24

*But those who wait for the Lord [who expect, look for, and hope in Him] will gain new strength and renew their power.*

ISAIAH 40:31 AMP

Do you expect God's best for your life? Do you expect God's best for your children's lives? As moms, we sometimes put our dreams and desires on the back burner, and we forget to expect God for good things in our lives. Well, I am here to reawaken those dreams and desires today. I want you to grab a sheet of notebook paper and a pen and jot down your dreams. I want you to jot down the dreams you have for your children. Now I want you to thank God in advance for bringing those things to be in your life. Believe God big-time!

Don't let your lack of expectations set the limits for your life. If you never expect anything good, you're never going to receive anything good. If you don't expect things to change for the better, then nothing will ever get better. Start expecting to overcome every challenge in your life. Live every day filled with anticipation of what God is going to do in your life and your children's lives. He wants to bless you abundantly above all you can ask or think. So start expecting today!

---
## MOM TO MASTER
---

*Lord, I am relying on You for big things.*
*I praise You for working on my behalf today! Amen.*

*Don't use foul or abusive language.*
EPHESIANS 4:29 NLT

Do your children look for the best in people? Or are you raising "Chris and Christina Critical"? Kids are brutally honest. Sometimes they are critical without even meaning to be.

Once when we were leaving a shopping mall in Indiana, we saw one of the largest men I've ever seen. He looked like one of those people you see on talk shows—the ones who are so large they can't leave their house. Anyway, it was hard not to stare at him. I was cringing inside, just knowing that my toddler, Abby, would say something. She was such a curious child. Well, sure enough, Abby said, "Mommy, look how *big* that man is!" (At least she didn't say fat!)

Being the diplomat, I said, "Yes, this is a big *mall*." I hoped the man hadn't heard her critical comment, but I'll never be sure.

As my kids have grown older, I've been amazed at how accepting they are of people. Sure, they have their faults, but making fun of others isn't one of them. In fact, they are usually pulling for the underdog in every situation. I'm thankful for that. If your children are critical, believe God that His love will fill them up and negate that critical spirit. Soon they'll be "Polly and Peter Positive."

——————— MOM TO MASTER ———————

*Lord, help me to raise positive children—kids*
*who look for the best in everyone. Amen.*

# October 26

*"Get wisdom, get understanding;*
*do not forget my words or turn away from them."*
PROVERBS 4:5

Could you use some more wisdom today? Me too. This is especially true when it comes to parenting. You could ask ten people the best way to potty train a child, and you'd hear ten different theories. No matter what the topic, you'll find "experts" who hold opposing views, and each one will have data and research to back up the findings. One year, breastfeeding is better for babies. The next year, bottle-fed babies tend to be more well adjusted. Ahhh! It's all so confusing. We want to get it right, but it seems so hard to navigate the right path.

I'm so thankful that I can go to God for my answers. He is the ultimate expert. He doesn't have to consult with anyone to give you an answer—He *is* the answer!

No matter what you need today, you can go to God and seek His counsel. He wants you to! Proverbs 4:5 says to "Get wisdom, get understanding." He wants us to hunger and thirst after Him. He wants us to seek Him. He wants to share His wisdom with us. So go ahead, take your questions and concerns to the Father. He's ready, willing, and able to answer.

——————— MOM TO MASTER ———————

*Lord, I am seeking Your wisdom today.*
*Thank You for freely giving me all that I need. Amen.*

# October 27

*He will not allow your foot to be moved;*
*He who keeps you will not slumber.*
PSALM 121:3 NKJV

I think the world needs more rocking chairs. We were at Cracker Barrel one time and had to wait for a table. So we all went outside and plopped down in our own rocking chairs. I hadn't sat in a rocking chair since my girls were babies.

With each swaying movement, I was taken back to a precious memory of holding baby Abby and baby Ally in my arms. As they grew older, they didn't sit on my lap as often. They were far "too cool" for that. Sometimes I long for those rocking chair days. Rocking chairs force you to slow down and enjoy the moment. It's almost impossible to be stressed out while rocking. Sitting in a rocking chair is like cozying up to a close, old friend. There's something very comforting and comfortable about spending time in a rocking chair.

You know, even if you don't have a rocking chair at your house, you can spend some quality rocking time in God's rocker. When I pray to the Father, I always picture Him sitting in a big, wooden rocking chair and beckoning me to sit on His lap. If you need to de-stress today, crawl into your heavenly Father's lap and rock awhile.

## — MOM TO MASTER —

*Lord, I need to spend some quality time just rocking with*
*You today. Thanks for loving me. Amen.*

# October 28

*"I will dwell in them and walk among them.*
*I will be their God, and they shall be My people."*
2 CORINTHIANS 6:16 NKJV

Are your kids independent? As my girls approached middle school, they became more and more independent. I used to help them pick out their outfits, but now they wanted to choose their own clothes. I used to fix their hair each morning, but now they wanted to do it themselves. And they rarely wanted me to pack their lunches anymore. They were growing into very independent girls.

My mom always used to say, "You're as independent as a hog on ice." I never really got that expression, but the visual was pretty funny! Well, now my girls are little piggies on ice, and I'm not too happy about it. I sometimes feel as if they no longer need me. Have you ever experienced those same feelings?

I bet that's how God feels whenever we try to do everything on our own without asking for His help or His intervention. You see, being independent isn't always a good thing. We should rely on God all the time. We should have our faith so far out there that we can't make it even one step without God. If you've become "a hog on ice" in the spiritual sense, come back to God. Ask for His help. He's happy to oblige.

——————— MOM TO MASTER ———————

*Lord, help me always to depend on You. Amen.*

# October 29

*But the fruit of the Spirit is love, joy, peace, forbearance,*
*kindness, goodness, faithfulness, gentleness and self-control.*
GALATIANS 5:22–23

I was in line at the grocery store, and I only had two items in the "20 items or less" lane. The man in front of me had the maximum amount of items, and he very kindly asked if I'd like to go ahead of him. That really made my day.

Wouldn't it be nice if all people in life were that kind, always thinking of others' needs above their own? Wouldn't it be nice if we could teach our children to be that kind? Well, we can! As Christians, we can have all of the fruit of the Spirit operating in our lives. We can claim that promise for ourselves and our children.

Put Galatians 5:22–23 in action today. Why not offer to carry someone's groceries? Why not send a card of appreciation to your pastors? Maybe you could bake some cookies for your neighbors. Or perhaps you could offer to call on a few shut-ins in your community. Ask your kids to help you, and you can work on growing more fruit of the Spirit together.

—————————— MOM TO MASTER ——————————

*Lord, change my heart so that I might show kindness to my*
*family, my friends, and to strangers. Thank You for*
*always showing kindness to me. Amen.*

# October 30

*"Give, and it will be given to you."*
LUKE 6:38

Doesn't it feel good to give? As moms, we're programmed to give. We give up our figures to carry babies in our bellies. We give up yoga classes for Baby and Me sessions. We give up golf for playgroup time. We give up sleep for nightly feedings. We give up a lot! But we also get so much in return.

In one of my favorite movies, *The Thrill of It All* starring Doris Day and James Garner, there's a great line describing motherhood. James Garner plays Dr. Boyer, an adorable obstetrician, and one of his patients says to him, "I don't know when I've been so happy. I guess there's nothing more fulfilling in life than having a baby."

I suppose that's true, although there are days when you haven't had a shower or any sleep that you might question that statement! Being a mother is a great honor and an awesome undertaking. It requires a great deal of giving—giving love, giving praise, giving encouragement, giving spankings, giving wisdom—giving it all! But we don't have to go it alone. On the days when we have nothing left to give, God does. He will supply all of our needs. He will give to us so that we can give to our families.

—————— MOM TO MASTER ——————

*Lord, help me to never grow weary of giving. Amen.*

# October 31

*So we say with confidence,*
*"The Lord is my helper; I will not be afraid."*
HEBREWS 13:6

What's on your agenda today? Are you facing some big challenges? No matter what you're going to be up against today, God has you covered. He says in Hebrews that He will be our helper. We don't have to be afraid.

I don't know about you, but I sometimes feel afraid. Sure, I put on a good outward appearance, but on the inside I feel insecure. I wonder if I'm doing a good enough job as a mom. Do you ever wonder if you're measuring up? I especially feel that way when I am around moms who are doing everything right. You know, the really cool mom who has a clean house, all of her laundry folded and put away, no dirty dishes in the sink *ever*, well-mannered children, and a perfect figure too! I want to be a mom like that someday.

But until then, I am declaring that "I will not be afraid." God did not give us a spirit of fear, but of love and of power and of a sound mind. We are up to any challenge. We can do all things through Him. We can be confident in Him today and every day.

--- MOM TO MASTER ---

*Thank You, Lord, for helping me every single day of the year.*
*I couldn't do it without You. I love You, God. Amen.*

# November 1

*"Then if my people who are called by my name will humble themselves and pray and seek my face and turn from their wicked ways, I will hear from heaven and will forgive their sins and restore their land."*

2 CHRONICLES 7:14 NLT

When terrorists attacked on September 11, 2001—it rocked the very foundation of America. I'll bet you remember exactly where you were when you first heard that the World Trade Center had been hit. For days, Americans were glued to CNN. And for days, we hugged our children a little tighter and prayed a little harder.

People all over the world hit their knees, seeking God's face, asking for wisdom, and praying for protection. Prayer became a priority from sea to shining sea. I know our family prayed longer and harder during those days following 9/11.

Now, several years since that fateful day in September 2001, the ribbons have come off the antennas on our vehicles and the patriotic clothing trend has died down, but the prayers are still going up on a regular basis. People have embraced this Bible verse and turned their faces toward heaven and prayed for this precious country. As Veteran's Day approaches, let's also pray for the men and women who have given their lives so that we might enjoy freedom. God bless America!

---

## MOM TO MASTER

*Thank You, Lord, for America. Please direct and guide our leaders, and protect those men and women who protect us. Amen.*

# November 2

*Our Father which art in heaven, Hallowed be thy name.*
*Thy kingdom come, Thy will be done in earth, as it is in heaven.*
*Give us this day our daily bread. And forgive us our debts,*
*as we forgive our debtors. And lead us not into temptation,*
*but deliver us from evil: For thine is the kingdom,*
*and the power, and the glory, for ever. Amen.*

MATTHEW 6:9–13 KJV

Do you remember learning the Lord's Prayer when you were just a little girl? I remember sitting in a Sunday school classroom when I was only seven years old, reciting the words to the Lord's Prayer so that I could earn a Tootsie Roll pop. (Candy was a good motivator!) I am so thankful to that dear woman who gave up her time to teach our first-grade Sunday school class. It was the first time anyone had really taught me to pray.

Once I learned the words to the Lord's Prayer, I was so excited! Sure, I was thrilled to earn the candy, but that wasn't the only reason I was excited. Just knowing that I could pray a prayer that Jesus once prayed seemed very cool to my seven-year-old mind. It still seems very cool to me more than twenty-five years later. If you haven't taught your children the words to the Lord's Prayer, why not begin today?

--------- MOM TO MASTER ---------

*Thank You for the Lord's Prayer. Amen.*

# November 3

*"Your Father knows exactly what you
need even before you ask him!"*
MATTHEW 6:8 NLT

Have you ever been so distraught that you didn't even know what to pray? I think we've all been there at some point in our lives. After my father had his first stroke and they didn't know if he would live through the night, I became numb. It was touch and go for several days, and all I did was drive to and from the hospital. On those forty-minute drives, I would try to pray, but all I could do was say the name of Jesus. Thankfully, that was enough.

In Matthew 6:8, the Word tells us that God knows what we need even before we ask Him. That's good to know, isn't it? Even when we can't pray what we want to pray, God knows our hearts. He knows what we need. If we simply call on the name of Jesus, He is right there beside us.

No matter how desperate you are today. No matter how hopeless you feel. No matter how far from God you think you are. . .God loves you. He wants to help you. He wants to help your children. He wants to bring you through this difficult time. Call on Him today.

—————————— MOM TO MASTER ——————————

*Thank You, Lord, for knowing me so well
and hearing my heart. Amen.*

# November 4

*Rejoice always, pray continually, give thanks in all circumstances;*
*for this is God's will for you in Christ Jesus.*
1 THESSALONIANS 5:16–18

There is a lot of good advice packed into the above scripture. Think about it. If we're joyful always, pray continually, and give thanks in all circumstances, we're going to enjoy life no matter what!

One of the happiest people I've ever known was a man named Ivan Hunter. He taught children's church at the church I attended as a little girl. Ivan loved to sing about Jesus. He loved to talk about the goodness of God. Even as a little girl, I sensed how deeply he loved the Lord. It wasn't until I became a grown woman that I learned that Ivan's life had been filled with much heartache. He and his wife had lost a child. He'd been in a serious accident and lost several fingers. And he had battled cancer for years. Still, if you asked Ivan how he was doing, he'd praise the Lord and share how wonderful Jesus had been to him. He truly gave thanks in all circumstances.

I want to be more like Ivan. I want my children to be more like Ivan too. Let's go into this Thanksgiving season with true gratefulness in our hearts. Let's look for opportunities to praise the Lord—like Ivan always did.

———————— MOM TO MASTER ————————

*Lord, help me to have constant joy,*
*pray continually, and give thanks to*
*You no matter what. Amen.*

# November 5

*Very early in the morning, while it was still dark,*
*Jesus got up, left the house and went off*
*to a solitary place, where he prayed.*
MARK 1:35

Are you a list maker? If I don't have a to-do list for the day, I feel lost. It's sort of my map for each twenty-four-hour period. Of course, I rarely accomplish all of the things on my daily list, so I carry over the remaining items to the next day, thus beginning my new to-do list. It's an obsession, really. Maybe you can relate.

You know the problem with making lists? If I don't write it on my list, I don't do it. So I've started adding "pray daily" to my list. Then, as I am checking off the things I've already accomplished, such as "Do two loads of laundry, work out, pick up dry cleaning, etc.," I see my "pray daily" entry. It's a great reminder.

You can pray all the time—continually—as 1 Thessalonians says, but you can also set a designated time for really intense, focused prayer. Mark 1:35 tells us that Jesus chose to do His praying in the very early morning, while it was still dark. Well, I'm not really a morning kind of gal, so I pray in the afternoon. Do whatever works for you, but just do it. Make prayer a priority in your life today.

———————— MOM TO MASTER ————————

*Lord, help me to make time for prayer. Amen.*

*And he said: "Truly I tell you, unless you change and become like little children, you will never enter the kingdom of heaven."*
MATTHEW 18:3

When Allyson was a preschooler, she loved to pray over our meals. She couldn't wait until that part of the day. I'd always ask, "Who wants to pray over our food?" Allyson would beam and shout, "Me! Me! Me!" And then she'd begin, "God bless Mommy, Daddy, Sister, Max (our dog), Ma-maw, Papaw, Nana, Granddad, Aunt Martie, Uncle Jan, Mandy, Autumn. . ." By the time Allyson finished her prayer, the food was totally cold. Still, there was something very sweet about her prayers. They were full of thanksgiving, humility, and genuineness.

I've learned a lot about prayer from my children. Both Abby and Allyson taught me to pray with enthusiasm, thanksgiving, and expectation. When Abby was only five, she prayed for her goldfish to live, and let me tell you, Bubbles was on his last fin. He was sort of swimming sideways in the bowl. He was fixing to go to the big fishbowl in the sky. But Abby prayed, and that little fish lived another two months. It was a miracle! She never had a doubt.

As moms, we need to have that same thankful heart and expectation when we pray to our heavenly Father. Learn from your little ones. They truly know how to pray.

——————————— MOM TO MASTER ———————————

*Lord, help me to pray like the little children. Amen.*

# November 7

*Pray continually.*
1 THESSALONIANS 5:17

I once read that Billy Graham said he prays without ceasing. In other words, he is in constant communication with God. He has a dialogue going with the Lord all day. I figured if Billy Graham thought that was a good idea, I'd do the same. After all, he is Billy Graham—one of the greatest men of God of all time!

So I have endeavored to continually dialogue with God ever since that revelation. At first, it seemed a bit awkward. I struggled with it, wondering what to say. But after a while, it became kind of second nature. I'd start praying without even realizing it.

Not long ago, we had one of those Texas "toad stranglers" come upon us on our way to gymnastics. I could hardly see to drive. The rain was intense. The sky was dark. And I was nervous. After a few moments, Abby asked, "Who are you talking to?" Her question made me realize that I'd been praying to the Lord, asking Him to make the rain subside, without even realizing I was praying. It had become my first instinct. Yay! I am making progress. I'm certainly no Billy Graham, but I am enjoying this continual conversation with God. If you haven't tried talking to God throughout your day, go for it! Talk to Him about everything. It's a wonderful way to live.

—————— MOM TO MASTER ——————

*Lord, help me to pray all the time. Amen.*

# November 8

*"Again, truly I tell you that if two of you on earth agree about anything they ask for, it will be done for them by my Father in heaven."*
MATTHEW 18:19

Did you know that you don't have to call a prayer line to get an answer to prayer? Growing up, my mother was on our "church hotline" phone list. Every other night, she'd get an urgent call from another lady on the prayer chain. Together they'd go over an updated list of prayer concerns from people in our congregation. Sometimes my mother would be on the phone for over an hour. Wow! That's a lot of prayer needs, isn't it?

From that experience, I grew up thinking that if I had a really urgent prayer request, I would need to call the local body of prayers or perhaps call a prayer line listed at the bottom of a Christian program I was watching. Somehow I thought they had a better chance of getting an answer than I did. Silly, isn't it?

According to this verse in Matthew, if *any* two agree on something and ask the Father, it will be done. Well, I have good news—we qualify as any! So the next time you have an urgent prayer request, grab your kids and ask them to agree with you as you lift up your request to heaven. Your family's prayers availeth much!

———————— MOM TO MASTER ————————

*Lord, help my family to establish our own prayer hotline. Amen.*

# November 9

*My help comes from the LORD, the Maker of heaven and earth.*
*He will not let your foot slip—he who watches*
*over you will not slumber.*
PSALM 121:2–3

Texas has terrible storms. Last summer we had a really scary storm. The sky was dark and a tornado warning was in effect for much of the area. Normally I don't panic when it storms, but Abby wasn't at home. She was with a friend at an amusement park. I tried calling her over and over again, but I couldn't reach her. By 9 p.m. I was hysterical. By 11 p.m. I was ready to drive through the torrential rain and search the entire Dallas–Fort Worth Metroplex for my little girl. I wanted to call several of my "prayer partners" from church, but it was too late to disturb them. It was so comforting to know that God wasn't asleep. He was waiting up with me. He heard every word I prayed.

As it turns out, the phone service was out in much of the area, which is why Abby couldn't call me and I couldn't call her. She had been safe at her friend's house for hours. God answered my prayers. He will answer your prayers too no matter what time of day you pray. He is on call all the time!

--- MOM TO MASTER ---

*Thank You, Lord, for always listening*
*to my prayers. Amen.*

# November 10

*Devote yourselves to prayer, with an
alert mind and a thankful heart.*
COLOSSIANS 4:2 NLT

Do you ever fall asleep during your prayer sessions? Be honest. It's okay—I sometimes catch a few z's during prayer time too. I don't intentionally sleep, but I occasionally drift off into dreamland.

As moms (especially new moms), we get so few hours of sleep that once we're still for just a few moments, we tend to fall asleep. When my girls were both babies (and on different sleep schedules), I always used to fall asleep during my devotional time. But I knew that God understood. He isn't some big ogre in the sky just looking for a reason to bop us on the head. He knew I needed the rest, and He wasn't mad at me. If you have trouble staying awake during your prayer time, God isn't mad at you either.

Ask God to help you be alert during your prayer periods, just as Colossians 4:2 says. He will help you. And even if you still fall asleep, God will be waiting when you wake up. He's not offended. He's ready to talk to you whenever you're ready.

--------------------- MOM TO MASTER ---------------------

*Thank You, Lord, for understanding when I fall asleep
during our conversations. Help me, God, to stay awake
and be more alert when I pray. I love You. Amen.*

# November 11

*Count yourself lucky, how happy you must be—*
*you get a fresh start, your slate's wiped clean.*
PSALM 32:1 MSG

Whenever we played board games at our house, it turned out that my children hated to lose. Yes, they are poor sports—wonder where they get that? Okay, they inherited it from me—the biggest sore loser of them all. I am *way* too competitive for my own good! But so are they. Here's how it usually goes down. If Jeff or I get too far ahead, the girls want to start over. They want to wipe the slate clean and start a new game. Typically, we won't start over because we want to instill good qualities in our children, building their character even when we're just having fun playing games. But sometimes we'll go ahead and start over. We show mercy, just like God.

Isn't it nice that with God we always get to start over? No matter what we've done. No matter how badly we've acted. No matter how disappointed we are in ourselves, God still loves us and forgives us. And the best part is that we get to start over! We get to wipe the slate clean! All we have to do is repent, and then we get to move forward with our heavenly Father. With God, we always win!

--- MOM TO MASTER ---

*Lord, thank You for always wiping my slate clean.*
*I love You. Amen.*

# November 12

*O God, let me sing a new song to you.*
PSALM 144:9 MSG

Is your prayer life in a rut? Do you pray the same words over and over, day after day, month after month, and year after year? If so, you're in a prayer rut. And the only way out of a prayer rut is to sing a new song. Praise the Lord with a new song, as it says in Psalm 144. Don't just ask God to bless everyone from your husband to your pet fish, Bubbles. Instead, spend some time just worshipping the Lord. Tell Him you love Him because He gave you wonderful children. Tell Him you adore Him for putting a roof over your head. Praise Him for the food He gives each day. Most of all, praise Him because He died on a cross so that you might live.

God is a good God. He is worthy of our praise. If you have trouble thinking of things to praise Him for during your prayer time, use the Bible to help. Quote scriptures, such as "You are worthy of my praise for Your mercy and goodness endure forever." Praise Him from the bottom of your heart, and put that prayer rut behind you once and for all.

——————— MOM TO MASTER ———————

*Lord, thank You for all of the blessings in my life,*
*but most of all, thank You for just being You. Amen.*

# November 13

*Faith shows the reality of what we hope for;
it is the evidence of things we cannot see.*
HEBREWS 11:1 NLT

Prayer works. It doesn't just work once in a while. It doesn't just work when you pray at a certain time of day. It doesn't just work when a minister prays for you. Prayer works all the time. There's only one requirement—have faith. If you're praying without any faith, then you might as well forget it. You have to believe in the Lord's ability to answer your prayers. You have to know that He is willing and able to meet your needs—no matter what they are. You have to know that He is all-powerful, all-knowing, and altogether merciful.

When Abby and Allyson were very little, I desperately wanted to work from home, but I couldn't see any way financially that we could make it without my source of income. We were living from paycheck to paycheck at the time. But God knew. I cried out to Him, and I told Him I knew He was able to supply all of our needs. It wasn't long before several freelance writing opportunities fell into my lap and I was able to quit my full-time job and see my children more. God heard and answered my prayers. He will do the same for you if you'll only have faith.

———————— MOM TO MASTER ————————

*Lord, help me to pray faith-filled prayers. Amen.*

# November 14

*Do not be anxious about anything, but in every situation,*
*by prayer and petition, with thanksgiving,*
*present your requests to God.*

PHILIPPIANS 4:6

I had a friend who prayed for her children's future spouses every day. And her children were only four and six! I hadn't ever considered doing that, but the more I thought about it, the more it made sense to me. So I began praying for my girls' future husbands on a regular basis. I prayed that they were being raised in Christian homes, learning about the things of God, and growing up to be godly men. Of course I never told my daughters I was doing this, because they would totally freak out. It was God's and my little secret. But someday when they get ready to walk down the aisle with the men of their dreams, I'll be able to share my secret prayers with them.

My friend who opened my eyes to praying for my children's future spouses has taught me many things about prayer. She prays about absolutely everything. She prays about things that I wouldn't think to bring before God. But she is seeing great results. She has challenged me to pray more—even about little things—and I'm excited to see God's manifestation in my girls' lives. I challenge you to pray more too. Don't think it's too insignificant to bring before God. He wants to hear it all!

—————— MOM TO MASTER ——————

*Thank You, Lord, for caring about*
*every detail of my life. Amen.*

# November 15

*Now when Daniel learned that the decree had been published,
he went home to his upstairs room where the windows opened
toward Jerusalem. Three times a day he got down on his knees
and prayed, giving thanks to his God, just as he had done before.*

DANIEL 6:10

Are you too busy to pray? Do you run 100 mph all day long? I
am so there with you, sister! That's why we need to take a lesson
from Daniel. Daniel was a wise man. He learned that in order to
hear from God, he needed to slow down. As you can read here
in the sixth chapter of Daniel, he stopped and dropped to his
knees three times a day to pray to God. He knew that he needed
to hear from God before continuing on.

We should realize that same truth too. No matter how busy
we become with our motherly duties, we need to take time to
pray. We need to seek His face on a regular basis. If we don't,
we'll just be spinning our wheels. So don't neglect your prayer
time. Give time to God, and He will give time back to you. He
isn't working against you, He is working *for* you. And together,
the two of you can't lose!

--- MOM TO MASTER ---

*Lord, help me to slow down in order
to hear from You. Amen.*

# November 16

*Then Jesus told his disciples a parable to show them*
*that they should always pray and not give up.*
LUKE 18:1

Are you waiting for God to answer a very important prayer request? Are you getting weary of praying about this matter? Do you ever feel like God has forgotten you and your request? Well, He hasn't. And He won't. He tells us in Luke 18 that we should always pray and not give up. So keep praying! Don't give up! Your answer, your ultimate victory, may be right around the corner.

I once interviewed a woman who had always longed to meet her birth father. He left when she was just an infant, and she'd never been able to track him down. She had cried out to God many times to help her in her search. Then, finally, after more than forty years, everything fell into place, and she was reunited with her father. It was a glorious reunion. Immediately, they established the relationship that had been lost due to unfortunate circumstances. God brought them back together, and they are definitely making up for lost time.

This woman shared with me that she never gave up. Every year, she'd say, "This will be the year I'll find Daddy." What if she had quit believing that after only thirty-nine years? So don't give up. Don't quit. Keep praying, because God is still listening and working on your behalf.

——————— MOM TO MASTER ———————

*Lord, help me never to give up. Amen.*

# November 17

*If we don't know how or what to pray, it doesn't matter.*
*He does our praying in and for us, making prayer*
*out of our wordless sighs, our aching groans.*
ROMANS 8:26 MSG

I once read this beautiful statement: "God hears more than words. He listens to the heart," and I've always remembered it. I love that thought. That means even if I can't communicate with words, God knows my heart. He hears my heart cries.

When my best friend had a stillborn baby, I couldn't get to her that night. I felt a million miles from her, and I wanted to be with her. I cried out to God, but I couldn't figure out what to pray. I was so heartbroken for her and her family. I couldn't believe that the baby we had been preparing for all of those months had already gone to heaven. I couldn't find the words, but the Holy Spirit prayed through me. After a few minutes of praying, I felt a sort of release. The heaviness left me, and I knew my friend was going to be okay. I knew her baby was sitting on the Father's lap and that someday we'd be able to hold that precious baby. If you're hurting today and having trouble knowing what to pray, just cry out to God. He understands.

## MOM TO MASTER

*Thank You, Lord, for hearing my heart. Amen.*

# November 18

*"If you stand your ground, knocking and waking all the neighbors, he'll finally get up and get you whatever you need."*
LUKE 11:8 MSG

I really don't like having to ask for favors from my friends, because I never want to inconvenience them in any way. I don't want them to see my phone number on caller ID and think, *Oh, it's Michelle. I'd better not get that. She may want something.* But sometimes we have to ask for help. Not long ago, I was stuck in Dallas traffic, and I knew I wouldn't be able to get to the school by 3 p.m. to pick up my girls. I was in a mess. I finally broke down and called my friend Karen. She usually lets her daughter ride the bus home, but after my call of desperation, she said she'd be happy to swing over to the school and pick up our girls. Whew!

As I was thanking her profusely, she said, "Michelle, it's no problem. I know you'd do the same for me." And that was it. She didn't feel put out or inconvenienced at all! I was so glad I had called her. She was a lifesaver that day.

Isn't it good to know that our prayers never inconvenience God? We can call on Him for help any time of day for any reason at all. Let Him be your lifesaver today!

--- MOM TO MASTER ---

*Thank You, Lord, for always being there for me. Amen.*

# November 19

*"That's why I urge you to pray for absolutely everything, ranging from small to large. Include everything as you embrace this God-life, and you'll get God's everything."*

MARK 11:24 MSG

Do you pray specifically or do you pray big, broad, general prayers? If you're praying general prayers, you're missing out. God wants us to pray specifically about small and large matters. He wants us to bring everything to Him, but not all at once. Think of it this way. It'd be like going into a department store and saying to your husband, "Buy me something pretty." You may be longing for a pretty ring, but he buys you a pretty scarf. You didn't get what you wanted because you didn't ask specifically for a pretty ring. It's the same way with God.

Instead of just praying for world peace, why not pray for peace in your home? Instead of only praying for the economy to turn around, why not pray for your family to become debt-free? Instead of praying for your children to be happy, why not pray for your children to walk in the plans that God has for them?

You have to give God something to work with. Be specific. Find scriptures to stand on. Confess those daily. Praise God for the expected answers to your prayers and get ready for your miracles!

―――――――― MOM TO MASTER ――――――――

*Thank You, Lord, for being concerned about the big and small things in my life. Amen.*

# November 20

*Then they brought him a demon-possessed man who was blind and mute, and Jesus healed him, so that he could both talk and see.*

MATTHEW 12:22

When people came to Jesus for healing, He didn't say, "Well, I'll be sure to put that on My prayer list." No, he acted then and there. Sometimes He laid hands on them. Other times He simply spoke words of healing to them. And one time He even spit in the dirt and made a mudlike substance and put it on a blind man's eyes.

You see, sometimes prayer is the best we can offer. But other times, we need to pray and *act*. When a missionary comes to your church in need of financial support, it's good to pray that his needs are met, but it's also good to drop some money into the offering plate for him. Praying and acting will bless him more than just praying for him. In other words, don't use prayer as an excuse not to take action when you know that you should do something.

Follow the Holy Spirit's leading and act on His Word. Notice the Bible says, "Do unto others. . ." Doing means acting. Praying for someone is always a good thing, but don't stop there. Go that extra mile and be a part of the solution.

--- MOM TO MASTER ---

*Lord, help me to be compassionate*
*enough to pray and act. Amen.*

# November 21

*When you ask, you do not receive,*
*because you ask with wrong motives.*
JAMES 4:3

Sometimes our prayers aren't answered because it's not in God's timing. Other times our prayers aren't answered because we haven't prayed in faith. Still other times, our prayers aren't answered because we're praying with the wrong motivation.

I have been guilty of this. A few years ago, I had been praying every day that my children's books would become *New York Times* bestsellers. That's every author's dream! I had confessed it in faith, and I just knew it was going to happen. Then one Sunday during praise and worship, the Holy Spirit asked me a question: *"What's your motivation for publication?"* No, I didn't hear a loud, booming voice. I simply heard that small, inner voice asking me over and over again, *"What's your motivation for publication?"* I had to repent. I knew my motivation had been wrong. Instead of praying that my children's books touch kids' hearts around the world, I'd been praying for *New York Times* bestsellers. I was ashamed.

It's easy to fall into the wrong thinking, which leads to the wrong kind of praying. So if you're not seeing any answers to your prayers, check your motivation. That may be holding up your miracle.

## —————— MOM TO MASTER ——————

*Lord, help me to always pray with a pure heart. Amen.*

# November 22

*It is good to praise the LORD and make music to your name,*
*O Most High, proclaiming your love in the morning*
*and your faithfulness at night.*
PSALM 92:1–2

If you're like me, mornings always come too early. I am a night owl. I love the midnight hour when everyone in the house is asleep. At that time, it's just me, God, and my little dachshunds. The wee hours of the morning (which I consider late, late night) are perfectly wonderful for talking with God.

Whether you're a wee-hours-of-the-morning kind of gal or a first-thing-in-the-morning person, use that time to praise the Lord. Psalm 92 tells us that it's good to proclaim God's love in the morning. Spend those first few minutes of each day praising the Lord. If you can't think clearly enough to thank God for specific things He has done for you, simply read various psalms out loud. Tell God, "I praise You today because Your mercy endures forever and ever!" Sing a song of praise, such as, "I love You, Lord, and I lift my voice to worship You, oh my soul rejoice. Take joy my King in what You hear. May it be a sweet, sweet sound in Your ear." Give God praise in the morning, and you'll have a much better day.

## ———————— MOM TO MASTER ————————

*Lord, I praise You for who You are today! I love You! Amen.*

# November 23

*Is anyone among you in trouble? Let them pray.*
**JAMES 5:13**

When I learned that Allyson would have to have her tonsils out, I was less than thrilled—especially after I read through all of the bad things that could happen. It was quite scary. The more I thought about it, the more I worried. I asked my parents to pray that the surgery would go okay. I asked my friends to keep Ally in prayer. I put Ally on our church's prayer line. In fact, I did all of those things before I actually hit my own knees on behalf of my daughter. Isn't that pathetic?

Is prayer your first instinct? James 5:13 tells us that if we're in trouble, we should pray. It doesn't say to call your best friend and have her pray. It doesn't even say to call your pastor and have him pray. It says for *you* to pray. It's okay if we have others supporting us in prayer as long as we also pray.

If our children see us turning to prayer as our first line of defense, they'll do the same. They will hit their knees in prayer at the first sign of trouble. If we can teach them to do that, they'll forever be all right.

――――――― MOM TO MASTER ―――――――

*Lord, help my first instinct to be prayer. Amen.*

# November 24

*"When I fed them, they were satisfied;*
*when they were satisfied, they became proud;*
*then they forgot me."*
HOSEA 13:6

When you were pregnant, didn't you pray for that little baby growing inside of you every single day? When my first pregnancy became high risk due to preterm labor, I prayed almost nonstop. But guess what happened when Abby was born perfectly healthy and I had survived the ordeal? I quit praying so often. The scary crisis was over, so my prayers became fewer and far between. I was guilty of the common "run to God in bad times but ignore Him when things are good" syndrome.

Have you ever been guilty of that syndrome? We all have. Even the Israelites, God's chosen people, were guilty of this syndrome. They cried out to God when they needed freedom from Pharaoh, but after they were safe and sound and out of Pharaoh's reach, they started worshipping other gods. They built idols. They ignored the very One who had freed them in the first place.

Any way you look at it, that's lame. And here's something else to chew on—we need God in bad and good times. Even if we don't feel like we need God in the good times, we do. Keep in touch with Him all the time. It's the only way to live.

— MOM TO MASTER —

*Lord, thank You for being there for me in*
*the good times and the bad times. Amen.*

# November 25

*In him and through faith in him we may*
*approach God with freedom and confidence.*
EPHESIANS 3:12

Do you know what really gets on my very last nerve? Those automated telephone systems.

One time Abby started having a little trouble with her eyesight (indicating she was probably ready for a new eyeglass prescription). Since we were on a new insurance plan, I wasn't sure if eyeglasses were covered—so I called our insurance provider to ask a few questions. Of course, a recording answered and listed nine options, and the nightmare began. For twenty-five minutes, I was lost in a maze of numbers.

"Press 1 to talk to an insurance expert. Press 2 to talk to claims. Press 3 if you're a pharmacist." I was on the phone so long that my ear grew hot! Finally, I was transferred to my intended destination only to discover that the office was closed. I proceeded to yell into the phone, "It wasn't closed twenty-five minutes ago when I first called you!"

I'm so thankful that God doesn't have an automated answering system. Can you imagine if He did? "Press 1 to praise. Press 2 to submit a prayer request. Press 3 to repent. Press 4 for wisdom. Press 0 if this is a real emergency." Hallelujah, our heavenly Father is available 24-7! Call on Him today!

---

## MOM TO MASTER

*Lord, I am thankful that I can come into the*
*throne room at any time. I appreciate You. Amen.*

# November 26

*Do not be anxious about anything, but in every situation, by prayer*
*and petition, with thanksgiving, present your requests to God.*
*And the peace of God, which transcends all understanding,*
*will guard your hearts and your minds in Christ Jesus.*

PHILIPPIANS 4:6–7

When you go into the throne room and enter the inner sanctum of God, do you crawl in on your belly, bawling and belly-aching, or do you walk in and kneel before the Father with thanksgiving in your heart? If you're like me, it would depend on the day. But we should never crawl in and whine our way to Jesus. Philippians 4 tells us that we are to present our requests with thanksgiving.

I have a friend named Tracy who is a nurse, but she isn't just your typical nurse. She prays over all of her patients. Of course, she always asks permission first, but not one has refused her yet. She doesn't pray prayers of desperation or hopelessness. She prays with faith and thanksgiving, and her patients have a tremendous rate of recovery.

What kind of prayers are you praying? What kind of prayers are you teaching your children to pray? Begin praising the Lord for the victories that are on the way. Don't beg God to answer your prayers, present Him with scripture to back up your requests. Like Tracy, pray faith-filled prayers, and you'll begin to see results!

———————————— MOM TO MASTER ————————————

*Lord, I praise You that my answers are on the way. Amen.*

# November 27

*And my God will meet all your needs according
to the riches of his glory in Christ Jesus.*
PHILIPPIANS 4:19

"Mom, can I have five bucks?"

"Mom, can I go to the movies with Macy?"

"Mom, can I ride my bike?"

"Mom, can you help me with my pioneer report?"

Are there days when you'd like to change your name from Mom to any other name? Be honest. There are days when you grow weary of hearing, "Mom. . . ," hollered at you, right? I think every mom feels that way once in a while. When I reach that point, I always answer, "Mommy is off duty. Please leave a message and find the father figure of the household. His shift just began." My children, of course, ignore my sarcasm and continue bombarding me with requests. But that's okay—it's all part of a mother's calling, right?

That's one of the reasons I am so thankful for God. He *never* tires of our requests. We can call on Him all the time, and He never gets sick of it! In fact, He wants us to bring all of our concerns to Him. Philippians 4:19 says that God will answer "all" of our needs, but He won't answer all if we don't bring all of them to Him. So go ahead. Call on God right now!

—————— MOM TO MASTER ——————

*Thank You, Lord, for never tiring of my questions. Amen.*

# November 28

*Yes, you will lie down and your sleep will be sweet.*
PROVERBS 3:24 NKJV

Once I read the cutest saying. It went something like this: "When you can't sleep, don't count sheep. Talk to the Shepherd instead." Isn't that great? I typically don't have trouble sleeping, but once in a while, I have encountered sleepless nights. This is especially true when there's unrest in the household—when my children are sick or they are struggling in school or they are hurting inside from losing a friend. At those times, it's easy to trade in restful nights for sleepless ones.

As moms, we want to make everything all right for our children. It's what we do. But as hard as we try, we can't fix everything. And worrying about the things we can't fix doesn't help either. It just causes us to lose sleep and require wood putty to cover our dark circles!

So the next time you're up worrying, stop worrying and start praying. Call on the Good Shepherd. He's always awake and ready to respond. Give it to God and then go to sleep. Follow the wisdom that's in a song that Bing Crosby sings in the classic movie *White Christmas*: "When you're worried and you can't sleep, just count your blessings instead of sheep, and you'll go to sleep counting your blessings."

— MOM TO MASTER —

*Heavenly Father, I thank You for sweet sleep
and answered prayers. Amen.*

# November 29

*"But when you pray, go into your room, close the door
and pray to your Father, who is unseen. Then your Father,
who sees what is done in secret, will reward you."*

MATTHEW 6:6

Have you ever heard the expression, "Kneeling keeps you in good standing with the Father?" We need to find time to pray every day. That may take some planning on your part—especially if you still have little ones running around your house. When Abby and Allyson were toddlers, I used to retreat to the bathroom just to have a few moments alone with God. I didn't have a prayer closet—it was more like a prayer bathtub. Still, it worked for me. I was able to steal some time away with the Father in the sanctuary of our pink ceramic tub.

If you're having trouble finding quality time to spend with God, get a plan! You may not be able to read the Word and pray first thing in the morning. The best time for you may be when the kids are down for their afternoon nap (assuming they all nap at the same time!). Or maybe you can spend some time with God after you put them to bed each night. Find a time that works for you and stick to it. The Father is waiting. . . .

—————————— MOM TO MASTER ——————————

*Heavenly Father, help me to take advantage of every
moment we can spend alone. I love You. Amen.*

# November 30

*But Jesus Himself would often slip
away to the wilderness and pray.*
LUKE 5:16 NASB

"Retreat and replenish." Remember that phrase? It's helped me a lot over the past few years. Every time I feel I have nothing left to give, Jesus reminds me that it's time to retreat and replenish. By spending time on my knees and in His Word, I am refilled with God's love, power, strength, joy, and energy. I give God all of my worries, sickness, concerns, tiredness, and grouchiness, and He gives me all the good stuff. What a deal, eh? Even Jesus recognized the need to retreat and replenish. After He had healed many people and driven out demons, He needed to retreat and replenish too.

If you're feeling worn out today, turn to God. Let Him reenergize you. Let Him refuel you with His love so that you'll have love to give your children. As moms, we have to refuel so that we are ready to minister to our families.

As moms, we set the tone for the home. If we're stressed out and drained, our homes will be full of stress and confusion. So do yourself and your family a favor and retreat and replenish. God is ready to fill you up!

--- MOM TO MASTER ---

*Lord, fill me up with Your love and
strength and joy. I love You. Amen.*

# December 1

*If you'll take a good, hard look at my pain,*
*if you'll quit neglecting me and go into action for me by*
*giving me a son, I'll give him completely, unreservedly to you.*
*I'll set him apart for a life of holy discipline.*

1 SAMUEL 1:11 MSG

Though I've never personally struggled with infertility, I have a very dear friend who has. She was able to get pregnant and have a baby some years ago, but she hasn't been able to conceive again. She and her husband originally wanted a household of children, but they are content to have what God has given them. They thank God for their little girl every day. Infertility has been a difficult road to walk, but they haven't walked it alone.

God has been with this loving couple every step of the way. Through the medical dilemmas, the expensive infertility treatments, the ongoing disappointment, and the ultimate decision to quit trying to have another child—God has been there.

Infertility is a very common problem. Last year alone, there were more than two million infertile couples across the United States. Let's pray today for those who are experiencing infertility. God is still a miracle-working God. We stand with them for their miracle!

———————————— MOM TO MASTER ————————————

*Thank You, Lord, for giving me children. I pray for those*
*who are still trying to conceive or adopt. Please give them*
*peace and patience as they wait for their miracle. Amen.*

# December 2

*Hannah did not go. She said to her husband,*
*"After the boy is weaned, I will take him and present him*
*before the Lord, and he will live there always."*
1 SAMUEL 1:22

I love the story of Hannah. She so badly wanted to have children. She saw that her husband's other wife, Peninnah, was able to have many children, yet Hannah could not conceive. Can't you just imagine how painful it was for Hannah to see Peninnah pregnant over and over again? As if that wasn't hurtful enough, Peninnah taunted Hannah for being childless. Hannah cried out to God, and He heard her prayers, causing her to conceive.

Hannah had a son and named him Samuel. He was the answer to her earnest prayers. But now she had to give Samuel back to God because she had promised God that she would. Can you imagine how hard that would have been to do? But she did. She gave Samuel to God, as she'd promised, to be raised in the synagogue. Later God gave Hannah three more sons and two daughters. He honored her because she honored Him.

Are you honoring God today? Have you given your children to God? After all, He gave them to you. Giving your kids to God is the best thing you could ever do for your children. Give them to God today and every day.

--- MOM TO MASTER ---

*Thank You, Lord, for my children.*
*Help me never to take them for granted. Amen.*

# December 3

*Glory in his holy name; let the hearts
of those who seek the Lord rejoice.*
1 Chronicles 16:10

I remember when my daughters were in the tween stage—in between being kids and being teens. It was an exciting age, full of adventure and fun. But it was also a difficult age. Maybe you have children who are tweens too. If you do, then you are in the "uncool" club with me. Suddenly, everything I suggest or say is totally uncool.

I don't know how it happened, but I have become the embarrassing mom who picks out nerdy clothes for her daughters and comes up with lame party games. Just when I thought I was totally hip, the rug was pulled out from under me. Sure, my girls still needed me, but not as much as they used to. There were days when I felt totally useless and sorry for myself.

When I had one of those blue days, I ran to God. In His presence, I felt complete and useful once again. He built me up, giving me the joy and strength I needed to move forward. He reminded me of His promises. He helped me to see a true picture of myself. He made me feel loved again. So if you're in a blue funk, go to God.

—————————— MOM TO MASTER ——————————

*Thank You, God, for loving me and building me up. Amen.*

# December 4

*If I give all I possess to the poor and give over my body to hardship that I may boast, but do not have love, I gain nothing.*

Have you read those wonderful children's books by Laura Numeroff? You know the ones—*If You Give a Moose a Muffin* and *If You Give a Pig a Pancake.* There's a lot of truth to those little books. Sometimes you give and give, and it never seems to be enough. If you're like me, you give until you get angry over your giving. Then you give some more but in the wrong spirit. Ever been there?

We threw a Build-a-Bear party for Allyson's ninth birthday. We paid enough so that every child could get a fifteen-dollar animal and one five-dollar outfit. One little girl who attended the party kept begging for more money. She *really* wanted the cheerleading outfit for her fifteen-dollar bear, but it was fifteen-dollars too. She dropped hint after hint, and then she finally flat-out asked me for more money. I, of course, said no because it wouldn't have been fair to the other kids. Her ungrateful spirit really perturbed me.

It got me thinking, *I wonder if God ever feels that way toward us?* He gives and gives and gives, and then we say, "God, I *really* want the fifteen-dollar cheerleading outfit for my bear. Could You give some more?" No matter what, we should always keep a grateful heart. Greediness is ugly any way you look at it.

---

## MOM TO MASTER

*Thank You, God, for giving so much to me. Amen.*

# December 5

*"If you, then, though you are evil, know how to give good gifts
to your children, how much more will your Father
in heaven give good gifts to those who ask him!"*
MATTHEW 7:11

Don't you love to give good gifts to your children? Moms are natural-born givers. We simply love to bless our kids. But you know what I have discovered over the years? We can bless them in many more ways than simply giving them stuff that we buy. Some of the greatest gifts my parents gave me growing up didn't cost a thing, but I'll cherish them for a lifetime. For instance, my parents gave me an appreciation for Frank Sinatra music. I grew up singing along to "Fly Me to the Moon," "All of Me," and "New York, New York." My father taught me ballroom dancing to Mr. Sinatra's music. Today I have an extensive collection of Frank Sinatra music and movies, and I'm educating my children in "Sinatra 101."

Giving me an appreciation for "Ol' Blue Eyes" is something I'll forever be thankful for, but of course, the greatest gift my parents gave me was a love for Jesus. I grew up in a Christian home, knowing who God is and what Jesus did for me. See, we don't have to have a lot of money to give good things to our children. If we teach them about Jesus, we've given them the greatest gift of all!

--------- MOM TO MASTER ---------

*Lord, help me to teach my children about
You so that they'll forever love You. Amen.*

# December 6

*Those who know your name will trust in you, for you,*
*LORD, have never forsaken those who seek you.*
PSALM 9:10

Do you trust God? Do you really trust Him? As Christians, we're supposed to trust God. Our money even says, "In God We Trust." Maybe you trust God in some areas of your life but have trouble trusting Him in other areas. That's where I am. I struggle a little bit when it comes to trusting Him with my children. I have to daily declare, "Lord, I trust You with my kids, and I thank You for taking such good care of them today."

It's not that I think I can do a better job than He can. That would be downright ridiculous. I just have trouble giving up control. You see, trusting means giving God your kids. It means giving God all of your worries and fears concerning your kids. And it means giving God all of the dreams that you have for your children.

If you're having trouble trusting God with your children, get back in His Word. Read over all of the promises. Hold on to those promises. You can trust Him with everything—even your children.

## ——— MOM TO MASTER ———

*Lord, I give my kids to You. I give You all of my worries*
*concerning my kids, and I give You all of the*
*dreams I have for my children. Amen.*

# December 7

*Those who give to the poor will lack nothing.*
PROVERBS 28:27

It's almost Christmas. One step into the mall, and you'll know that it's Yuletide time. Muzak renditions of "Jingle Bells" and "White Christmas" play throughout the department stores, while shoppers hustle and bustle to finish their shopping. (In case you haven't finished buying for everyone on your list, this is for you: "Attention, shoppers! Only eighteen days of Christmas shopping left!")

We are all in that gift-buying mode. It's fun! It's busy! It's tradition! And it's not an activity that everyone can afford to do. The holidays aren't so happy for those who are needy. They aren't able to buy the latest toys for their children. They can't buy those designer sweatshirts and matching hair accessories for their little girls. They may not even have money to buy all the fixin's for a Christmas dinner.

If you know a family that fits this description, why not "adopt" that family this holiday season? Get your children involved in shopping for each adopted family member. Have your kids help you bake Christmas cookies for them. Make it a fun activity that your family can do together, bringing the true meaning of Christmas to the forefront of this holiday season. Give love this Christmas. It truly is the gift that keeps on giving.

--- MOM TO MASTER ---

*Lord, help me to never lose sight of the true meaning of Christmas. Amen.*

# December 8

*"For God so loved the world that he gave his one and only Son, that whoever believes in him shall not perish but have eternal life."*
JOHN 3:16

Do you give God your best? Do you give Him your best praise? Do you give Him your best attention? Do you give Him your best effort? Do you give Him your best love?

If you don't, you're not alone. We all fail to give God the very best of ourselves. Instead of giving Him the best that we have, we offer Him our leftovers.

Especially at this time of year, when giving is such an important part of the holiday season, we need to make sure we're giving God our best. We need for our children to see us giving God our best. Let them see you getting up thirty minutes early in the morning to spend time with God. Let them see you dropping more money into the offering plate. Let them see you praising the Lord at every given opportunity. Let them see you being kind to strangers. If they see you serving God wholeheartedly, they will want to do the same.

Give God your best today. After all, He gave us His very best when He sent Jesus more than two thousand years ago. He certainly deserves our best.

―――――――――― MOM TO MASTER ――――――――――

*Heavenly Father, help me to always give You the best of me. Help me to put You first in every situation. I love You. Amen.*

# December 9

Following September 11, 2001, my girls desperately wanted to do their part to heal America. They had heard on the radio that people could give blood at the American Red Cross in order to help, and both Abby and Allyson begged me to take them. I was touched by their enthusiasm, but I had to explain to them that they were too young to donate blood. Saddened that they couldn't help in that way, the girls came up with another plan. They set up a lemonade and cookie stand in front of our house. Ally held up the patriotic poster while Abby poured the pink lemonade. At the end of the day, they had collected a whole sock full of change that we could send to the American Red Cross.

Their enthusiasm to help really inspired me. I thought, *Wouldn't it be great if all of us lived every day like that. . .just looking for any way to help others?* It challenged me to think of others' needs before my own. I hope you'll be challenged to do the same. Let's not wait for another tragedy to bring out the best in us— let's start giving of ourselves today.

———————— MOM TO MASTER ————————

*Lord, help me to live to give, and help me to
teach my children to live to give too. Amen.*

# December 10

*"As for God, his way is perfect: The LORD's word is flawless;*
*he shields all who take refuge in him."*

2 SAMUEL 22:31

We do the best we can do as Christian moms. Like the Bible says, we train up our children in the ways of the Lord, and we pray for them on a regular basis. We take them to church. We offer words of wisdom whenever the opportunity arises. We try to set a good example for them. But in all of that doing, guess what? Our children will still make mistakes. They will still disappoint us. Why? Because they are only human. And though we like to think our little bundles of joy are perfect, they are far from it. They are no more perfect than we are. That's a scary thought, eh? There's only One who is perfect, and as long as we point our children toward Him, then we've done the very best we can do.

And just as the Master forgives us when we stray, we need to do the same for our kids. We need to be merciful and loving like our heavenly Father. In fact, we need to emulate Jesus so that our kids will want to serve the Lord. So do your best and let God do the rest!

———————— MOM TO MASTER ————————

*Lord, help me to always point my children*
*toward You and Your Word. Amen.*

# December 11

*"It would be better for him if a millstone were hung around his neck, and he were thrown into the sea, than that he should offend one of these little ones."*

LUKE 17:2 NKJV

How is your witness? Do you know that everywhere we go, we are witnessing? We are witnessing all the time—either glorifying God or portraying a poor reflection of Him. And here's the kicker: our children are taking it all in. They are like little sponges, absorbing everything we do and say, all the time. Wow! Have you ever thought about that reality? Our kids may be basing their view of Christianity on how we behave? Oh my!

I first realized that fact when Abby was just a toddler. She was a miniature parrot. She repeated absolutely everything I said—good or bad. Once I was on the phone with my mother, and I said that someone had acted like a horse's behind. Later that night when Allyson drooled on one of Abby's favorite dolls, Abby said, "You are a horse's behind!" While it was funny, it was sad too. I knew exactly where she had heard the expression— from me!

So like the song says, "Be careful little mouth what you say," and go forth and give a good witness. You have an attentive audience nearby.

─────────────── MOM TO MASTER ───────────────

*Lord, help me to be a good reflection of You all the time. Help me to point my children toward You. Amen.*

# December 12

*But Jesus said, "Let the little children come to Me,*
*and do not forbid them; for of such is the kingdom of heaven."*
MATTHEW 19:14 NKJV

Parents today are quite proactive. They have their unborn babies on waiting lists for the top preschools in the area. They have college funds established before their children have ever spoken their first words. Parents today are really thinking and planning ahead. That's a good thing; however, many parents are neglecting the most important part of their children's lives— their salvation.

While it's wonderful to put so much thought into the proper preschool for our little ones, it's much more important to make sure we're attending a church that will nurture and encourage our children's spiritual development. If you're in a church that doesn't have a strong children's ministry, it may be time to seek God for a new place of worship.

Ask the Lord to help you find the best church for your children's sake. If you're attending a church that simply entertains and babysits the kids, then start looking for another church. Let's face it, being a good dodge ball player isn't going to help our children when they are facing peer pressure. Let's be proactive about our children's spiritual lives. There's nothing more important.

─────── MOM TO MASTER ───────

*Lord, please direct me to a church that will*
*best minister to my children. Amen.*

# December 13

*"For the LORD does not see as man sees; for man looks at the outward appearance, but the LORD looks at the heart."*

1 SAMUEL 16:7 NKJV

How many times have you heard the phrase "heart of the matter" in your lifetime? Probably hundreds. But have you ever considered its meaning when it comes to your spiritual life? If not, you should. It could totally change the way you pray and the results your prayers receive.

I used to pray for the Lord to make my daughters quit fussing all the time. I'd cry out, "God, they are driving me crazy! Please make them stop fighting and love one another." After months of praying this prayer, the Lord convicted me. In that still, small voice, He whispered, *"Your heart is wrong. You're praying selfishly."* I wanted God to cause my girls to stop fighting just so I could get a break—not for their benefit. My heart motivation was wrong, which caused my prayer to be useless.

Once the Lord pointed out the real "heart of the matter," I was able to pray more effectively and thus see results almost instantly. I had to get my heart right in order to get my prayers right. Maybe you need to do the same thing. If you're not seeing results in your prayer life, ask the Holy Spirit to do a heart check on you. Your motivation might be off!

——————— MOM TO MASTER ———————

*Lord, help my heart to be pure before You. Amen.*

# December 14

*As each one has received a gift, minister it to one another.*
1 PETER 4:10 NKJV

When I was a little girl, I used to love to go into our local five-and-dime store. Mom would give me a dollar, and I could shop forever. Today the five-and-dime stores are pretty much a thing of the past, but we do have lots of dollar stores around. And I enjoy buying stuff in there too. My children were especially amazed that the same stuff they found in other stores for three and four dollars cost only one dollar in the "Everything Is a Dollar!" store. In fact, they embarrassed me sometimes by asking the clerk, "How much is this?" He just pointed to the large sign overhead that reads, EVERYTHING IS A DOLLAR.

The girls quickly learned the value of a dollar. When they earned an allowance, they realized how hard it is to make money and how easy it is to spend it. That's a valuable lesson. I wanted my girls to grow up and be wise shoppers. I took advantage of every opportunity to share shopping tricks with them.

As moms, we need to give our children little tidbits of truth every day. Maybe you can teach them how to shop more wisely. Maybe you can teach them to grow their own veggies. Give them your knowledge, and watch them grow. It's exciting!

---

## MOM TO MASTER

*Lord, help me to recognize opportunities to teach. Amen.*

# December 15

We must pay the most careful attention, therefore,<br>
to what we have heard, so that we do not drift away.<br>
HEBREWS 2:1

When Allyson was born, Abby was already off the bottle. But guess what happened when Abby saw Allyson drinking juice from a bottle? That's right, Abby started crying for her "bah bah" too. "Where'd my bah bah go?" she'd ask, hands on her hips. If she didn't get the answer she wanted, she'd simply walk over, snatch Allyson's bottle, and be on her way.

It's a common occurrence for an older child to regress a bit when a new baby enters the picture. We certainly struggled with it, and maybe you did too. You know, children aren't the only ones who struggle with this problem. As Christians, we sometimes go backward too.

My father always used to say, "If you aren't moving closer to Jesus, then you're moving farther away because it's impossible to stay in the same place." He's right! If you get busy with the children and neglect your time with the Father, you won't stay the same; you'll drift away. Pretty soon you'll be off the meat of the Word and back on the milk. Don't let that happen. Make time for God so that you will move forward with Him every day.

---
## MOM TO MASTER
---

*Lord, help me to move forward with<br>
You every single day. Amen.*

# December 16

*In the same way, the Spirit helps us in our weakness.*
ROMANS 8:26

When I was in eighth grade, I got my very first perm. Remember the '80s big hair? Oh yeah, I wanted that look. Well, the hairdresser rolled my hair on the really small rods, so you can imagine what happened. My hair came out looking like I'd stuck my finger into a light socket. It was so curly! As with all bad perms, it took many months to grow out. Once it finally grew out, I vowed never to get another one. Then, the summer of my freshman year in college, I let a friend talk me into getting another perm. We went together and both came out of the salon looking like pitiful poodles.

Why did I let myself get talked into something so stupid again? Call it perm peer pressure, but I let my buddy totally talk me into something that I knew wasn't good for me.

Guess what? Our children will fall for the same stuff if we don't give them a heads-up before it's too late. Today it's not just perms—it's belly button piercings and tattoos. Before they grow up and want to pierce every body part, let's give them 101 reasons not to go there. And then let's back it up with prayer.

—————— MOM TO MASTER ——————

*Lord, help me to help my children be strong
in the face of peer pressure. Amen.*

# December 17

*Jesus Christ is the same yesterday, today, and forever.*
HEBREWS 13:8 NLT

Consistency. That's why athletes are so strong and perform so well—they train consistently. Unlike me, they don't run two miles one day and then skip four or five days until they can find time to work out again. It's a part of their daily schedule. Being consistent makes the difference between a casual jogger and an avid runner.

It's the same way in our parenting efforts. If we give unconditional love one day and yell and scream the next day, our kids become confused. If we enforce the rules in one situation and bend the rules the next time, we lose our kids' trust and confidence. If we say one thing and do another, we place doubts in our children's minds. We need consistency in every part of our lives.

Hebrews 13:8 tells us that Jesus Christ is the same yesterday, today, and forever, so He is the ultimate when it comes to consistency. Since we are commanded to be like Him, we have a right to ask God to help us in this area of consistency. The Holy Spirit will help you with this aspect of your parenting. It's not easy. It takes effort, but if you'll commit to being consistent in your parenting, your children will become consistently happier kids.

—————————— MOM TO MASTER ——————————

*Lord, please help me to be consistent as
I discipline and love my children. Amen.*

# December 18

*My son, pay attention to what I say; turn your ear to my words.*
*Do not let them out of your sight, keep them within your heart.*
PROVERBS 4:20–21

Have you ever been listening to the radio, and a song comes
over the airwaves, and all of a sudden, you start singing every
word, and you didn't even know that you'd ever heard that song
before? Isn't that wild? That happened to me just the other day.
A song called "Somebody's Watching Me" came on, and as soon
as that first note came through the speakers, I remembered.

I've often thought I was a lot like Cliff on *Cheers*—full of
tons of useless factoids and trivial information. Are you also a
junior Cliff Claven? Well, don't feel too badly. That can actually
be a good thing. If we can retain all of that useless information,
that means we are also capable of retaining large amounts of
the Word. We just have to program the Word into our system
so that it's there when we need it.

If you're spending a great deal of time transporting your
children to one practice after another, use that car time as
Word time. Get yourself the Bible on CD and start program-
ming your mind with some useful information. C'mon, Cliff,
you know you want to!

—————— MOM TO MASTER ——————

*Lord, help me to retain the good stuff and share*
*it with others—especially my children. Amen.*

# December 19

*. . .that you do not become sluggish, but imitate those
who through faith and patience inherit the promises.*
HEBREWS 6:12 NKJV

Patience. Ugh! It's so hard to have patience, isn't it? As mothers, we are doers. Our motto is "Just do it!" We don't wait for somebody else to act on our behalf or take care of the situation. We just press forward and accomplish the task. But what happens when the situation is out of our hands? What happens when we can't solve the problem? That's where patience comes in.

Patience is power—did you know that? It gives us the strength to hold strong when our prayers aren't being answered immediately. Patience undergirds our faith until the miracle is manifested. Maybe you've been praying for your children to come back to God. Maybe you're standing in faith for your child's healing. Maybe you've been praying to conceive another child. Whatever it is, hold fast.

If you have been praying for something for quite some time, and the answer hasn't come, have patience. God hasn't forgotten you. He's heard your prayers. Stand your ground in faith, knowing that your answer is on its way in His perfect timing. Don't give up. Don't back down. Press on in patience.

--------- MOM TO MASTER ---------

*Lord, help me to stand in patience until the answer comes.
I love You and trust You. Amen.*

# December 20

*So do not throw away this confident trust in the Lord.
Remember the great reward it brings you! Patient endurance
is what you need now, so that you will continue to do God's will.
Then you will receive all that he has promised.*
HEBREWS 10:35–36 NLT

Are you problem-centered or solution-centered? When you look at a glass that is half full of milk, do you see it as half empty or half full? In other words, are you a Polly Positive or a Nelly Negative? Well, if you're feeling more like Nelly than Polly today, let me encourage you with a few promises from the Word of God.

"You are strong, and the word of God lives in you, and you have overcome the evil one" (1 John 2:14).

"But thanks be to God! He gives us the victory through our Lord Jesus Christ" (1 Corinthians 15:57).

"What is impossible with man is possible with God" (Luke 18:27).

You see, no matter what you're facing today, God has given you a promise to handle it. Don't dwell on the problem. Meditate on the Master. He has made you more than a conqueror and has already guaranteed your victory. So don't fret. Rejoice! You have much to celebrate!

--- MOM TO MASTER ---

*Father God, help me to become a more positive person. Help me, Lord, to be Word-centered, not problem-centered. Amen.*

# December 21

*"I will prevent pests from devouring your crops, and the vines in your fields will not drop their fruit before it is ripe," says the LORD Almighty. "Then all the nations will call you blessed, for yours will be a delightful land," says the LORD Almighty.*

MALACHI 3:11–12

*Ch-ching!* How is your bank account? Are your credit cards smoking from Christmas shopping? Are you in debt up to your eyeballs? If so, you're not alone. Almost one out of every hundred households will file for bankruptcy, and 43 percent of all US households will spend more money than they make this year. It's a sad fact, but it's a reality for many families.

Here's another reality for you: God is vitally interested in your finances. He wants to free you from debt and protect your finances, but you have to give Him that opening. The only way to open that door is through tithing. When you tithe, you give God the legal right to intervene in your financial situation. As it says in this passage in Malachi, God will prevent the pests from devouring your crops. In other words, when financial tragedy strikes, God will be there to rescue you. So start giving today. Teach your kids to give 10 percent to God, and secure their financial future too!

——————— MOM TO MASTER ———————

*Heavenly Father, thank You for promising to provide for me. I trust in You. Amen.*

# December 22

*"Do not despise these small beginnings,
for the LORD rejoices to see the work begin."*
ZECHARIAH 4:10 NLT

I have discovered that I often don't give my children enough credit. Instead of expecting them to make the right choice or do the right thing, I often worry that they won't. Then, once in a while, God will give me a glimpse of who they are in Christ Jesus, and I am truly humbled.

This happened one time with Abby. Her good friend won a writing contest that Abby had hoped to win. Instead of acting ugly when her friend's name was announced, Abby jumped up from her seat and cheered for her buddy. There was no resentment or jealousy—just pure joy for her friend. I couldn't have been prouder of Abby even if she had won the contest. I am so glad that God gave me a glimpse of Abby's precious heart.

Sometimes we get caught up in the parenting and forget how precious our kids are. We need to give them more credit because they are awesome creatures. Even when they are having "off days," we need to see them through our eyes of faith. Ask the Lord to help you see your children as He sees them. They are precious in His sight!

— MOM TO MASTER —

*Heavenly Father, thank You for my precious children.
Help me to always see them as You see them. Amen.*

# December 23

*Because of that experience, we have even greater confidence*
*in the message proclaimed by the prophets. You must pay*
*close attention to what they wrote, for their words are*
*like a lamp shining in a dark place—until the Day dawns,*
*and Christ the Morning Star shines in your hearts.*
2 PETER 1:19 NLT

When my girls were little, they would only sleep in their rooms if the nightlights were plugged in and shining brightly. If the lights wouldn't work, or if I forgot to plug them in, the girls were quick to point out the lack of light in their bedrooms. They would not stay in a room that was without light.

We are people of light. We like light. We're sort of like moths—if a light is on, we're drawn to it. That's a good thing. We should want to head for the light. Of course, Jesus is known as the Light of the world. And Psalm 119:130 says that the entrance of God's Word into our hearts brings the insight we need. In other words, the Word sheds light on every situation we could ever have.

If you're struggling with something today, head for the light! God's Word will shed light on your situation and drive out the darkness of confusion. C'mon, step into the light today.

—————— MOM TO MASTER ——————

*Heavenly Father, thank You for the light of Your Word.*
*Help me to turn to Your Word in every situation. Amen.*

# December 24

It's all about family this time of year, isn't it? I'll bet your family has wonderful holiday traditions. Every Christmas Eve, we head to my parents' house and spend the night there. We play games and eat lots of fattening stuff, and we allow every person to open just one gift. (Okay, sometimes we talk my mom into letting us open two gifts on Christmas Eve, but usually she's a real stickler on the "one gift rule.")

It's my favorite night of the year. It's not because of the board games or the yummy sweets or even the gifts. It's my favorite time of year because we're all together. After everything settles down and the kids are not so "sugared up," my father always reads the Christmas story. And even though we've heard it a thousand times, it's just as exciting every year. And sometimes we'll have a spontaneous testimony service where every person shares something he or she is most thankful for that year. It's very special.

Whatever your traditions, I hope you'll include Jesus as part of them. Don't let Santa and his reindeer take center stage. Give your children the true meaning of Christmas this year. Jesus is the reason for the season.

## MOM TO MASTER

*Heavenly Father, thank You for sending
Jesus as a baby some two thousand years ago. Amen.*

# December 25

*Then Peter came to Jesus and asked, "Lord, how many times shall I forgive my brother or sister who sins against me? Up to seven times?" Jesus answered, "I tell you, not seven times, but seventy-seven times."*
MATTHEW 18:21–22

Christmas is the time of year when we give lots of presents. It's also a time when family members get together—maybe the only time of year when everyone is together. If you've been harboring unforgiveness against someone in your family—maybe a sibling or a cousin or a parent—give the gift of forgiveness this year.

Maybe you thought you'd forgiven that family member, but every time you think of that person, a little tinge of "ickiness" fills your heart. Get rid of those icky feelings today. Forgive that person.

You might say, "Michelle, that person isn't even sorry!" That's okay. That person doesn't have to be sorry in order for you to forgive. Ask God to help your heart to forgive and your head to forget so that you can start the next year free from any baggage.

Give the gift of forgiveness and you'll receive gifts too—freedom, love, joy, and more! It's time to forgive and forget. Let Jesus fill your heart today so there's no room for any hurt. And have a merry Christmas!

——————— MOM TO MASTER ———————

*Lord, thank You for forgiving me.*
*Help me to forgive others. Amen.*

# December 26

*"I am the vine; you are the branches. If you remain in
me and I in you, you will bear much fruit;
apart from me you can do nothing."*

JOHN 15:5

The presents are all unwrapped. The Christmas programs are over. The carolers are hoarse. The children are already bored with their new toys, and you're pretty sure you put on five pounds in the last two weeks. I'm there with you, sister! I feel like singing a rendition of "The Party's Over." The excitement of Christmas shopping, wrapping presents, and baking cookies is over, but there are always the after-Christmas sales to hit! Oh yeah!

Seriously, aren't you glad that Christmas is about so much more than presents, carols, cookies, and Santa? If it weren't, we'd be so let down on the day after Christmas. But we can celebrate Christmas all year long because Jesus lives inside of us! We can look forward to getting out of bed each day just to see what He has in store for us.

If you know someone who is depressed this time of year, why not share Jesus with that person? Get your children involved. Go witnessing as a family. Give the gift of Jesus—the gift who truly keeps on giving.

―――――――――― MOM TO MASTER ――――――――――

*Lord, thank You for giving me a reason to celebrate
every day of the year. I love You. Amen.*

# December 27

*But the fruit of the Spirit is love, joy, peace, forbearance, kindness, goodness, faithfulness, gentleness and self-control.*
GALATIANS 5:22–23

I was at a local department store, and the cashier behind the counter was totally stressed. I thought she was going to throttle the woman in front of me. They had ugly words with one another, which didn't help this cashier's mood.

*Oh great,* I thought, *and I've got an exchange. She's going to love dealing with me.*

"Do you have your receipt?" she barked.

"No, it was a gift," I said perkily.

"You didn't get a gift receipt?" she snapped.

"Uh. . .no."

"Well, I'll have to give you the sale price then," she explained, which was practically nothing.

"Fine," I said. "I understand."

Then I proceeded to ask her about her holidays. I complimented her beautiful rings, and we had a pleasant conversation. She just needed someone to be nice to her. See, I had a choice to make. I could've become ugly over the sale price refund, but I chose to let Jesus shine through. (Now, I don't always make the right choice—trust me.) Every day we have opportunities to share joy or share ugliness. Choose joy. Our joyful spirits will win others for Jesus. They'll want whatever it is we have! So go forth and be joyful today!

——————— MOM TO MASTER ———————

*Lord, help me to share joy with others. Amen.*

# December 28

*I will be glad and rejoice in you;*
*I will sing the praises of your name, O Most High.*
PSALM 9:2

As the year draws to an end, you're probably reflecting on the past twelve months. It's a good time of year for reminiscing and reflecting, as long as those mind activities don't lead you down the paths of regret and guilt. Hey, we've all made mistakes this year. Yes, even Christian moms occasionally do things that displease the Lord. But don't let those mistakes haunt your holidays. If you've repented for those misdeeds, God has already forgiven them and forgotten them. So you need to do the same. God says in His Word that He has removed your sin as far as the east is from the west—and that's a long way!

Instead of feeling guilty or regretful over past mistakes, take this time to think on the good things God did through you and in you and for you this year. Think on all of the miracles He performed on behalf of your family.

If you keep a journal, take a few minutes to read through it, and like the song says, "Look what the Lord has done!" Praise God for the victories—both big and small. Let Him know that you appreciate Him today. Give Him praise today! That's the way to close out one year and begin another—praising God!

## MOM TO MASTER

*Lord, I praise You for all You've done*
*and all You're going to do. Amen.*

# December 29

*I can do all this through him who gives me strength.*
PHILIPPIANS 4:13

Is there something you've been putting off? Have you been neglecting your time with God because you're too busy? Have you been putting off starting that diet and exercise program because you're afraid of failing again? Have you been putting off organizing your house because you just don't think it's possible to have closets that don't explode when you open them? Have you been putting off having a family devotional time even though you know your kids need it?

Whatever you've been putting off, it's time to get to it! And here's the best part—you don't have to do it alone. God is right there beside you, ready, willing, and more than able to help you. The task may seem big, but nothing is too big for God. Just call on His expertise. If it's willpower you need to stay on a healthy eating program, ask God to change your taste buds to crave only healthy food. If you need more time to accommodate a family devotional time, ask the Lord to help you better organize your day. He will help you. All you have to do is ask.

——————— MOM TO MASTER ———————

*Lord, I need Your help today. Help me to accomplish _____ that I've been putting off for too long. I can't do it alone, but I know You will help me. Amen.*

# December 30

*"Submit to God and be at peace with him."*
JOB 22:21

This time of year, you hear a lot of talk about peace. People send out holiday greeting cards that say, "Peace to your family." All of the networks run season's greetings commercials proclaiming "Peace on earth." Peace is very popular during the holidays, but as Christians, we can enjoy peace throughout the year. And, as moms, we need peace in the worst way, because if we aren't peaceful, our homes won't be peaceful. We set the tone for our homes. We need to let peace rule our hearts, our homes, and our children.

If we let God in and give Him total control of our lives, we are guaranteed peace. He is the giver of true peace. God's kind of peace isn't a temporal thing. It isn't affected by the outside world. It's a peace that passes all understanding. When God takes control of your circumstances, your challenges, your situations, and your messes, He brings peace on the scene. Jesus wasn't just called "the Prince of Peace," He *is* the Prince of Peace. Turn to Him today. Give peace priority in your life.

—————— MOM TO MASTER ——————

*Thank You, God, for bringing peace to my heart and my life. Help me to walk in that peace every single day of the year. I love You. Amen.*

# December 31

*But the fruit of the Spirit is love, joy, peace, forbearance, kindness, goodness, faithfulness, gentleness and self-control.*
GALATIANS 5:22–23

Did you get a fruit basket this year for Christmas? How about a fruitcake—did you get one of those? (If not, I'll send you one of the fruitcakes I received—yuck! I am not a fan of fruitcake.) But maybe you like fruitcake. Or maybe you enjoy giving fruit baskets to your friends and family members at Christmastime.

Let me tell you what's even better than giving a fruit basket or a fruitcake—giving the fruit of the Spirit. And we don't have to just give love, joy, peace, forbearance, kindness, goodness, faithfulness, gentleness, and self-control during the holidays— we can radiate those qualities year round!

Our children need to see us walking in these qualities. They need to feel that love, joy, peace, forbearance, kindness, goodness, faithfulness, gentleness, and self-control operating in our homes. Sure, we're going to miss it once in a while, but as long as we're growing in those things, that's all that counts. God isn't keeping score on how many times we lose self-control; rather, He is celebrating with us as we grow in every fruit. So go on. Radiate good fruit today, and if you must, send out a fruitcake or two!

—— MOM TO MASTER ——

*Thank You, God, for the fruit of the Spirit.
Help me to grow in each fruit this coming year
so that I'll become more like You. Amen.*

## About the author

**Michelle Medlock Adams** is an award-winning journalist and bestselling author, earning top honors from the Associated Press, the Society of Professional Journalists, and the Hoosier State Press Association. Author of nearly five dozen books, Michelle has written more than a thousand articles for newspapers and magazines since graduating with a journalism degree from Indiana University. Her book *Divine Stories of the Yahweh Sisterhood* was named a Family Christian Bookstores Premiere Pick in 2006, and her children's book *My Big Book of Prayers* won the SELAH Award for best children's book of 2012. When not working on her own assignments, Michelle ghostwrites books for celebrities and some of today's most effective and popular ministers, assisting with a *New York Times* bestseller in 2008. Michelle is a much sought after teacher at writers conferences and universities around the nation, and she loves speaking to women's groups, youth groups, and congregations, encouraging others to discover their destinies in God. Michelle is married to her high school sweetheart, Jeff, and they have two college-age daughters, Abby and Allyson, as well as a small petting zoo. When not writing or teaching, Michelle enjoys cheering on the Indiana University basketball team and the Chicago Cubs. Visit her website: www.michellemedlockadams.com.

# Scripture Index